THE ✤ LEGEND ✤ OF
HALLIBURTON

THE ✦ LEGEND ✦ OF
HALLIBURTON

Jeffrey L. Rodengen

Also by Jeff Rodengen

The Legend of Chris-Craft

IRON FIST: *The Lives
of Carl Kiekhaefer*

*Evinrude-Johnson and
The Legend of OMC*

*Serving The Silent Service:
The Legend of Electric Boat*

The Legend of Honeywell

The Legend of Dr Pepper/Seven-Up

The Legend of Briggs & Stratton

The Legend of Ingersoll-Rand

The Legend of Stanley

The Legend of Applied Materials

The Legend of York International

The Legend of Amdahl

Run with it: *The Legend of AMD*

The MicroAge Way

Publisher's Cataloging in Publication
Prepared by Quality Books Inc.

Rodengen, Jeffrey L.
    The legend of Halliburton /Jeffrey L. Rodengen.
    p. cm.
    Includes bibliographical references and index.
    ISBN 0-945903-16-2

1. Halliburton Company. 2. Petroleum industry and trade—United
States. I. Title

HD9560.9.R64 1996   338.7'6223'38'0973
                        QBI96-20244

WRITE STUFF

Write Stuff Syndicate, Inc.

1515 Southeast 4th Avenue • Fort Lauderdale, FL 33316
1-800-900-Book (1-800-900-2665) • (305) 462-6657

Library of Congress Catalog Card Number 95-062227

ISBN 0-945903-16-2

Completely produced in the United States of America

10 9 8 7 6 5 4 3 2 1

iv

Table of Contents

Foreword

EVEN THOUGH I have been associated with Halliburton for a relatively short time, I remember watching Halliburton trucks rolling across the highways as a boy growing up in Wyoming. As the congressman from Wyoming for 11 years, I learned about the public policy issues that affected those trucks and the energy industry in general.

But over the past year I have had the opportunity to witness firsthand the creativity, drive and determination of the employees, managers and officers of this organization. Throughout this book, you will read about many of these people, beginning with the entrepreneurial spirit evinced by the founders: Erle Halliburton and the Brown brothers, George and Herman, and you will see how that spirit still thrives today.

There is a dynamic evolution — maybe even revolution — that is occurring within our industry today. From the outside, there seems to be a simple relationship between the price of oil and the prosperity of the industry. The more valuable the barrel of oil, the greater the opportunity for those who provide essential services for the industry. What has happened is that the pressures of the market have forced fundamental change. It is no longer simply a matter of reacting to the cycles — making money one year and not the next — but rather a strategy to provide a broader range of customer-focused and integrated services less sensitive to the cost of oil.

In the beginning, Erle Halliburton forged a leadership role in the industry with a philosophy of "You call, we haul." Though we continue this same tradition of responsive service to customer needs, we have learned to anticipate the needs of our customers to a much higher degree. We are in the middle of a major and fundamental restructuring of the business, a critical process that is also being undertaken by our customers and by our competition.

A case in point: we recently completed a reorganization of our energy group to achieve the synergy between all of our energy-related business units, including our most recent acquisition of Landmark Graphics Corporation. Halliburton Energy Services, Landmark, Brown & Root Energy Services and Halliburton Energy Development, which are now positioned together under a new energy group, can provide customers with the broadest possible range of services and expertise.

But no matter how well we position ourselves in the market, I am struck by the extent to which the success or failure of a project is as much of a political decision as it is an engineering decision. Many times the engineering and technical aspects of a project can be relatively easy but the project may be thwarted by unresolved political issues. A good example is the tremendous potential for the development of resources in the former Soviet Union, confounded by regional unrest, poverty, lack of infrastructure or an inability to develop a political consensus. Energy issues for producers and for consuming countries are issues of strategic importance. Just as I used to deal with people in the Middle East concerning military matters, it turns out that often the same people are involved in strategic energy issues.

The Middle East will still be the world's prime source of crude oil in the 21st Century. I made a tour of the region recently, visiting everywhere from New Delhi to Cairo and all points in between. They all have significant projects on the drawing boards, great expectations and are all anxious to be able to expand their capacity for the long term. Some of these projects are massive, the kind of work for which Brown & Root is especially qualified, particularly since the subsidiary has been refocused on its core strengths. Other initiatives will require the

ongoing and long-term expertise and combined efforts of the Halliburton Energy Group. And as we continue forward with challenges overseas, we will also remain ready for new opportunities in our largest market — the United States — where 50 percent of our revenues are generated.

Throughout both of their histories, Halliburton and Brown & Root have made significant contributions to both the science and the craft of their respective industries. As the growing global community prepares to embark on even more bold energy, engineering and construction initiatives, these proven organizations are ready to meet the challenge.

Dick Cheney, Chairman, CEO and president of Halliburton, served as Secretary of Defense under President George Bush from 1989 to 1992. He also served as White House Chief of Staff under President Gerald Ford in 1975, and was Wyoming's sole representative — becoming minority whip — for six consecutive terms.

Introduction

A STUDY OF Halliburton Company reveals an intrepid and dynamic organization. Workers improve products, corporate structures adapt to new challenges, leaders change titles and responsibilities. In fact, as this book was being written Halliburton Company completed its acquisition of Landmark Graphics Corporation, one of the first companies to develop ways to interpret and integrate crucial geophysical information for oil and gas exploration. Halliburton also completed a major shift in the way its energy services segments conduct business, centering its vast array of resources under a new group called the Halliburton Energy Group.

But even as Halliburton Company, founded by Erle Halliburton in 1919, continues to evolve its mission remains the same: maintain leadership, develop integrated solutions for customers and, above all, never rest. Halliburton Company's energy services segment provides a broad range of services and equipment critical to the exploration, development and production of oil and natural gas.

Brown & Root, Inc. mirrors the vitality demonstrated by the energy segment. The engineering and construction segment of Halliburton Company, has soared, burrowed and built itself into the record and history books. It is one of the world's largest providers of engineering, construction, project management, operation, maintenance and environmen-

THE FIRST
OFFSHORE OIL WELL
First producing offshore oil well out of sight of land was completed Nov. 14, 1947 in the Gulf of Mexico forty-three miles South of Morgan City, Louisiana

tal services. The 60,000 employees comprising all sections of Halliburton Company work in more than 100 nations, building and developing new devices, methods and facilities that affect just about every industry.

Products introduced by Halliburton to the oil and gas industry have improved efficiency many times over. For example, the TRACS stabilizer, used in directional drilling equipment, have enabled operators to drill faster, farther and with greater precision to reach reservoirs. The stabilizers helped set a record when used for the first time for accuracy and speed. The well was located on BP Exploration's Wytch Farm operations in southern England. The stabilizer allowed drillers to extend the horizontal well to more than 24,000 feet. The well led to a reservoir underneath environmentally-sensitive Poole Bay without disturbing the bay itself.

Hard work and grit characterize the rise of both Halliburton Energy Group and Brown & Root, Inc. The similarities between the two are not coincidence. In the early 1960s, the aging Brown brothers, Herman and George, wanted to sell Brown & Root to a company that maintained the same core values that had helped them build the company from a tiny road-construction operation into a world presence. In Halliburton, the brothers found kindred values. Both Brown & Root and Halliburton got their start in 1919. Both fought mud, economic uncertainty and even worn-out mules to emerge as leaders in their fields.

Like Erle Halliburton, George and Herman Brown created a company-family atmosphere, which fostered intense loyalty. Like the Browns, Erle Halliburton seized opportunity and embraced new challenges in areas where others saw only risk. Although the two companies merged in 1962, they operated autonomously. As former Halliburton Chairman and CEO Thomas Cruikshank described it, "Halliburton and Brown & Root had totally different cultures. Our philosophy at Halliburton was that when we acquired something, we wanted it with 'stand-alone' management."

Keeping with this philosophy, Halliburton evolved into nine oil field-related companies in the 1960s and 70s, in addition to Brown & Root. The oil field service companies were soon grouped under Halliburton Energy Services. Corporate leaders such as Thomas Cruikshank, Dave Lesar, Ken LeSuer, Al Baker, Dale Jones, Zeke Zeringue and Les Coleman brought these companies into a closer working relationship with one another. Zeke Zeringue said the goal was to develop a "fully-integrated, seamless organization," working in partnership with customers to find total solutions to their needs. Halliburton Company made a major stride toward this goal in July 1996. Halliburton Energy Services and Brown & Root announced that they would jointly develop a natural gas field in the Bay of Bengal, a job that takes advantage of the expertise of both organizations. Brown & Root is in charge of the surface construction, while Halliburton Energy Services will perform the subsurface work. The work will be completed under the newly-created unit called Halliburton Energy Development, part of the newly-created energy group. This group aligns all of the upstream energy-related units — Landmark Graphics, Halliburton Energy Services, Brown & Root Energy Services and Halliburton Energy Development — to achieve the synergy envisioned by Chairman and CEO Dick Cheney.

Regardless of the company's structure, however, the people of Halliburton Company are committed to serving customers' needs no matter how tough the job. In a remote area of Venezuela, Halliburton engineers struggled to design a fracturing technique to prevent the wells from plugging up. A combination of fluids and 3-D computer-imaging software, known as FracPro, provided production results that exceeded expectations.

Erle Halliburton revolutionized the oil field service field by working in partnership with his principal customers, the forerunners to today's major oil companies. Halliburton Company continues that tradition by providing the energy industry with the service and information it requires to meet the changing needs of an increasingly industrialized world.

Acknowledgments

A GREAT MANY individuals and institutions assisted in the research, preparation and publication of *The Legend of Halliburton.* The development of historical timelines and a large portion of the principal archival research was accomplished by my valued and resourceful research assistants, Joan Thompson and Douglas Long. Their thorough and careful investigation into the early years of Halliburton and Brown & Root have made it possible to publish much new and fascinating information on the origin and evolution of both historic and dynamic organizations.

However, without the cooperation and dedicated assistance of the organizations' executives, employees and retirees, this book would have been impossible to produce. Principal among these are Steve Moore, director of corporate communications and Brandon Lackey, public relations manager for Halliburton. Their patience in answering questions in layman's terms, assistance in finding artwork and prominent records and individuals is greatly appreciated. The historic photographs and research material cheerfully supplied by Pee Wee Cary provided valuable background information highlighting the unique history of Erle Halliburton and his company. I would also like to thank Tommy Knight, former president of Brown & Root, Inc. for the unexpected and generous loan of the key to the Browns' fabled 8-F suite, as well as Mr. Knight's enjoyable anecdotes and insights.

The interviews provided on relatively short notice by Landmark Graphics President and CEO Robert Peebler and Hank Holland, executive vice president of Integrated Solutions, were especially helpful in describing the acquisition and role of their company in the Halliburton family. The interest and courtesy of the many interview subjects for the book was most gratifying. Particularly helpful were Chairman Dick Cheney, Halliburton's chief executive officer, whose insight and vision was most appreciated and helpful. Thomas Cruikshank, former Chairman and CEO of Halliburton, and Chief Financial Officer Dave Lesar were also extremely helpful. I would also like to thank the retirees whose recollections about the earlier days of Halliburton brought Erle Halliburton's personality to life in the book: former CEOs Ed Paramore and Jack Harbin; former COO W. Bernard Piepe; Malcolm Rosser, longtime advertising manager; Bob Diggs Brown, former vice president of sales and advertising; and Bill Taylor former president and CEO of Halliburton Services and Welex; Gary Montgomery, recently retired as vice president of Brown & Root Energy Services; Of the many employees and officers who were instrumental, I would particularly like to thank: Dale Jones, vice chairman of the board; Ken LeSuer,

CEO of Halliburton Energy Services; Zeke Zeringue, president of HES; Guy Marcus, vice president of investor relations, Halliburton Company; Jerry Blurton, vice president and treasurer; Jimmy Cooper, vice president and chief environmental officer of Halliburton Energy Services; Dale Davis, director of strategic and business management, HES; Greg Loyacano, vice president of Sales and Marketing, HES; B.N. Murali, vice president of technology, HES; Robert Nash, senior vice president, HES; Peter Arrowsmith, vice president of Brown & Root Environmental; Jack Browder, vice president of business development, Brown & Root, Inc.; B.K. Chin, vice president of Brown & Root Energy Services; Randy Harl, president of Brown & Root Government Services; Jim Jacobi, vice president and chief information officer, Halliburton Company; Gary Morris, senior vice president of Shared Services, Halliburton Company; Larry Pope, president of Brown & Root Engineering and Construction; Les Coleman, executive vice president and general counsel, Halliburton Company; John Redmon, vice president and COO of Brown & Root Engineering and   Dr. Jay Weidler, senior vice president of Brown & Root Energy Services; Stephen Zander, senior vice president and regional manager — Americas, Brown & Root, Inc.; Susan Keith, vice president, secretary and corporate counsel, Halliburton Company; Marion Cracraft, manager of corporate communications, Halliburton Company. I would also like to extend my appreciation to the legendary Red Adair, whose colorful stories paint a romantic picture of the oil industry.

Finally, a very special thanks to the dedicated staff at Write Stuff Enterprises, Inc. and key consultants, especially my executive assistants and office managers Bonnie Bratton and Linda Manis, Karine N. Rodengen, Executive Editor Karen Nitkin, Associate Editor Alex Lieber, Creative Director Kyle Newton, Art Director Sandy Cruz, Production Managers Ray Mancuso and Peter Ackerman, Marketing Director Christopher Frosch, Logistics Manager Raphael Santiago and office mascots Kodak and Butterscotch.

This book is a project of Write Stuff Syndicate, Inc., and Jeffrey L. Rodengen, its president. It is not a Halliburton Company publication, Neither Write Stuff Syndicate, Inc., nor Jeffrey L. Rodengen, nor any othe Write Stuff personnel, are employees or agents of Halliburton Company, or otherwise affiliated with Halliburton Company. The author wishes to thank Halliburton Company for its cooperation throughout the project, and particularly for making its pictorial and editorial archives available for use in researching and art preparation for the book.

Erle P. Halliburton around 1920, watching as his company's new well-cementing methods become popular. A memorial statue erected in Memorial Park, in Duncan, was cast from this photograph.

Cementing the Future

"[Halliburton] instilled an attitude to fight the competition and out-perform them. Not undercut them but ... outperform in services."

— John P. "Jack" Harbin, 1995[1]

WILLIAM G. SKELLY, president of the Skelly Oil Company, had a problem. An oil well was gushing out of control in the Hewitt Field near Wilson, Oklahoma. Skelly had tried to control the well every way he knew how, but every effort had failed. The thick plume of oil continued to spurt toward the sky.

Then Skelly got a call from Erle Palmer Halliburton. Erle promised that he could get the well under control, or he wouldn't charge Skelly a dime. He planned to use a procedure known as oil well cementing. He would force cement down a pipe that ran the length of the well, using so much pressure that the cement would be pushed out the bottom of the pipe and forced up the outside, between the pipe and the bare walls of the hole. When the cement dried, the pipe would be held securely in place, and the flowing oil would be protected from water and other contamination. The secured pipe could then be fitted with devices that regulated the flow of oil.

Skelly had nothing to lose, so he told Halliburton to give it his best shot.[2] It was January 1920, and few people in the mid-continent oil fields gave oil well cementing much thought. There was so much oil flowing, and so many people were making so much money, that ideas about conservation and efficiency got pushed into the background. If oil well cementing was considered at all, it was usually rejected. Most oil men thought the process was useless at best, and damaging to the oil wells at worst.

Erle, however, believed that his future and the future of the oil business lay in oil well cementing. Though Erle was small in stature, there was something about his self-assured manner that made people stop and listen. And there was nothing in his nature that allowed him to quit. Controlling the well was more important to Erle Halliburton than it was to Bill Skelly, whose oil company, founded in 1919, would become one of the most important in the nation. It was Erle's big chance to prove the value of cementing. When he successfully gained control of Skelly's wild well, people noticed. After years of struggle, Erle and his methods had finally gained credibility.

The Early Years

Erle P. Halliburton was born September 22, 1892, on a farm near the town of Henning, Tennessee, about 50 miles north of Memphis. His

---

An Oklahoma oil well in the early 1920s. Erle revolutionized methods to drill and cement wells.

father, Edwin Gray Halliburton, was a graduate of Vanderbilt University and had, at various times, been a teacher, writer, merchant and farmer. During the fall and winter, Erle attended school in Ripley, a town north of Henning, and in the summer he attended a country school near his home. He was a good student, completing both elementary and high school in just eight years. Even when he was very young, Erle was curious about the operation of mechanical devices. He liked to fix things. If they weren't broken, he would take them apart anyway, just to see how they worked.

When Erle was 12, his father died, and Erle, his mother, his sister and his four brothers plunged into desperate poverty. In 1906, when Erle was 14, he left home to find work to help support his family. According to legend, he vowed not to return until he had made a million dollars. It was an absurd boast for a poverty-stricken boy, but one that he apparently took seriously.[3]

Between 1906 and 1915, Erle held no fewer than a dozen jobs and managed to see much of the world. His first job was in the commissary at a railroad construction camp. Soon, he was assigned to drive a small locomotive. Next, he took a job operating a steam crane that loaded logs onto barges on the Mississippi River. Then he worked in Brooklyn, New York, as a salesman of automatic stokers and smoke consumers for W.D. Mayo, who later became chief engineer for the Ford Motor Company.[4]

During this time, Erle traveled to San Diego, California, where he shipped out as a merchant seaman on a six-month cruise to Manila, China and Honolulu. He also worked for several months as a steam shovel operator in Fresno, California, and operated a steam crane in Durant, Oklahoma.[5]

In 1910, at age 18, Erle enlisted in the United States Navy. He was trained in engineering and hydraulics and operated the Navy's first motor barge. He served two tours and was honorably discharged in July 1915.

In the autumn of 1915, Erle arrived in Los Angeles, where he became the superintendent of water distribution for the Dominguez Irrigation Company, at that time the largest pressure irrigation project in the world. He was paid $100 a month, plus room and board. That year, in Riverside, California, Erle P. Halliburton married Vida Taber. Vida would provide a wellspring of

1919: Erle Halliburton goes into business as the New Method Oil Well Cementing Company.

1921: Erle pawns his wife's wedding ring to build the Halliburton Measuring Line.

1920: Erle proves his ideas work by getting William Skelly's oil well under control.

support in both good times and bad, and would prove to be Erle's most valuable business partner.

The Oil Business

Halliburton's next job was with the Long Beach Chemical Company, a producer of strontium nitrate crystals.[6] Finally, after nine years of travel and job-hopping, Erle seemed to find his niche in 1918 when he went to work as a truck driver for the Perkins Oil Well Cementing Company, owned by Almond A. Perkins. Perkins had invented and patented a method of cementing oil wells that would grow increasingly important as the oil business developed. His technique was to mix cement with water to form a slurry, which was pumped down a pipe to the bottom of the well, then forced back up between the wall of the hole and the pipe. This technique was a considerable improvement over previous methods, which generally called for filling the drill hole with slurry first, then lowering the pipe before the cement hardened.[7]

Erle was a quick study and a hard worker, and he was soon promoted to cementer. But his constant stream of ideas put him in conflict with

One of the first trucks used by the young Halliburton Oil Well Cementing Company, around 1919.

his boss, who did not want to be given advice on how to run his business. Finally, Perkins grew so irritated at Erle's suggestions that he fired

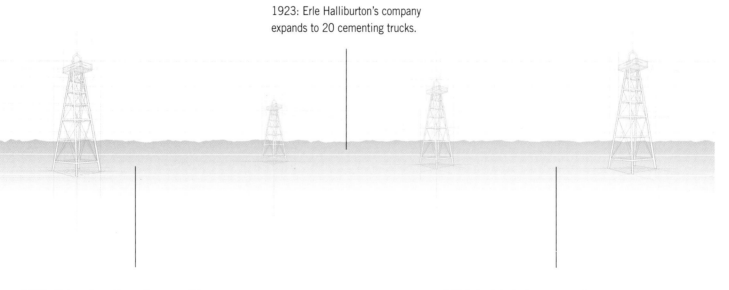

1923: Erle Halliburton's company expands to 20 cementing trucks.

1921: Going where the action was, Erle moves his family and business to Duncan, Oklahoma.

1924: On July 1, the company incorporates as the Halliburton Oil Well Cementing Company.

HALLIBURTON CO.

Erle Halliburton's moment of truth. He would demonstrate that his new methods to bring wild wells under control actually worked. William Skelly, center, watches as Erle, far left in dark suit, directs his men. From this beginning, the Halliburton Oil Well Company would grow into international prominence.

Halliburton. Years later, Erle would say, "The two best things that ever happened to me were being hired, and then fired, by the Perkins Oil Well Cementing Company."[8]

Working for Perkins seemed to put the oil business into Erle's blood. Halliburton went immediately from California to Wichita Falls, Texas, a town full of wildcatters and roughnecks working the drilling boom at the nearby Burkburnett and Waggoner fields. In 1919 alone, these fields produced 40 million barrels of oil. It took only a few relatively shallow probes to bring oil gushing from the ground.

Erle went into business by making a deal with his neighbor. The neighbor would have use of Erle's outdoor privy, and Erle would have use of the neighbor's wagon and team of horses. Erle then borrowed a pump, purchased some hoes, built a mixing box, and proceeded to inform all within earshot that he was in the oil well cementing business. Despite Erle's feverish belief in the value of cementing, nobody exactly beat a path to his door.[9] The oil men in Wichita Falls were too busy cutting deals, counting their money and cleaning the black goo off their clothes and out of their hair to ponder the benefits of oil well cementing.

Even though nobody else seemed to agree with him, Erle stubbornly believed in cementing, and he formed a company based on that conviction. Halliburton persuaded four friends to invest between $250 and $1,000 each, for a collective 50 percent interest in his New Method Oil Well Cementing Company. Customers were scarce, and

Right: A 1920 cementing wagon. Erle borrowed from both friends and creditors to buy some of his first equipment.

Below: Main Street of Duncan, Oklahoma, in 1920. Erle Halliburton moved to Duncan in 1921.

HALLIBURTON CO.

Erle struggled to remain a step ahead of his creditors. He decided to move his family and company to a more promising location.[10]

About 60 miles northeast of Wichita Falls, near Wilson, Oklahoma, new fields were being drilled. Erle put his wife and two children on the train to Wilson while he drove the muddy roads. More than 25 years later, Vida reminisced about the experience.

"In 1919, Hubby and I decided to go to the new field at Wilson. Hubby drove the car and I took the two children on the train. Erle Jr. was three and Zola was one year old. When I arrived in Wilson, Hubby was not there, so I got a room in the hotel and started looking for a house. There was none to be had, but I found an oil field shack, the worst I had ever seen, for $50 a week. I had weathered the oil boom in Taft, California, and the one in Wichita Falls, Texas, but I had really seen nothing. I stayed on at the hotel until Hubby arrived. He was tired and dirty, as he had to dig the car out of one mud rut after another. There were no paved roads in Oklahoma then."[11]

Days before, on a scouting visit to Wilson, Erle had bought a wagon and a pump, and also some lumber and hardware to build an office, a garage, and a supply house. These he planned to build on a lot he rented just outside town on the highway toward the oil fields. But Wilson had become a boom town so quickly that, by the time the Halliburtons arrived, the only homes available were the dirtiest, dilapidated shacks, offered for rent at extravagant prices. So the lot, lumber and hardware became the Halliburton home, a one-room house built by Erle and a carpenter in two days. The house had

MAIN ST. DUNCAN OKLA.

STEPHENS COUNTY HISTORICAL MUSEUM

Above: Harvey Breashears, one of the earliest employees of the Halliburton Oil Well Cementing Company in 1920. Breashears is standing in front of the company's first cementing wagon.

Right: Halliburton employees proudly stand in front of the company's second cementing wagon.

two jobs coming up that needed plugs and belting, and we needed money to hire a team to haul the equipment to the field.

"The conversation had drifted from the lack of a bank account to a new idea on how to cement an oil well using a measuring line to tell just how far down the well the cement was. I was thrilled with the idea and was busy drawing every word Hubby said. It must have been about 1 a.m. then, and I was using my left hand. The lamp shone on my ring and I sat there admiring it when the thought came to me, 'here is the money we need.' At first Hubby would not listen to me. The very idea! But I argued we could get it back, so we went to sleep all thrilled with the new idea of cementing, the new means of getting jobs and the money."[14]

no water, gas or electricity, but it was solid, especially compared to the tents that were serving as homes to newer arrivals.

"A few blocks away ... was a hydrant," Vida recalled. "If you ever want to realize how much water you use, just start hauling it in a bucket."[12]

The Halliburtons installed a telephone, and so the tiny home became an office. During the days, Erle worked in the fields while Vida tended to the house and handled business calls. In the evenings, the young couple worked over the company's books. But no matter how many times they added the numbers, the bottom line remained the same. Money was tight, as Vida recalled.[13]

"We started on the books, which was our bank account. It was low, seriously low, and we had

Erle pawned the ring the next day, and bought the materials necessary to make his first measuring line, a device that continually measured the depth of the cement as it was pumped down a well. Halliburton had come up with the idea in the Tonkawa Field of Oklahoma, when he marked a clothesline with Roman numerals and lowered it into a well to measure the depth of the cementing operation.[15]

It was a simple idea and it worked. Halliburton integrated the measuring line into the mechanics of the cementing equipment and received a patent. The only downside was that the white chalked numerals had to be laboriously cleaned after each use so that the line could be marked again in the future. When the company incorporated, it purchased the patent from Halliburton for $2,000.[16]

Some Bad Roads in Tonkawa Oil Fields

Above: Erle and his men often came home caked in mud after they mired their cementing wagons in an unforgiving soupy mud.

Below: The simple but highly innovative — and quickly patented — Halliburton Measuring Line. Erle and wife Vida devised the tool to measure the depth in oil and gas wells.

"Because the measuring line is made of material with practically no stretch, and because of the precision of the depth meter at the surface, the Halliburton measuring device has become the standard for accurate measurement of depth in oil and gas wells," noted the *Duncan Banner* in 1934.[17]

On another occasion, the Halliburtons did not have enough money to meet the payroll. "Then we thought of the lovely four rooms of furniture we had in storage in California. ... We wired the storage company and sold the furniture, dishes, and silver to them, lock, stock and barrel," recalled Vida. "Pleased and proud as punch with ourselves, we handed each man his paycheck when it was due."[18]

The Breakthrough

The financial situation dramatically improved in January 1920, when The New Method Oil

HALLIBURTON CO.

Well Cementing Company got its big break. Once Erle proved that he could control Skelly's wild well business began to pour in. With the fee paid by Bill Skelly, Erle bought his first cementing wagon and hired several full-time employees. Suddenly, Vida Halliburton was very busy taking messages and scheduling cementing jobs for her jubilant husband.[19] As the company became more successful, Mrs. Halliburton's life became busier, she later recalled.

"More jobs meant more telephone calls, more people coming to the house, more reports to make out and file, more bills to pay, more money to keep track of, and more supplies to order. This was my end of the job. All this, added to the regular cooking, keeping house, and caring for two small children. ... The idea that we had not even been to a movie or out on any pleasure trip in over a year never occurred to either of us — we were too interested in the development of our new enterprise to think of pleasures."[20]

As the company grew, Erle searched for ways to increase the efficiency of the well-cementing process. Mixing cement with water could be done only in small batches, with workers stirring each batch with hoes and shovels.

Mixing enough cement and pouring it down the pipe before the cement began to harden was as difficult as it was critical. To speed the process of mixing and pouring, Erle invented what he called the Jet Mixer, or the Halliburton Cement Mixer. Using this device, workers had only to empty bags of cement into a large tub. The Jet Mixer would automatically add water and stir. From this device the cement was pumped directly into the well pipe.[21]

"The first outstanding development of Halliburton in his field was the simple and rugged little device known as the Halliburton Cement Mixer," noted the *Duncan Banner* in a 1934 retrospective of the company's first ten years.

"Weighing less than 150 pounds, this simple device was recognized immediately as the fastest known method of mixing cement. ... Prior to the introduction of the Halliburton Cement Mixer, cement was mixed in boxes by hand. The limitation of box methods of mixing became very evident when *attempts were made to place the proper amount of cement behind casing in deep wells. Speed became the essential requirement. The Halliburton Mixer amply met this demand for speed, one of the most necessary factors in the long string of mechanical details in the successful cementing of oil well casings at the present extreme depths of almost two miles."*[22]

The Jet Mixer did the job so well that it created another problem. Cement was available only in sacks small enough for one strong man to handle, but the Jet Mixer could consume a thousand sacks in only a few minutes. No man, regardless of his strength, could open sacks fast enough to keep up with the Jet Mixer. Erle solved the problem by inventing the Sack Cutter, which quickly and conveniently opened the sacks and dumped the cement into the mixer.[23]

"I Started in Business Infringing"

Erle's early success might not have been possible if he had not infringed on the patents of Almond Perkins, the man who had fired him years earlier. According to Earl Babcock, a patent attorney with the Halliburton Company from the 1930s onward, Erle never denied patent infringement, and in fact often said to Babcock, "Don't ever tell me I cannot do something because it will infringe somebody's patent. I started in business infringing."[24]

This rather brazen business philosophy caught up with Erle in 1922, when Perkins'

STEPHENS COUNTY HISTORICAL MUSEUM

As business began to boom in the Oklahoma oilfields, Erle Halliburton experimented with faster and more efficient cementing methods. He developed the Halliburton Jet Mixer, which consumed thousands of sacks within a few minutes, and then invented the Sack Cutter.

patent attorney, Leonard Lyon, arrived in Duncan, Oklahoma, and announced that Perkins would no longer tolerate the theft of his ideas. The matter was settled in a mutually beneficial deal that gave Halliburton an exclusive license on the Perkins patent for the mid-continent, and gave Perkins an exclusive license on the Halliburton Jet Mixer for California and the surrounding states.[25]

Although Erle embued his company with many traits and practices, infringement was one that did not endure.

By the end of 1920, Erle and his rugged band of cementers had worked on some 500 wells, driving from one site to another in one of the company's three cementing trucks. Meanwhile, the cementing business was slowing down in the fields around Wilson and new fields were opening around Duncan, some 50 miles to the northwest. Erle moved his wife, his two children, and his business to Duncan on March 21, 1921.

The move proved to be a wise one, and business increased as word of Halliburton's services spread. To keep up with demand, Erle expanded the business by acquiring five Army surplus trucks. He fitted them with pumps and pneumatic tires and used them to work the fields around Duncan, as well as new strikes in Mexia and Corsicana, in Texas; the El Dorados, in Arkansas; Tonkawa and Seminole, in Oklahoma; and other locations within a 500-mile radius of Duncan. By 1923, the business had grown so much that it required a fleet of 20 cementing trucks.[26]

The Halliburton Oil Well Cementing Company

Though the New Method Oil Well Cementing Company was larger than ever, operations were still fairly informal. Business deals were most often sealed with a promise and a handshake, and promises were casually broken if the oil well proved disappointing. The money flowed in fits and starts, sometimes forcing Erle to scramble to make payroll. In 1924, however, this financial instability came to a sudden end.

In a breathtakingly shrewd move, Erle proposed to seven large oil companies, his most reliable customers, that he and they form a corpora-

tion. The companies accepted his proposition because they needed his patented service. Erle formed the Halliburton Oil Well Cementing Company (Howco) on July 1, 1924 under the laws of the state of Delaware. Stock was authorized at $100 per share for 3,500 shares. Suddenly, Erle's biggest customers became his partners.

The original stockholders of Howco were major oil companies, including Magnolia (later Mobil), Texas Company (later Texaco), Gulf (later Chevron), Humble (later Exxon), Sun, Pure (later Unocal), and Atlantic (later ARCO).

Six of these companies — Magnolia, Texas, Gulf, Humble, Pure and Atlantic — bought 200 shares each. Sun took 100 shares. Together, the oil companies held 1,300 shares, while Erle and Vida owned 1,700 shares. Five hundred shares, owned by the corporation, were held in trust and voted on by the Republic National Bank of Dallas. If the bank and the oil companies disagreed with Erle about the operation of the corporation, their combined 1,800 shares would be decisive in a vote. As it turned out, such a circumstance never occurred.[27]

The Halliburtons contributed no cash to this arrangement. Instead, they received $130,000 from the oil companies on July 23, 1924, to use Halliburton cementing equipment and patent rights to the cementing process.[28]

Howco began with three corporate officers. Erle P. was president and chief executive officer, with a salary of $15,000 per year. H.C. Gloeckler was vice president, with a salary of $4,200, and H.T. Crain was secretary-treasurer, also earning $4,200 per year.[29] The new company employed three office employees, 17 shop employees and 37 field workers.[30]

Howco's first directors were W.B. Pyron, L.C. Hawkins, W.S. Farish, H.C. Gloeckler, L.L. Humphries, Wirt Davis, and, of course, Halliburton himself. Farish resigned August 16, 1924, and was replaced by W.W. Fondren.[31] The board of directors met once a year at the renowned Magnolia Building in Dallas. Stockholders met once a year at the Howco office in Duncan. In a few short years, Erle Halliburton had come a long way. But his success story was just beginning.

One of Erle Halliburton's trucks at work in front of a typically flimsy oil derrick in the early 1920s.

CHAPTER TWO

From Oil Wells to Airplanes

"We intend to build up and maintain a complete organization. We will cover all phases of oil well cementing service. We will maintain an aggressive and sustained program of research. We shall give uniform quality and service. We'll get there somehow, regardless of location."

— Erle P. Halliburton,
July 1, 1924, day of incorporation[1]

IN 1924, THE OIL FIELDS of Oklahoma and Texas were awash in opportunity, and Erle P. Halliburton was in the thick of it all. One of the first business transactions of the new Halliburton Oil Well Cementing Company, Inc. (Howco) was to buy a one-room house across the street from the Halliburton home in Duncan, Oklahoma.[2]

The modest wooden structure became Howco's first corporate headquarters. Erle could finally clear his spare room of the papers and receipts that had accumulated during four years of doing business there. Vida Halliburton's day-to-day role in the company was taken over by professional accountants, bookkeepers and secretaries. Yet, as she wrote in 1949, "I have never been relieved completely of all my duties and have continued to work for Howco for the past 29 years, only my paychecks have been in the form of dividends."[3]

As president and chief operating officer, Erle P. Halliburton was the driving force behind Howco. His ambition, confidence and energy set the tone and standards of the new corporation. The company's policies, established by Erle, demonstrated his high expectations.

"We intend to build up and maintain a complete organization. We will cover all phases of oil well cementing service. We will maintain an aggressive and sustained program of research. We shall give uniform quality and service. We'll get there somehow, regardless of location."[4]

Halliburton knew that Howco had to remain at the forefront of well cementing technology in order to succeed. He never stopped designing new equipment and pioneering new methods of production, and he was fiercely protective of his ideas. Edwin Paramore, president of Halliburton in the 1970s, said Erle also possessed foresight for business opportunities.

"He could look into the future and see what was coming better than any other man I ever met. He could tell what was going to happen with cement. ... And he could look into the future and see what you almost had to have to survive."[5]

From One Boom Town to Another

From the beginning, Howco boasted that it would provide the same high-quality service regard-

A 1930s Halliburton oil well cementing crew. Halliburton maintained legendary faith in his workers and considered them part of his family.

The first office of the Halliburton Oil Well Cementing Company began as a one-room, single-story wooden building across from Erle's home. Over the next four years, two one-story additions were built. The two-story addition was built in 1928.

July 1924: Erle becomes partners with seven large oil companies, forming the Halliburton Oil Well Cementing Company.

1926: Handing a $15,000 check to inventor John Simmons, Erle purchases the Simmons Drill Stem Tester.

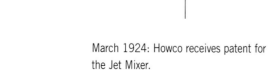

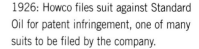

March 1924: Howco receives patent for the Jet Mixer.

1926: Howco files suit against Standard Oil for patent infringement, one of many suits to be filed by the company.

less of the well's location. Howco employees traveled from one boom town to another, finding work wherever the latest oil strike had occurred. "The booms in those days were short-lived," explained Jeff Watters, an early Howco employee.

"They'd last maybe three months, and then everybody would move on to the next boom. You knew everybody in the field no matter where you moved. Everyone picked up and moved from boom to boom — the tool pushers, the roughnecks, the hashers in the eating places, and the service crews like Halliburton."[6]

Getting from place to place could be extremely difficult. In the 1920s, paved roads were still a rarity in the United States. Before Route 66 was commissioned for construction through the center of the nation in 1926, only about 2,500 miles of road existed in the entire continental United States. About 800 miles of them were paved.[7] In Texas and Oklahoma, most roads were simply dirt tracks, and getting to an oil well in a truck heavy with cement could mean slogging through quagmires, on the road and in the oil field.

HALLIBURTON CO.

A Halliburton air compression truck from the 1920s.

January 1927: Howco stock dividend reaches $100 per share. Business is booming in oil industry.

1927: Erle forms the SAFEway airline. The Depression soon forced him to sell it, however.

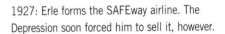
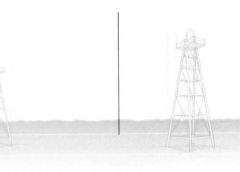

1927: The semi-professional baseball team, the Cementers, is formed.

HALLIBURTON CO.

Above: With few paved roads in the nation, scenes such as this, a Howco truck imprisoned by quicksand-like mud, were common. Mules were sometimes required to extricate the trucks.

Left: Erle equipped his four-wheel-drive trucks with pneumatic tires to better fight the mud.

"In those days, the trucks had no starters and no heaters," Watters explained. "There was no such thing as antifreeze, and we used an old, heavy oil. So, in cold weather, you never killed the engine on a truck from the time you left camp until you got back."[8]

In the early twenties, Erle Halliburton purchased five Army surplus trucks and a Ford Model B four-wheel-drive truck, fitting them with pneumatic tires for better traction and weight-bearing capacity.[9] Even with the special tires, the Ford would sometimes get stuck in the mud, and on more than one occasion mule teams had to be hitched to the vehicle to pull it free.

One popular story that has survived in oral tradition tells of Howco men driving on a plank road along a swamp in Louisiana on their way to a cementing job. When the driver hit the brakes too hard, the truck slid off the rough boards, coming to rest with one side of the truck on the road and the other side stuck fast in swamp mud. The men jumped out of the truck and watched in horror as two wheels sank into the swamp and the truck flopped onto its side. Soon a Halliburton supervisor happened upon the scene. "Well, boys," he was reported to say, "while she's in that position, you might as well grease her."[10] Once the truck was serviced, the Halliburton men righted it and continued to the job site.

A more verifiable story occurred in 1931, when a crew of Howco men drove five days and four nights from Duncan to control a wild well in Pennsylvania. Howco had no qualms about sending crews 1,000 miles or more to cement a single well.

Halliburton men earned a reputation for being tough, dedicated and dependable. Erle Halliburton expected his men to work hard because he worked hard. And he trusted them. He had to, because his men were often hundreds of miles away, setting up makeshift operations wherever the current boom was taking place. J. Evetts Haley, who wrote *A Genius With Cement*, explained that the men in charge of these traveling operations would simply rent a shack or house, set up a telephone, and start soliciting business. It was not easy work.

"He had to be something of a skilled mechanic, but also a seasoned cementer with some rudimen-
tary knowledge of the geological problems involved. He had to be able to boss independent crews of roughnecks. He had to be something of an enterpriser, selling and expanding their services.*

"He had to keep accounts, care for his men, credit them when they were broke, and maintain equipment at a time and place that seemed to care little for men and nothing at all for machines. He operated under certain rough policies laid down in Duncan, and looked to shops there for replacements and parts, for the prices to be charged, and wages paid.

"But when he rolled his cementing truck out to a job, he was completely on his own. Since cement brooks neither indecision nor delay, when once the work was started there could be

A late 1920s Howco cementing truck. No job was too far away and the red trucks soon became a common site in oilfields throughout the country.

Grimy, gritty and tough, this Halliburton crew takes some time out from a 1929 cementing job near Oklahoma City.

no hesitancy, no seeking of advice from head-quarters. Of necessity these cementers had to be tough-fibered, resourceful and independent!"[11]

The faith that Halliburton had in his men was legendary. On one occasion, Halliburton discovered that three men had stolen tools from the company. When they were caught, a supervisor fired them. At a company gathering a short time later, Halliburton, speaking to the assembled crowd, wondered aloud if anyone in the room had taken something from the company. Surely, somebody in the room had stolen a pencil or envelope at one time or other. He noted that even the best people in the company make mistakes. Then, in front of everyone, he publicly welcomed the three men back into the company.[12] Malcolm Rosser, former editor of the Howco publication, *The Cementer,* remembered the incident.

"Erle P. said, 'Well, nobody's perfect,' and gave all three their jobs back, and one of the three stayed in spite of that. I don't think the other two could actually face him. Somebody who had helped him cement a well in 1919, he always had a job for them."[13]

Halliburton was a diminutive man, but his energy and self-confidence made him seem larger than life. Nora Cunningham, an early Howco employee, described Halliburton's leadership style during the 1920s and 1930s.

"He often wandered through the shops and offices visiting with employees and asking questions about the work they were doing. On one such occasion, one of the newer employees remarked to an older hand, 'If that little pest doesn't quit bothering us at our work, we're going to get fired. Who is he, anyway?'

"His fellow worker replied, 'That's Erle Halliburton.' "[14]

From the very beginning, Howco turned a profit and stock dividends were impressive.

On March 15, 1925, Howco paid $30 per share. On October 1, it paid another $50. The following April, the dividend was $20, and four months later it was $75 per share. On January 1, 1927, the Howco dividend per share was $100.[15] Erle and Vida Halliburton collected dividends on 1,700 shares and did so in an era when income tax was a few pennies on the dollar.

Howco's first overseas venture was in 1926, when the company sold five fully outfitted cementing trucks to a British firm for use in Burma. From that point, the company's export business enjoyed increasing success.

Another venture that Halliburton established, independent of Howco, was the Halliburton Oil Well Cementing Company, Ltd., of Canada. In 1926, two of Erle's younger brothers, Paul and George Halliburton, went into business in the Turner Valley field in the Province of Alberta. With Erle's backing, they operated two steam-powered pump trucks and enjoyed increasing success. Tragically, George was killed in a 1936 truck accident. Erle filled the void by becoming vice president of the Canadian company. Howco would later buy the Halliburton Canadian business in 1948.[16]

Erle had become a wealthy man, and his wealth encouraged him to seek opportunities

Above: Erle Halliburton stands with friend and eventual neighbor Will Rogers around 1930. Erle's personal pilot, Bob Cantwell, stands to the right of Rogers.

Below: Erle, dressed in black, stands with pilot Bob Cantwell in 1928, in Duncan, Oklahoma. Charles Lindbergh's flight that year sparked Erle's interest in aviation.

STEPHENS COUNTY HISTORICAL MUSEUM

Erle's SAFEway planes flew to points east and west without radar, radios or current weather reports. The airline nevertheless maintained an impressive safety record.

to invest his assets outside the oil business. One such opportunity was in the developing aviation industry.

SAFEway

Since the mid-twenties, Halliburton had been flying from Duncan to the various distant drilling sites served by Howco, riding in the back seat of two-seater biplanes. His interest in air travel grew in 1927, when Charles Lindbergh flew *The Spirit of St. Louis* solo across the Atlantic, from Long Island, New York, to Paris. Convinced by that historic flight that air travel was commercially viable, Halliburton purchased eight Ford Tri-Motor

passenger planes and went into business as Southwest Air Fast Express, or SAFEway. The airline's busiest routes linked Tulsa, Oklahoma City, Wichita Falls, Abilene and Sweetwater.

Even though the planes were without radios or radar, and weather information was passed from airport to airport by telegraph, SAFEway's safety record was impeccable. The business ran into financial trouble during the Great Depression because few people could afford air travel.

Halliburton knew that the only way to keep SAFEway solvent was to win a contract with the United States Postal Service to fly airmail. SAFEway bid for an airmail contract but was refused because the bid was too low.[17] An incredulous Erle Halliburton went to Washington, determined to convince the government to reverse its decision. He spent weeks knocking on doors and talking with politicians and bureaucrats, but to no avail. From that moment on, Erle Halliburton distrusted

"those people in Washington," as he derisively referred to them. He sold the airline, and it merged with others to ultimately become American Airlines.[18]

The airline business led Halliburton toward another independent venture. He had been impressed by the strength and lightness of the aluminum alloy used for structural elements and for the skin of the Ford Tri-Motors. Using this alloy, he manufactured a line of luggage.[19] Today it is used widely, and though no longer owned by a Halliburton company, the line is known as Zero-Halliburton.

Fighting Against Imitators

Though Halliburton frequently boasted that he had started his own business by improving on the ideas of the Perkins Oil

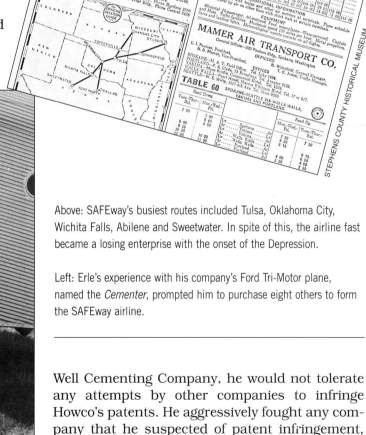

STEPHENS COUNTY HISTORICAL MUSEUM

Above: SAFEway's busiest routes included Tulsa, Oklahoma City, Wichita Falls, Abilene and Sweetwater. In spite of this, the airline fast became a losing enterprise with the onset of the Depression.

Left: Erle's experience with his company's Ford Tri-Motor plane, named the *Cementer*, prompted him to purchase eight others to form the SAFEway airline.

Well Cementing Company, he would not tolerate any attempts by other companies to infringe Howco's patents. He aggressively fought any company that he suspected of patent infringement, and he usually won.

The first such fight involved Halliburton's Concrete Mixer, also known as the Jet Mixer, which had received a patent on March 18, 1924.[20] When Halliburton learned that a group of

Caring For
Frank "Heavy" Kempf

From the beginning of the Halliburton Oil Well Cementing Company, Erle and his wife, Vida, considered employees a part of their family. They were committed to the workers' welfare and often took care of them when they were sick. In the 1949 issue of the *Cementer*, Vida revealed how seriously she and Erle felt about taking care of loyal workers.

"It was during this epidemic that Frank Kempf got smallpox. He was in a rooming house and had no one to care for him. So, I cooked his meals, and either Hubby or I took them to him and nursed him as best we could. Somehow, we managed to get him well and back to work.

Now the smallpox epidemic was over, but it left a typhoid epidemic in its wake. This meant boiling all the water that was used, and on that smelly, slow old kerosene stove it was a full-time job. Boil water late at night so the canvas water sacks could be filled for the men in the field the next day. ... We

felt that by cleaning them and boiling the water we were protecting our men from typhoid. This epidemic was over without the loss of one of our men."[1]

In another account, Vida and Erle took in employee Slats Endicott, who was run over by a cementing truck. The hospital had written off Endicott as a dead man when Erle's brother Paul offered to pay for treatment, Vida wrote.

"The hospital told [Paul] to take Slats off as he would be dead before morning anyway. Paul and one of the men who was asleep at the Bunk House carried the cot into the office which was inside Erle and Vida's small house, and now we had a hospital. We called

Dr. Williams out. We had several employees now and yet the relationship seemed more like one big family, than that of employer and employee. Slats was a member of that family so I took care of him. He was seriously ill for a long time and not able to move. Finally he got well, and when he tried to get up, it was discovered that one of his arches was broken. This set him back again, but not for long. He finally got well and remained working for Howco until he recently passed on."[2]

blacksmiths in Guthrie, Oklahoma, had copied his design and was manufacturing the mixer, he promptly filed suit for infringement.

The day before the trial date, Halliburton and his attorney, Leonard Lyon, arrived in Guthrie and checked into a local hotel. In the evening, they descended the stairs from their second-floor rooms, on their way to the main-floor dining room. But before they reached the landing, four burly men blocked their path. Halliburton and Lyon, thoroughly outweighed by these four thugs, retreated to their rooms, where they meekly ordered sandwiches for dinner.

Halliburton telephoned one of his employees, a formidable cementer named Frank "Heavy" Kempf, and told him to travel to Guthrie that night. The next morning the four men were again at the bottom of the stairs when Halliburton, Lyon and Heavy Kempf appeared. Heavy looked at the roughnecks and said, "Well, if you are going to start anything, start it now, and if that ain't soon enough, set your watches ahead." The

STEPHENS COUNTY HISTORICAL MUSEUM

four men retreated, and Halliburton and Lyon made it to court on time. The trial was over before noon, with the judge finding in favor of Halliburton and putting the infringers immediately out of business.[21]

Sometimes the infringer was considerably more powerful than the upstarts in Guthrie. In 1926, Howco filed suit against Standard Oil of Louisiana, charging that the company had infringed on Howco's exclusive rights — in states other than California, Arizona, Nevada and Oregon — to use the Oil Well Cementing Process, patented by Perkins. Standard settled the case by paying Howco $75 for every oil well deeper than 200 feet that it cemented with this patented process. This settlement remained in effect until December 12, 1928, when Howco's exclusive rights to the Perkins process expired.[22]

Above: A 1925 photograph of a Halliburton crew: left to right, A.H. "Dago" Baugh, Dick Blevins and Charles Russell.

Below: By the late 1920s, the Halliburton Oil Well Cementing Company yard and shops in Duncan took up more than a city block.

HALLIBURTON CO.

The Simmons Drill Stem Tester

In 1926, Erle Halliburton heard about an invention that seemed likely to be valuable to an oil well servicing company. It was on display in the lobby of the Garrett Hotel in El Dorado, Arkansas. Halliburton went to El Dorado and viewed the invention. He was so impressed that he decided to seek out the inventor, John Simmons, and found him there in El Dorado. Halliburton and Simmons sat down that evening for a few drinks and some discussion, and Simmons left the meeting with a check from Halliburton for $15,000 as payment for the invention. Thus Erle Halliburton acquired the Simmons Drill Stem Tester, a device that saved oil companies time, effort and money in the search for oil.

Inside a Howco shop in the late 1920s, employees work on oil well cementing plugs.

Once down the well hole, a valve in the device would open and close to capture fluid and bring it to the surface for analysis. The drill stem tester was clearly a valuable device, capable of saving considerable time and expense. Halliburton brought the device back to Duncan, where he and his chief engineer, A.D. Stoddard, tested it in a hole owned by George Pace. The test was a success, but unfortunately, Stoddard and Halliburton could not remove the device from the hole in the ground. Pace sued, claiming that he had expected the well to be a fine producer, and Ben Saye, general counsel for Howco, settled the case out of court. The device remains in that hole to this day.

Chief Engineer Stoddard altered the Simmons design and built another device. This one worked perfectly, and with it, Halliburton established a drill stem testing company, separate from Howco. A 1941 Halliburton Oil Well Cementing Company catalog offered a brief perspective on the stem tester, which became known as the Stop Cock Halliburton Tester after it was acquired by Howco.

"Before the discovery of the Howco method of testing the productivity of a formation while drilling a well, it was necessary to set a string of casing above the formation and then bail out the drilling fluid. Oil, water or gas flowed from the formation into the empty casing, thereby giving the operator a productivity test, both as to kind and quantity of production.

"If the test by the casing-bailing method showed oil or gas in commercial quantities, the expense of setting the casing was not wasted. But, more frequently, tests showed oil or gas in insufficient quantity, or salt water, or just plain dry. In those cases, the setting of casing was an expensive loss and deeper drilling was restricted because of the smaller hole which could be drilled below the casing.

HALLIBURTON CO.

"Therefore, the invention of a simple, effective and inexpensive method of testing the productivity of formations that does not require setting casing and bailing marks an important step in the art of drilling wells. This very desirable step was accomplished by a method first introduced to the trade in the spring of 1926 by Erle P. Halliburton."[23]

In 1932, Howco purchased the drill stem company outright. There would, however, be a lengthy legal battle over patent rights on the Simmons Drill Stem Tester, lasting until the end of the decade with a decision by the U.S. Supreme Court.[24]

When Halliburton applied for a patent on the device in 1926, others were applying for patents on similar devices. The Patent Office set up something called an Interference Proceeding, in which all the patent applicants offered testimony explaining why the patent should be awarded to them. Halliburton needed John Simmons to testify that he had sold the device to Halliburton for $15,000, but Simmons had mysteriously disappeared. Halliburton's lawyer, Ben Saye, wrote a letter to Mrs. Simmons and received a discouraging reply. It seemed that Mr. Simmons had always wanted to travel, and with the money paid to him by Halliburton, he had departed on a tour

of the world. According to Babcock, Mrs. Simmons wrote:

"He was never a good husband, but he did give me money sometimes for myself and my large family. Now he has run off and left me entirely, and it is all Mr. Halliburton's fault."

Mrs. Simmons' next letter, addressed to Halliburton, thanked him for the generous check he had apparently sent her. Still, nobody could locate John Simmons.[25]

Meanwhile, Halliburton reluctantly prepared to testify at the Interference Proceeding without Simmons. He signed a statement about the date of invention, based merely on what Simmons had told him over drinks on the night of the purchase. Then, out of the blue, word of John Simmons arrived in a letter from Simmons himself. He was in Australia, had spent all his money, and was wondering if Halliburton could possibly send him enough cash to return to the States. Halliburton paid for Simmons' passage home, Simmons testified at the Interference Proceeding, and the Patent Office awarded priority of invention to the drill stem tester he had invented. Halliburton gave Simmons a job and sent him to work in Illinois. This, however, was not the end of the patent dispute.[26]

Among those who had contested the patent on the drill stem tester was a man named E.C. Johnston. Relying on the drill stem tester, Johnston had built up a thriving business testing wells in Texas. Even though patent rights had been awarded to Halliburton, Johnston continued to test wells with the drill stem technology.

Halliburton sued Johnston in federal district court. The court found in favor of Halliburton and

John Halliburton, shown above as a Cementer playing in left field, would eventually succeed his brother Erle as Howco president.

enjoined Johnston, forcing him to stop using the tester. Johnston, however, found a way to get around the court ruling. Though he was not allowed to use the tester, his brother, M.O. Johnston, in California, had no such order against him. E.C. Johnston shipped his tools to his brother, and M.O. was soon engaged in a thriving well-testing business.[27]

It is possible to imagine steam issuing from the ears of Erle Halliburton. Despite all the trouble he had endured to secure rights to the stem testing patent, his patent continued to be infringed. Halliburton embarked on a letter-writing and legal rampage. Every oil company in California doing business with M.O. Johnston received a threatening letter from Halliburton. The letter angered the oil companies and put them on the side of M.O. Johnston. Halliburton

filed suit in a federal district court in California against M.O. Johnston, and also against one of the oil companies, Honolulu Oil Corporation.[28]

Erle Halliburton served as his own expert witness on the techniques of drill stem testing. He proved to be as dynamic on the witness stand as he was in business. On at least one occasion the judge felt compelled to instruct Halliburton to "Sit down! Sit down, I tell you! And stop pounding the bench with your fist!"[29]

The California court decided against Halliburton. Now two federal district courts were in opposition: the Texas court in favor of Halliburton, and the California court opposed. The next step for the case was the U.S. Supreme Court.[30] On April 17, 1939, after more than a decade of wrangling with the Patent Office and fighting in federal district courts, the Supreme

HALLIBURTON CO.

The Cementers, around 1930. Top row, left to right, Guy Simpson, Pop Laird, Brice Wininger, Peaches Davis, C.A. Parker, Dennis Assiter, John Jacobi and Dean Hanes. Bottom row: Raymond Emery, Jim Woods, Roy Tatum, Bob Cates, John Sharp, John Phipps and R.R. Emery. Bobby Cates was the batboy. The team played semi-professional baseball, winning the national championship in 1936.

Court held that the Simmons patent on drill stem testing, owned by Halliburton, was invalid. Infuriated by the decision, Halliburton remarked, "If the courts will not sustain my patents, I am not going to respect anybody else's."[31]

Meanwhile, Howco employees worked hard in the oil fields, laboratories and shops. When they had time off, they worked hard at having fun. The Howco semi-professional baseball team, the Cementers, was formed in 1927 after Erle purchased uniforms and a bus for the team. At first, the team was part of the local Twilight League, but it soon branched out to compete in state and national tournaments. Halliburton liked his relaxations but couldn't stand to lose, whether the game was on the ballfield or the oilfield. The Cementers played for 14 summers, winning the national semi-professional championship in 1936.[32] "He liked good Scotch whisky and good cigars, and hated the competition," said former Halliburton CEO John "Jack " Harbin.[33]

A 1930 oil well gushes wildly out of control.

CHAPTER THREE

Prosperity Amid Turmoil

"During the Depression, [Halliburton] hired 60 men to water a base-ball diamond, excavate for and put down sidewalks, clean out city culverts, and anything the city manager wanted done. He paid their wages himself because 'those fellows had to eat.' ... Many a doctor bill in Duncan has been paid for by Halliburton, because he knew a needy family's circumstances."

— Duncan Daily Banner, 1948[1]

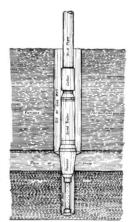

ON OCTOBER 29, 1929, the stock market plummeted to an unprecedented and spectacular loss. Black Tuesday, and the Great Depression that followed, turned a prosperous nation into a land of beggars and paupers.

Though the economic crisis seemed to touch every nook and cranny of American life, the Halliburton Oil Well Cementing Company remained profitable even during the worst years. The number of oil wells being drilled in the United States dropped dramatically, yet Halliburton was never in danger of going out of business.

In 1929, the year of the stock market crash that heralded the start of the Depression, 26,356 new oil and gas wells were drilled in the United States. Howco's net profit that year was $715,914.46. In 1931, with the nation deep in the Depression, the number of wells decreased to 12,432, and Howco's net profit dropped accordingly, to $286,980.85.

Yet in 1933, the very worst year of the Depression as measured by the Gross National Product, Howco's net profit actually increased to $449,282.66, even though only 12,312 wells were drilled. In 1934, the number of wells drilled increased to 18,197, and Howco's net profit exceeded $1 million for the first time. Not until 1937 did drilling exceed the 1929 level, with 31,622 wells drilled. That year, Howco's net profit exceeded $2 million.[2]

How did Howco succeed when so many other companies failed? Howco had built a strong reputation for reliable, high-quality work. It offered volume discounts. It enjoyed a virtual partnership with major oil companies, whose representatives sat on the Howco board of directors. Howco's success also had to do with its innovations in materials and methods. The company poured hundreds of thousands of dollars into research and development, and continually brought new technology to the cementing industry.

Erle P. Halliburton was acutely aware that other people did not share his good fortune. Though he had a gruff exterior, Erle was an exceedingly generous man. During the Great Depression, he provided jobs and financial support for many residents of Duncan, recalled the local newspaper in a 1948 article.

"During the Depression, [Halliburton] hired 60 men to water a baseball diamond, excavate for and put down sidewalks, clean out city culverts, and anything the city manager wanted done. He

A drawing of a Howco drill stem tester from a 1937 export catalog.

paid their wages himself because 'those fellows had to eat.' ... Many a doctor bill in Duncan has been paid for by Halliburton, because he knew a needy family's circumstances."[3]

Bob Diggs Brown, who later became vice president of sales and advertising for Howco, grew up in Duncan during the Depression and remembers how grateful the town was to have the Halliburton Oil Well Cementing Company.

"When I was about 12 or 13 years old, I heard people talking about the Depression and how fortunate we were to have 70 or 80 employees working for this Halliburton."[4]

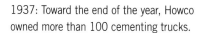

Above: A fleet of Howco's acidizing trucks in the 1930s.

Left: A 1937 lab at Duncan. Labs such as this helped to develop new ways to extract oil with the help of acid.

1934: In the midst of the Depression, Howco's net profit tops $1 million for the first time.

1937: Toward the end of the year, Howco owned more than 100 cementing trucks.

1934: Howco celebrates its 10th anniversary by throwing a party for the town of Duncan.

1938: Howco performs first offshore cementing job.

Technological Innovations

In January 1930, Howco established a chemical laboratory at Duncan under the direction of Hayden (Count) Roberts. Situated on the second floor of a building used to store trucks, the laboratory was used primarily to test the properties of various cement mixes. It was a modest beginning for what would become the industry's premier laboratory for chemical research and development, but Bob Diggs Brown said Halliburton knew research and development was vital to Howco's future.

"Roberts was the first chemist Mr. Halliburton had hired because Mr. Halliburton always believed that scientific advancement and chemistry were a vital part of the service business."[5]

In 1933, Roberts began investigating the use of acid to break down oil-bearing formations. He found that hydrochloric and other types of acid injected under pressure into limestone or carbonate formations would enlarge the pore spaces, opening larger passages that would allow the oil to flow more freely. This service, known as acidizing, was first offered by Howco in 1934. In years to come, acidizing would be as common to Howco services as the cementing of wells.[6]

Another item introduced in 1934 was a tester specifically designed for deep and crooked holes. Known as the J-Tester, the device was similar to the earlier Stop Cock Tester in that it collected fluid from the well so that it could be analyzed from the surface, revealing clues about the quantity and location of oil. The J-Tester, however, featured a differential piston that automatically compensated for varying depths, and a poppet-type valve. The value of this innovation was discussed in Halliburton catalogs.

"In producing fields, as well as in wildcat wells, by means of this testing method, many formations are being proven good producers, which would be passed as too doubtful in appearance to risk the expense of a test by setting casing. Also, there are cases in which a core taken in a well resembles cores taken in the productive formation in offset producing wells, but when this formation is tested, either water or an insufficient quantity of oil or gas is found."[7]

Also in 1934, Howco began offering electrical well logging services.[8] In this method, electrodes

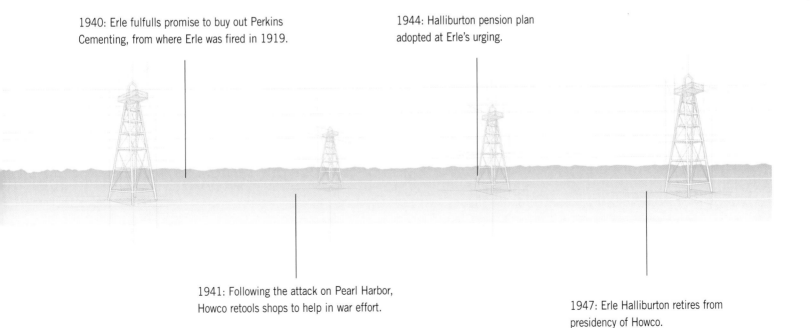

1940: Erle fulfulls promise to buy out Perkins Cementing, from where Erle was fired in 1919.

1944: Halliburton pension plan adopted at Erle's urging.

1941: Following the attack on Pearl Harbor, Howco retools shops to help in war effort.

1947: Erle Halliburton retires from presidency of Howco.

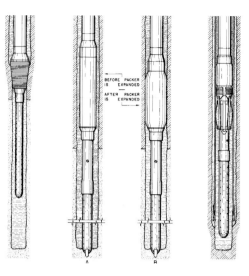

were lowered into a well hole via an electric cable to measure the resistance of formations. Because various formations and the amount of oil they hold have distinctive electrical characteristics, this method helps determine the location of oil-bearing formations. Electrical well logging would eventually lead to a legal confrontation between Howco and a major competitor, Schlumberger, a multi-

national oil field service company founded in 1919 and managed from Paris by Conrad Schlumberger.

Schlumberger's principal service was wireline logging, a process that could detect the presence or absence of oil through the use of a probe that measured electrical resistance beneath the earth's surface. In 1938, Schlumberger filed suit against Howco on two patents related to electrical measuring devices that could detect oil-producing formations in oil wells. Hoping to settle out of court, Schlumberger representatives traveled to Houston to meet with Erle Halliburton.

Above: A selection of oil well productivity testers advertised in the 1937 export catalog.

Right: A specimen chart taken from a pressure element in a Howco oil productivity tester.

Below: The first well logging truck.

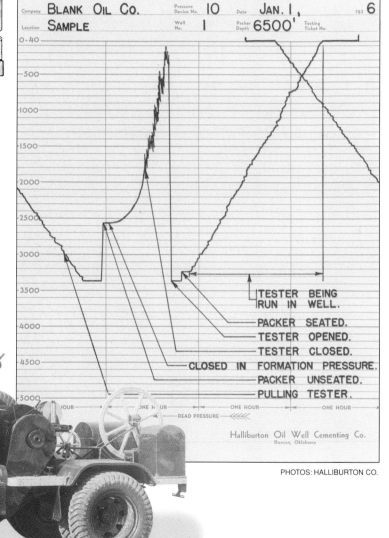

STEPHENS COUNTY HISTORICAL MUSEUM

The meeting was attended by several senior officials from each company. It began amiably enough, with a few words from a Schlumberger spokesman who expressed the necessity of settling the suit. All eyes turned to Halliburton, waiting for his response. Erle stood up, and in a voice that thundered through the quiet board room, said, "I'll tell you how to settle this lawsuit. You Frenchmen go back where you belong, and let Americans run American businesses!" That particular meeting came to an abrupt end, but the lawsuit continued into the 1940s. When it was finally settled on appeal, Howco emerged as the victor.[9] Schlumberger would remain one of Howco's most formidable competitors in the oil well industry. Former *Cementer* editor, Malcolm Rosser, recalled Erle's ill-will toward Schlumberger.

"He always resented the fact that while we were undoubtedly the leaders in cementing, in high-pressure pumping, Schlumberger dominated well logging. They dominated well log-

ging to more of a degree than we dominated cementing. He always wondered why."[10]

Early Success

In 1934, Howco celebrated its 10th anniversary with a day long celebration that included swimming in Duncan's municipal pool, leased from the city for the day, a bathing beauty revue for girls 2 to 10 years old, a swimming and diving contest for the boys, and music by the Halliburton Nut Busters Band. A picnic supper was served to an estimated 500 people.

In a single whirlwind decade, Howco had completed more than 75,000 oil well cementing

Above: Halliburton crews traveled hundreds of miles to do a job. Here, a crew works on a cementing job in California in the early 1930s.

Right: A 1938 Howco cementing truck could mix large amounts of cement right on the job site.

HALLIBURTON CO.

jobs. The company had grown from 57 employees to 432, and the volume of business had expanded accordingly.[11]

By the end of 1937, Howco owned more than 100 cementing trucks, most of which were painted red. The trucks were equipped with galvanized iron cement vats, cement mixers, pumps, measuring devices and an incredible assortment of rugged tools. In addition to headquarters in Duncan, Oklahoma, the company had a machine shop, a truck shop, an engine shop, an electric shop, a blacksmith shop, an erecting shop and a woodworking shop, all under one roof.

Thanks to Erle, cementing had become standard practice on oil wells in the United States and abroad. Once considered a luxury, it was universally recognized as a reliable way to stabilize the oil well, protect the oil from contamination, and protect nearby drinking water supplies. In addition to a rapidly expanding

HALLIBURTON CO.

export business, Howco was doing business in 17 states, as far west as California and as far east as Pennsylvania; as far south as Louisiana and as far north as Wyoming.[12]

Methods and equipment had improved substantially in the 13 years that Howco had been in business. The company now offered specialized services such as multiple stage cementing and full hole cementing. Multiple stage cementing, used on deeper holes, made it unnecessary to pump all the cement down the entire length of the casing and up behind the casing. "By splitting the total amount of cement into separate stages going out at different levels, the time is materially reduced during which the cement is subjected to the high temperatures from deep formations," noted a 1937 catalog.[13] Full hole cementing was touted as a "modern method of accomplishing an aim almost as old as the industry itself — larger drainage service — and at the same time reducing the initial investment per well and yielding greater ultimate profit."[14]

Halliburton was fiercely protective of the patents earned by his company. From the middle 1920s into the 1940s, Howco patent attor-

---

Above: A four–wheel drive cementing truck from the late 1930s. This fully equipped cementing truck cost $15,500.

Center: Oil crews use the Full Hole Cementing device to cement oil wells as deep as 9,600 feet.

neys continued to work feverishly, either filing or defending against suits, frequently settling out of court or actively litigating. In 1931, Howco brought suit against Owen Oil Well Cementing Process, Inc. in U.S. District Court, Western District of Oklahoma, for infringement of Howco's Concrete Mixer. The point of contention was the velocity of the water used in the Owen mixing process, a velocity that appeared to be in violation of the Howco patent. The suit was settled when Howco acquired several patents for $15,000, in effect dissolving Owen Oil Well Cementing Process, Inc. The Owen Cementing Corporation was formed in its stead, and Howco allowed it to use the Howco cementing process for $15 per well.[15]

Growth and Innovation

In 1938, Howco men floated a barge from Louisiana into the Gulf of Mexico, to a rig in the Creole field, and performed its first offshore cementing job.[16] Though it was a new procedure, the Howco crew was in familiar territory. For more than a decade, Howco men had been cementing wells in the swamps and marshes of Louisiana, working out of camps established by Howco in Thibodaux, Lafayette and Lake Charles. Working conditions were generally miserable, with boots sucking in the mud and trucks sinking into it. Mosquitos, snakes, heat and humidity enhanced the overall ambiance. In the swamps, Howco crews would drive their trucks onto shallow-draft barges, load the barges further with bags of cement, and float the barges to the site of the well.

Howco's first offshore cementing job was the beginning of what, after World War II, would become a fleet of oil well service ships.

As Howco's export business continued to grow, Halliburton decided in 1940 to establish an international office. Howco sent men and equipment to Venezuela to establish Howco's first overseas operation. The Howco board of directors had been advised that Venezuelan law was more favorable to domestic corporations than to foreign corporations, so on July 1, 1940, it authorized the use of $25,000, equivalent to 80,000 Venezuelan Bolivars, to form Compania Halliburton de Cementacion y Fomento.[17] Foreign operations were soon expanded to Colombia, Ecuador, and Peru. "It is not my idea to just make money out of a country," Erle Halliburton said, "but to develop it and to raise the economic standards of its people."[18]

Above: An oil well in the Gulf of Mexico, off the coast of Louisiana, in the early 1940s.

Halliburton trucks being moved by barge in Louisiana. The Louisiana oil project was Howco's first offshore cementing job.

ROBERT YABNAII RICHIE/
HALLIBURTON CO.

Above: The upper management of Halliburton in the
1930s: W.R. McClendon, Blackie Clark, L.B. "Preach"
Meaders, Jimmy Creed and Ty Wallace.

Right: Howco's superintendents gather from all over the country for a
photograph at their annual meeting, held in Duncan in 1938.

STEPHENS COUNTY HISTORICAL MUSEUM

Milestones

The year 1940 was a landmark year for the Halliburton Oil Well Cementing Company. On March 7, at a special meeting of the Howco board of directors at the Magnolia Building in downtown Dallas, Erle Halliburton's prediction that someday he would buy out Perkins Cementing, Inc., came true. The five board members present, Halliburton, John R. Suman, W.B. Pyron, Ben F. Saye and L.S. Sinclair, authorized the expenditure of $550,000 to "purchase and acquire all and singular the property, rights, privileges, franchises and assets" of Perkins Cementing, Inc. of California, and the Perkins Oil Well Cementing Company of Wyoming. The company at which Erle Halliburton had been introduced to the oil well cementing business, and from where he had been fired 22 years earlier, was now owned by his corporation.[19]

Also in 1940, Howco introduced an important new method to the oil well cementing business. By now, wells were being drilled deeper and into hotter zones. Various additives, developed in the labs at Duncan, had to be mixed with cement so that the slurries pumped into the wells could flow and set in whatever manner might be appropriate to the varying extremes of the well hole. Cement had always come in sacks, which were not only difficult to handle at 94 pounds each, but were inadequate for achieving a precise and consistent mixture of additives with the cement. Howco introduced a method called bulk cementing with the opening of a plant in Salem, Illinois. This new method was the beginning of ready-mix concrete, common today wherever cement is used.[20]

World War II

While 1940 had been a year of productive and sensible advancement for Howco, and of a kind of poetic achievement for Erle Halliburton with the acquisition of Perkins, 1941 would be a year of unpredictable changes. The following letter gives an indication of those changes.

Right: Howco workers building bulk cementing tanks in Bakersfield, California in June 1940. Such structures could be assembled quickly.

Below: The same California bulk cementing facility, completed in 1940. Bulk cementing was the beginning of ready–mix concrete, used today in construction projects.

HALLIBURTON CO.

Fort Bliss, Texas
June 21, 1941

Halliburton Oil Well Cementing
Company
Drawer 471
Duncan, Oklahoma

Gentlemen:

On account of the possibility of having to remain in the military service longer than one year, I hereby tender my resignation as a Director of the Halliburton Oil Well Cementing Company, with the definite request that Mr. Joe Russell, of the Gulf Oil Corporation, Houston, Texas, be made a director in my stead.

Yours very truly,

Walter B. Pyron[21]

On the day this letter was written, World War II was raging across the Atlantic. The Germans occupied Western Europe and North Africa. The day after this letter was written, Germany invaded Russia. The United States had cut off oil supplies to Japan to protest the nation's merciless aggression against China. Desperate to secure oil and other materials, Japan bombed Pearl Harbor, sinking or seriously damaging five American battleships, 14 other ships and killing more than 2,000 Americans. Within four days, the United States declared

STEPHENS COUNTY HISTORICAL MUSEUM

war on Japan and her Axis partners, Italy and Germany. America had joined the horrible fury of world war, and the possibility of Mr. Pyron remaining in the military service longer than one year would become a certainty.

In the next four years, many Howco men would be away at war, and Howco shops would work not only on the production and maintenance of oil field service equipment but also on the production of war materials. Halliburton made a personal contribution to the war effort in the form of his yacht, the Vida, which he donated to the military for use as a floating weather station in the far Pacific.[22]

While Howco continued to produce cementing equipment, the company expanded its shops at Duncan to produce gun mount bearings for the U.S. Navy. Howco engineers and technicians also produced electrical and mechanical equipment for the Aviation School of Medicine in San Antonio, and also electrical devices for ships. Howco expanded its engineering department to include a War Products Engineering Section. Out of this section Howco contracted to produce jigs, fixtures and dies for the Boeing plant in Wichita, Kansas, and these parts were used in the production of B-29 Super Fortress bombers. Beech Aircraft used the Howco Inspection Department to check aircraft parts. And Howco, in a project most in line with its expertise, developed a soil/cement process used by the Army Air Corps for landing strips.[23]

One of the materials that was most precious to America during the war was, of course, oil. Howco provided a tremendous number of products and services that made it easier to access and control oil production. Howco had refined well cementing significantly since it first went into business. The company now used retarded-set cements, which made it possible to fully cement the well before any of the cement hardened. To maximize oil flow, Howco offered gun perforating. Once the well was cemented, a cylindrical device, with holes for projectiles to pass through, was lowered into the hole. Once lowered, the device would fire steel projectiles through the casing and cement and into the oil-bearing formation, where it would allow oil to flow.

Products offered by Howco included high-pressure mobile pumping equipment; dump bailers, used to dump special material to seal, plug or tamp explosives into a well; the Echometer; retrievable cementers; calipers, used to measure the diameter of a wellhole; cement additives; and downhole tools.

With the acquisition of the Perkins company and its territory, Howco had expanded to the West Coast and the Rocky Mountains. The company was working at more varied tasks and over a greater geographic area than ever before.

These efforts were the topic of discussion at the July 1, 1943 meeting of the board of directors. At the meeting, Erle Halliburton noted that the workweek had increased from 54 to 60 hours, experienced personnel had been lost to the armed forces, and the duties and responsi-

O.L. Morisett in the Duncan laboratory. Labs such as these developed the formula that would evolve into ready–mix concrete.

Right: A Howco employee uses an Echometer to measure the depth of an oil well.

Center: A 1930s oil well pressure measuring device. An oil well needed to have the correct pressure for a smooth flow of oil to avoid an agonizing trickle or an out–of–control spray.

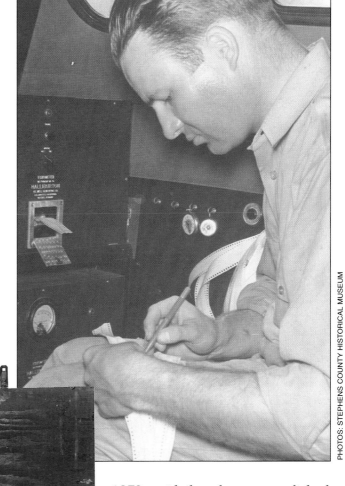

bilities of the corporate officers had increased. For these reasons, he proposed a pay increase for the company's officers. The salaries of the four vice presidents, John C. Halliburton (Erle's brother), A.D. Stoddard, C.P. Parson and W.R. McClendon, increased from $10,066.56 per year to $11,400. The salary of the secretary-treasurer, L.D. Campbell, increased from $8,866.56 to $10,200. The salary of the assistant secretary treasurer, Hugh H. Leonard, increased from $4,200 to $6,000. Only the salary of the president, Erle Halliburton, did not increase, but remained at $11,400.[24]

During the war, Halliburton made sure that employees in the field and shops would be taken care of when they retired. Back in 1938, Halliburton had recommended the establishment of a retirement plan for employees. Officers agreed to study the idea and return to the 1939 stockholder meeting with a recommendation.[25] But there is no mention of a retirement plan in the 1939 stockholders' minutes. The retirement plan wasn't discussed again until the stockholder meeting of July 1, 1944, and once again, it was Erle Halliburton who brought up the topic.

On this occasion, Erle demanded that a plan "was to be investigated and adopted." At a special meeting of stockholders on December 20, 1944, the Halliburton Profit-Sharing Plan and the Declaration of Trust for the Halliburton Employee's Benefit Fund were established. Thereafter, Howco employees could look forward to a more comfortable income in their retirement.[26] Jack Harbin, who became Chairman of the Halliburton Company in 1972, said the plan accomplished two of Erle Halliburton's goals.

"That was just the thing that kept the company non-union. That profit-sharing plan paid an amount equal to 17 to 18 percent of your salary. I saw many people retire and take out enough money to live on, and the value in the fund never reduced over a period of 10 years. That was the greatest plan in the world."[27]

Malcolm Rosser, former editor of *The Cementer* and longtime advertising manager, agreed.

"He set up this benefit package which was pretty generous compared to most types of pension plans and so forth. A lot of us retired very comfort-

ably. Very comfortably. ... Actually, I used to think we were a bank disguised as an oil field service company. There was a time when the profits were rolling from right to left. Everybody benefited."[28]

Howco spent a considerable amount of its own capital to finance the facilities and tooling required for war production. Although taxpayer money was available through federal defense plant loans, Howco never accepted a dime of it. Halliburton loathed the idea of taking money from the government because he loathed the idea of giving it to the government.[29] He built Howco up literally from the mud without help from the government, so he could not fathom why he should take money now that he was successful. In a 1949 issue of *The Cementer*, Halliburton railed against the rise in taxes and what he considered the decline of free enterprise.

"As the politicians have become more powerful, the operation of free enterprise and the things that we in our generation have tried to accomplish have become more difficult. ... If the trend continues ... the ingenuity and efforts of the next generation will be so sapped through taxation by the politicians that human progress will be reduced to the speed of a snail."[30]

The government and its way of wasting tax dollars was a frequent topic of conversation for Halliburton, whether he was giving a speech or just talking among friends. Halliburton passionately opposed what he perceived as creeping socialism and the redistribution of income. Bob

Diggs Brown said Halliburton would often wander through the offices and shops, ask how everyone was doing, then launch into a discussion about politics and business.

"He'd chitchat about a lot of different things like being conservative, about the waste of government spending money, taxes so dad-gum high that a 'guy like Bob Diggs over here could never, with taxation, reach the plateau of being an entrepreneur.' He was very radical and very outspoken on his political position."[31]

Post-War Growth

When the war ended, Howco was ready for a major expansion. Though much of the equipment had already been purchased during the war, Howco did not have the funds to pay for new facilities. Specifically, Howco needed $752,000 to expand bulk cementing

Above: A.D. Stoddard, chief engineer of Howco. Stoddard improved on the Simmons drill stem tester, a more accurate and cost-effective way to measure the amount of oil in a well. Halliburton formed a separate company to sell the tester.

Right: The Halliburton Oil Well Cementing Company office building in the 1940s. The building was a far cry from the days when Erle Halliburton ran the company with his wife, Vida, from their cramped, one-room house.

PHOTOS: STEPHENS COUNTY HISTORICAL MUSEUM

to the Gulf Coast, both inland and along the waterways; $640,000 to extend foreign operations, principally to Saudi Arabia; $2,270,000 for new equipment and supplies in the United States; and $600,000 to provide labor and materials for an export sales order. At the July 1, 1946, directors meeting, the directors authorized Erle Halliburton, president, and L.D. Campbell, secretary-treasurer, to borrow $3 million from Republic National Bank of Dallas.[32]

With this injection of capital, expansion was under way, most notably in south Louisiana. Howco bought an old shipyard at Harvey, Louisiana, across the river from New Orleans. Docks and shops were constructed. Howco purchased five military surplus Landing Craft Tanks, known as LCTs, which were outfitted with pumps and bulk tanks that could hold about 25,000 pounds of cement. These enormous carriers, big enough to carry trucks and heavy supplies of cement, became the first Howco fleet of marine servicing and cementing units.

In increasing numbers, oil companies were building offshore platforms. Howco provided service to these companies by building skid cementing units, which were essentially portable tanks and pumps that could be towed on a barge to the platform and

Erle Halliburton with his wife, and partner, Vida. Vida Halliburton once gave her wedding ring to Erle to pawn so he could meet the payroll. Vida eventually got the ring back.

installed upon it. These were either sold or leased to the drilling companies, though they were operated by Howco crews.[33] Ed Paramore, a longtime Howco employee and eventual Howco president, said Erle had sent him to south Louisiana in 1947 to find a way to cut costs.

> *"I said, 'Mr. Halliburton, I don't know anything about water.' ... But he said, 'That's exactly what I want down there, somebody who doesn't know anything about it. People down there think they know it all, and that's the reason we are losing our tail, so you're going.' "[34]*

While Howco was in the initial steps of huge expansion in 1947, Erle Halliburton was withdrawing from the day-to-day management of the

company. Though he was only 55 years old, Halliburton decided to retire from the presidency. His retirement involved a complicated financial transaction that took nearly one year to complete. In the end, 1,312,000 shares of Howco stock were made available to the public as common stock at a par value of $5 per share. Erle and Vida Halliburton sold 600,000 shares of stock to underwriters for this public offering. Another 50,000 shares owned by Erle and Vida Halliburton were made available directly to Howco employees. The Atlantic Refining Company provided 50,000 shares to the underwriters.[35]

Erle's younger brother, John Halliburton, was promoted from vice president to become the second president of Howco. Erle Halliburton was

elected to a new position as chairman of the company and provided a salary that by contract could range between $26,500 and $43,450 per year. Erle's salary as president in 1946 had been $35,000. His brother, John, was earning $30,000 as vice president, and the company's other vice president, W.R. McClendon, was collecting $25,000. Two other vice presidents, Parsons and Stoddard, left the company in 1946.

Halliburton would, according to the language of the corporate minutes, "accept posi-

A Howco machine shop, where parts are manufactured for cement mixers, measuring lines, pumps and other machinery.

tions as director and/or officer of the Company as he may, from time to time, be tendered by the Board of Director of the Company." He could be fired on 30 days written notice, with severance pay of one-half of the maximum annual salary.[36] Although Erle planned to keep a much lower profile in Howco, he could not help but stay involved in some of his favorite pet projects, such as the opposed piston pump. Bob Diggs Brown described how Erle resurrected the project, which his brother John tried to postpone indefinitely.

"Mr. Halliburton had gotten the idea that an opposed piston pump would pump at high performance, and he wanted one designed and tested, and Roy (Edwards) was selected as the engineer to do this work. But during 1947 or 1948, the oil industry went down. John, being conservative, he shut it down. (Erle) came in one day and asks, 'Roy, how are we getting along on that pump?' Roy told him, "Mr. Halliburton, we shut down. We're not working on that.' He said, 'You sit here just a minute, Roy.' They went on 24 hour days to get the pump completed."

Bob Diggs Brown said the pump didn't work as well as Erle hoped and the project was shelved.[37]

For the most part, however, the era of Erle Halliburton was at an end. He carried with him the aura of a self-made man, the very model of independence and entrepreneurial drive. Erle didn't need to cater to an executive board. "We didn't have board meetings. Mr. Halliburton did not like them," said Jack Harbin.[38] But with Erle's semi-retirement, the more officious and cautious era of the accountant, the banker, and the corporate lawyer had begun.

"Our feeling, as we complete a quarter-century of service, is one of deep-felt appreciation." As the decade drew to a close, Howco celebrated its 25th year by commemorating workers who were with Erle Halliburton from the time the company incorporated.

CHAPTER FOUR

New Methods &
Global Expansion

" ... The industry that we started 25 years ago is still young, vigorous and capable of continued growth."

— Erle P. Halliburton[1]

ON THE EVENING of June 30, 1949, in the back yard of W.R. McClendon's home in Duncan, Oklahoma, a celebration was under way. It was the eve of the 25th anniversary of the incorporation of the Halliburton Oil Well Cementing Company, and the celebrants were 23 men who had worked for the corporation since the day it began.

Erle P. Halliburton, founder and chairman of the company, flew to Duncan from his home in Los Angeles to attend the festivities. Surrounded by his original employees, Halliburton blew out the candles on the anniversary cake. In an apron and a chef's white hat, W.R. McClendon presided over the large, brick barbecue in his back yard, preparing dinner for the "25-year men," as Halliburton referred to those present that evening. McClendon had been an independent cementer in Mexia, Texas, in 1923, when Erle P. Halliburton lured him to Howco as a cementer. In 1925, he became manager of Howco's Gulf Coast operations, and in 1942, he went to Duncan to serve as general superintendent of Howco's field operations. A year later he became vice president of field operations. At the time of the barbeque, he was a vice president and director of Howco. In 1950, he would succeed John Halliburton as Howco president.

Also present was Frank "Heavy" Kempf, Halliburton's first employee, hired February 1, 1920, at Wilson, Oklahoma. He had been the driver of cementing wagon Number One, with Erle P. Halliburton as his cementer. Now he was a fieldman at Beaumont, Texas. Kempf had rescued Halliburton and his attorney from the roughnecks at the hotel in El Dorado, Arkansas, when the Simmons Tester patent had been in dispute.

Claud A. Murray, who began in 1924 as a sweeper in the shops at Duncan and was now an assistant shops superintendent, was there, along with Charlie Pressly, who had started out as a field worker and teamster in 1924, and was now in charge of the field office in Wichita Falls. And Ty Wallace, who began in 1922 as a cementer's helper, then became a cementer and then a tester, and was now testing superintendent at Houston.[2] At the event, Erle described what he and his men had accomplished in 25 years of business.

"We have helped to create wealth in a greater measure than we have used it. We have

Oil painting of Erle P. Halliburton at the time of Howco's 25th anniversary in 1949.

HALLIBURTON CO.

With his trademark Scotch whisky in hand, Erle P. relaxes with some of his men at a Howco 25th Anniversary party.

1947: Super-Cementer proves its worth in
a muddy Oklahoma field.

1953: Erle P. Halliburton Day declared on May 1
in Erle's adoptive hometown of Duncan, Oklahoma.

1949: Napalm, gasoline, crude oil and sand are used
in Howco's first commercial hydraulic fracturing job.

1957: Erle P. Halliburton dies. Howco worth
$190 million with camps all over the world.

helped to make this mechanical age possible."[3]

Ed Paramore, a former president of Halliburton, was a comparative newcomer to the company, and knew he stood on the bruised and overworked shoulders of those who came before him. He described the feeling of respect he and other newcomers had for the "old-timers."

"The old-timers had built the company as much as anyone else. I think you may hear that from other people. Whether you do or not, that's the way it was. They had something, or the company wouldn't have grown as fast as it did."[4]

These men and the others at the barbecue that evening shared more than a passing familiarity with backbreaking work. They had hefted 94-pound sacks of cement and carried them from the warehouse to the wagon or truck, and then from the wagon or truck to the ground beside the well, where the sacks would form a pile as tall as a man, and then from the pile to the cutting table, where the contents of each sack would be entered, one by one, into the

mixer. These men drove night and day through every kind of weather on every kind of bad road to reach the next booming field. They worked in the dark and in the daylight, in the heat and in the cold, and in the seemingly endless mud. The grueling task of cementing wells had evolved over 25 years, and perhaps no change was more dramatic than the progress that had been made in equipment. Bigger changes were still in the future.

The Super-Cementer

In the early days of oil well cementing, the pumps used to push the cement down the well could deliver 600 pounds of pressure per square inch, more than enough for the comparatively shallow wells of the time. Over time, wells became deeper and increased pump pressure became necessary. By October 1944, when Howco began

HALLIBURTON CO.

The logo for the worldwide and world-respected Halliburton Oil Well Cementing Company.

1957: Howco purchases Welex, which pioneered jet perforation.

1960: Stockholders change the official name from Halliburton Oil Well Cementing Company to the Halliburton Company.

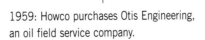

1959: Howco purchases Otis Engineering, an oil field service company.

Above: Weighing in at a powerful 22 tons, the Howco Super-Cementer provides the 12,000 pounds per square inch of pressure needed for deep well cementing.

Below: Howco's fleet of acidizing trucks, such as this one from the late 1940s, provided well stimulation services to customers in far-flung oil fields.

research and development on the Super-Cementer, maximum pump pressures ranged between 6,000 and 8,000 pounds per square inch. The T-10 series of pumps introduced by Howco was capable of producing more than 12,000 pounds of pressure per square inch. The Super-Cementer had two T-10 cementing pumps mounted on a truck equipped with two 123-horsepower diesel engines. Both engines could be used to either drive the truck or operate the cementing pumps.[5]

On the rainy morning of January 19, 1947, Howco's first Super-Cementer was introduced to the field at a site near Velma, Oklahoma. Bill Owsley, Howco's

chief engineer, parked the new truck next to W.F. Turner Well No. 5. With Owsley at the pump controls, a crew cemented the well. The Super-Cementer performed superbly. As it left the field, however, it got stuck in the mud. This was a fairly typical predicament, and the usual procedure was to pull the truck loose with a bulldozer. This time, however, Owsley put the two powerful diesels to the task, and the Super-Cementer rolled free.[6] In January 1948, Howco used the same T-10 pumps and diesel engines to build an acidizing unit. The acidizer was built on a YU four-wheel drive tractor, which pulled a 2,000-gallon tank mounted on a trailer.[7]

Hydraulic Fracturing

These new trucks represented a substantial advance in equipment. In 1949, the company introduced a substantial advance in methodology. At the end of World War II, the Stanolind Oil and Gas Company — a division of Standard Oil Company of Indiana — began developing a new method of stimulating oil and gas production in old wells. The method, which became known as hydraulic fracturing, called for pumping fluid into the well at extremely high pressure. The pressure opened cracks in the geologic formation, which became filled with the fluid. Carried with the fluid were "propping

agents" such as sand, walnut shells, or aluminum pellets which, when the hydraulic pressure was released, remained in the cracks and kept the cracks propped open. These cracks could then serve as channels through which oil and gas, previously captive in the rock, could flow. Stanolind used the trade name Hydrofrac for this process and granted Howco an exclusive license on its use.[8]

The investment was risky for Howco, with hundreds of thousands of dollars at stake. Bob Diggs Brown, former vice president of sales and advertising, said Howco's chief engineer, Bill Owsley, was convinced of the concept's potential.

"It wasn't a cheap prospect at a point in time when the process hadn't really been proved. But Bill Owsley, bless his heart, he's the man that had the concept that this was just right for Halliburton. He convinced Mr. Halliburton."[9]

A Howco plant in Salem, Illinois, would eventually be named Owsley Station for the chief engineer. Howco's first application of Hydrofrac was in 1949, on a well 4,882 feet deep, in Alma, Oklahoma. To hydraulically fracture the well, Howco used gasoline, napalm, crude oil, a breaking agent and 150 pounds of sand.[10] This was a modest beginning, given that future frac jobs could require more than 750,000 gallons of fluid, 2 or 3 million pounds of sand, and thousands of pounds of pressure per square inch.

STEPHENS COUNTY HISTORICAL MUSEUM

Above: A stream of innovative concepts and inventions flowed from the Duncan, Oklahoma, lab.

Below: Howco workers busy on a fracturing job. Fracturing enabled oil companies to reopen wells that appeared to have run dry long ago.

Hydraulic fracturing became enormously successful for all concerned. For Howco, it became a large part of its business, on par with cementing. For customers, the process rejuvenated scores of fields. One example of the benefits of the process occurred at the Gulf Naddell Ranch lease in West Texas. After numerous holes were drilled and found to be dry, the drilling company turned to hydraulic fracturing as a last resort before giving up on the field. As a result, 600 wells were eventually drilled, with each one producing between 500 and 700 barrels of oil per day.[11]

By many estimates, fracturing has increased recoverable oil and gas reserves in North America by as much as one-third.

Years of Expansion

In the years immediately following World War II, the demand for oil grew at an unprecedented rate, and Howco's oil field services were in greater demand than ever. Domestic demand was increasing by about 4 percent each year, and international demand was even

Above: A 1953 aerial view of the Halliburton yard and shops. New shop space, in the lower left, had been recently completed.

Inset: This new machine shop was completed in 1955, but Howco actually lost floor space due to a fire that year in another building.

stronger, increasing by more than 11 percent annually. Howco began an ambitious program of foreign expansion.

By 1951, Howco had service centers operating in Canada, Venezuela, Peru, Colombia, Saudi Arabia and Indonesia. By 1957, the company had wholly-owned subsidiaries in Mexico, Argentina and Italy; branches in Austria, West Germany, Cuba, Libya, Iran, Turkey and Alaska; and export sales offices in New York and Geneva, Switzerland. In 1951, Howco's foreign revenue was $7 million. By 1957, foreign revenue had nearly quintupled, to $32 million.[12]

By 1957, Howco operated 201 office and service locations in 22 states. Howco's total net revenue of $94.5 million in 1951 mushroomed to $194.1 million in 1957.[13] The headquarters in Duncan were also expanded, as a 1952 *Cementer* article explained.

"Work started early in September on a modern Technical Center at Duncan, President W.R.
McClendon announces. The six-acre Technical Center will house our engineering, laboratory and research facilities. Over one hundred engineers, chemists and other technical personnel will transfer to the center from Halliburton Plants One and Two.

"The first structure at the center will be the Engineering-Laboratory Building. The building will be an air-conditioned, two-story brick structure. The south wing will be especially designed for chemical research. ... First-floor rooms include Electrical Engineering, Bulk Cement Engineering, Cement-Hydrafrac Laboratories and administration offices. The second floor will have Organic and Analytical Chemistry Laboratories, conference rooms, technical library, General Engineering and Physical Chemistry Laboratories."[14]

This new building soon proved too small, and, in 1956, it was expanded with a three-story addition.[15] The Howco administration building, which had been built in 1935, expanded in 1942, 1944, and 1949; it was expanded again in 1954 and in 1956.[16]

In 1955, a 52,500 square-foot machine shop was completed near the administration building.

Almost before the paint was dry, the shop was found to be too small to meet the demands put upon it. To make matters more difficult, Howco actually lost floor space in 1955 when a fire destroyed the carpenter shop and the export shipping building. Planning was soon under way for the design of larger facilities.[17]

A New Generation of Leaders

These changes were taking place under the leadership of men who had been hired by Erle Halliburton and had risen through the ranks of Howco. In 1953, McClendon retired from the presidency, and the position was filled by L.B. "Preach" Meaders.[18] Meaders had started with Howco in 1928 as an equipment operator and had become a cementer, then a field supervisor, a fieldman and a district manager. In 1950, he succeeded McClendon as vice president for field operations, and three years later, he succeeded McClendon to the company's top post.[19] As president, and later as chief executive officer, Preach Meaders would oversee the phenomenal growth of Howco until his retirement in 1972.

PHOTOS: HALLIBURTON CO.

Above: Erle swaps ideas with protégé Preach Meaders, with hat, while they tour Howco's Gulf Coast facilities in the early 1950s.

Below: In appreciation for Erle Halliburton's accomplishments, the citizens of Duncan present Erle with a bust of himself.

Erle P. Halliburton was still chairman of Howco. On May 1, 1953, the citizens of Duncan, Oklahoma, honored him by declaring Erle P. Halliburton Day. At a dinner at the Duncan fairgrounds, attended by 400 friends and admirers and broadcast on local television, Halliburton was presented with a sculptured bust of himself. Oklahoma Governor Johnston Murray praised Halliburton as "an example of what a determined man can do under the great system of free enterprise in this country," and passed along congratulations from the governors of 22 other oil-producing states, plus Alaska, which was not yet a state.[20]

Erle passed away in 1957, six years after he lost his wife, Vida. When he died, Halliburton's personal fortune was worth millions of dollars and his 10,000-employee company was valued at more than $200 million. But Halliburton had achieved much more than material wealth. He had helped revolutionize the oil industry.

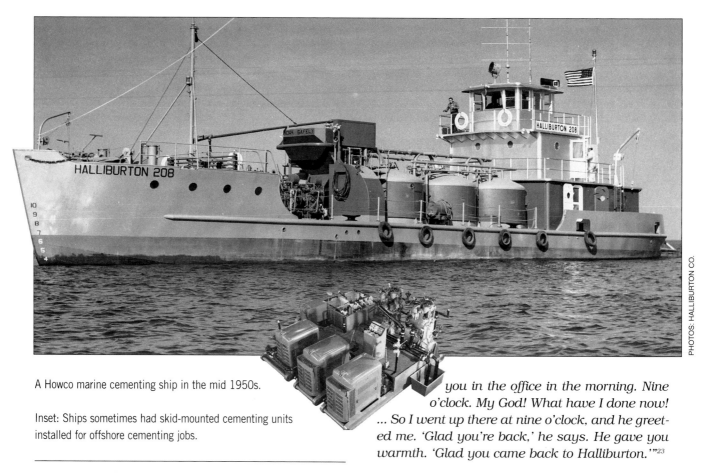

A Howco marine cementing ship in the mid 1950s.

Inset: Ships sometimes had skid-mounted cementing units installed for offshore cementing jobs.

you in the office in the morning. Nine o'clock. My God! What have I done now! ... So I went up there at nine o'clock, and he greeted me. 'Glad you're back,' he says. He gave you warmth. 'Glad you came back to Halliburton.'"[23]

In honor of his many achievements, Halliburton was inducted into the Oklahoma Hall of Fame shortly after his death.[21] About awards and recognition, Halliburton once said, "Early in life I formed a simple philosophy. All of the happiness I was going to get out of life would come through the hearts of others. I could have done nothing without the aid of my friends. When you honor me, you are honoring them."[22]

The men who worked for Halliburton never forgot his personal style of leadership or his devotion to his employees' well-being. Bob Diggs Brown recalled being called into Erle's office shortly after Bob Diggs Brown had returned to Howco from the Army in 1945. Erle wanted to ask Bob Diggs Brown a few questions related to the Middle East, where he had served.

"After the war, I hadn't been back over a month or two when Jimmy — that was his secretary — calls me and says Mr. Halliburton wants to see

There is a certain sense of the poetic in the timing of Erle P. Halliburton's death, the man who started a cementing company with a wagon and a borrowed team. In the final year or so of Halliburton's physical decline, his company also suffered a decline. The decline was little more than a bump in the road, yet it suggested a sympathy with the decline of the man. Howco would, of course, continue and succeed, endowed with the lingering spirit and philosophy of Erle P. Halliburton. The chairman's seat, which had been filled by Halliburton since he retired from the presidency in 1947, was taken over by Logan D. Campbell, who had been hired to handle the books for Howco in the 1920s.

A Strategy of Diversification

In 1957, Howco performed 20,000 fewer service jobs than it had in 1956, a decline of about 7 percent. Net income dropped by $796,823, a decline of about 4 percent from the previous year.

For the first time since the end of World War II, consumption of petroleum products in the United States had not increased, but had actually declined 7.4 percent, the sharpest drop since 1942.

Other sources of income were stronger than ever, however. Revenue from the sale of bulk materials such as cement and its additives, from equipment such as casing centralizers and wall cleaners, and from foreign operations, had increased by a combined average of 9 percent from 1956, cushioning the loss from domestic service jobs.

The drop in oil consumption prompted Howco executives toward a strategy of diversification. While Howco had acquired Perkins in 1940, and Halliburton Cementing of Canada in 1948, it had never acquired a company outside of the cementing field. On October 15, 1957, Howco exchanged 359,770 shares of its stock for the assets of Welex Jet Services, Inc., which specialized in an aspect of oil field service known as jet perforating. A wholly-owned subsidiary called Welex, Inc. was formed, and under this name, Howco joined its own wireline electric well services with Welex Jet Services.[24]

Welex had introduced jet perforating to the oil field after World War II. Jet perforating is a technique similar to gun perforating, except that in jet perforating, a shaped charge of high explosives is used rather than a simple projectile. The difference could be described as the difference between a simple bullet and a cannon shell. The idea for jet perforating, in fact, was inspired by the success of the World War II bazooka rocket, which featured a nose cone with a metal-lined, shaped charge. A small group of engineers in Fort Worth, Texas, including Henry Mohaupt and R.H. McLemore, realized that the principle of explosive

HALLIBURTON CO.

Above: A 1947 Welex Jet Perforating truck. Jet perforation used the same principle as a World War II bazooka rocket.

Inset behind the truck: The Welex logo.

Below: The Grumman Goose, capable of carrying six passengers. This plane was assigned to the New Orleans Division in the late 1950s. Pictured here is future Howco President Ed Paramore, standing in the middle, wearing a hat. Pilot D. Marsh stands to the left of Paramore and co-pilot L. Ybos stands to the right.

HALLIBURTON CO.

The famous fracturing crews, like the one on this HT-400 unit, stimulated wells all over the country, producing almost a third more oil from wells that were ready to be abandoned. Pictured here are: Ronnie Watkins, P.R. Fagan, John White, Bill Jiles, Paul Howell, James Johnston, J.F. Faught, David Parr, A.C. Stone and T.H. Lord. Standing in front are C.E. Taylor and J.H. Smith.

charges could work in oil wells. The engineers formed a company and manufactured the charges, but few in the industry bought them. The engineers then decided, in 1947, that the business would fare better if the product was delivered to the field as a service.

They formed Welex Jet Services, from WELEXplosives Inc., the name of the original manufacturing company. By 1957, when Howco acquired the company, Welex had about 400 employees, more than 30 service locations and the Jet Research Center, a manufacturing facility in Arlington, Texas, of which Howco bought a 50 percent share.[25]

In 1957, Howco introduced the HT-400 pump. For some years the venerable T-10 pump, which could pump up to 12,000 pounds of pressure per square inch and deliver about 10 barrels of slurry or acid per minute, had been the Howco workhorse. The HT-400, however, was a great improvement. It could pump up to 20,000 pounds per square inch and deliver as many as 24 barrels of slurry or acid per minute. The HT-

400 was the most powerful pump ever developed for cementing and fracturing.[26]

The oil business remained depressed into 1958, a year which also saw a general recession in the American economy. Revenue across the range of the company's products and services, foreign and domestic, declined. Net income in 1956, the last year of the post-war boom, was about $19.9 million. In 1957, net income edged down to $19.1 million, and in 1958, it slid to about $13.5 million. Because supplies of oil were abundant around the world, drilling dropped off everywhere. In Venezuela, drilling was down 38 percent, and if that weren't bad enough, the Venezuelan government enacted a retroactive income tax in December 1958 that nearly doubled Howco's tax burden in that country.[27]

Otis Engineering

The corporate emphasis in 1958 focused on costs. Between March 15 and August 15, working hours were reduced for 1,500 home office and plant employees. But by the end of 1958, the national recession was ending, and the oil business was also picking up.[28] Improvements continued into 1959, when well completions rose 4 percent and footage drilled increased 6 percent. Net income rose 9 percent, to about $15.8 million. The most notable event for Howco in 1959, however, was the acquisition of Otis Engineering Corporation, of Dallas, Texas.[29]

Otis Engineering was an oil field service and equipment company, specializing in the development of methods and the manufacturing of equipment that controlled pressures in oil and gas-producing wells. Otis equipment could prevent or stop blowouts, and could coax old wells back to life. The company had been founded by Herbert Otis, an engineer with the Arkansas Natural Gas Company. In 1928, a producing company in East Texas had advertised a reward of $1,000 to anyone who could control a certain wild well that had been blowing out of control for days. Accepting the challenge, Otis had run a small-diameter pipe into the well. The pipe circulated mud, and the mud brought the well under control. Otis pocketed the reward, patented the

Otis Well Tubing Process, and founded his own company, Otis Pressure Control.

The company's first base of operations was in Shreveport, Louisiana. In 1934, Otis moved to Dallas, where it could be close to the large oil fields of Texas and Oklahoma. By 1959, Otis had changed its name to Otis Engineering Corporation and was operating from six division offices — in Oklahoma City; in Lafayette, Louisiana; and in Houston, Odessa, Longview and Corpus Christi, Texas. Tools were manufactured and trucks were equipped at the Dallas facility. Otis operated outside the United States through subsidiaries in Canada and Venezuela, and through a sales office in Switzerland.[30]

The negotiations to purchase Otis were more complicated than those conducted to buy Welex. Former Howco Chairman Jack Harbin worked on both deals when he was senior vice president of finance. He said Herb Otis Jr., son of owner Herb Otis, wanted to remain in charge of the company and had scuttled an earlier deal. Harbin said L.B. "Preach" Meaders, a former Howco director, and the two Otis men sat down to discuss the demands.

"Herb Jr. presented his demands, and Preach Meaders said that was our final offer. 'We're going to buy the company. We will run it. ... Herb, if you do a good job then you've got the job. But no more. Either accept it or forget it.' So, Mr. Otis accepted that. ... Herb Jr. ... quit Otis of his own accord at a later date."[31]

Otis Engineering embodied many of the traits that Meaders and other Erle Halliburton protégés respected, such as an almost paternalistic concern for its employees. Karen S. Stuart joined Halliburton in 1965 and recently retired as vice president of administration. She was acquainted with Herb Sr., and his philosophy.

"He was a wonderful man. ... In the old days of Otis, the company was not able to make the payroll, and Mr. Otis met the payroll out of his personal funds to preserve the employees' welfare. ... He also liked to become familiar with the customer's problem, and mull over how to get that problem solved."[32]

While Halliburton's oil well services and products addressed the needs related to the drilling of wells, Otis's expertise was in keeping a well from going wild and in optimizing production of an existing well. With Welex, and now Otis, Howco was able to provide virtually all oil well services required by production companies.

Halliburton Company

By 1960, the Halliburton Oil Well Cementing Company had grown far beyond its roots. With the services of Welex and Otis, and with Howco's own expansion over the years into fracturing, acidizing, testing and the manufacturing of a

Above: The Otis Engineering logo. Otis was acquired in 1958 by Howco.

Right: The entrance to the new Halliburton Executive Offices in Dallas, established in 1961.

HALLIBURTON CO.

variety of service tools, the cementing of oil wells no longer accurately described the company. Howco management proposed to the stockholders at their annual meeting in June 1960 that the name of the company be changed to Halliburton Company. The new name was approved by the stockholders and became effective July 5, 1960.[33]

The name change became increasingly appropriate as Halliburton continued to grow beyond its original business. In 1960, the company expanded into grouting, a process of pumping cement or other materials into permeable or loose rock formations to reduce or eliminate leaks. This process was used on dams and mine shafts, for example, or to shore up the footings of foundations. The company applied its oil well stimulation processes to the stimulation of water wells.

Such diversification finally became an institution within Halliburton in 1960 with the formation of the Special Products Division. For the first time, equipment that had been developed for the oil field was marketed to other industries. For example, the Lo-Torq valve, developed to control high pressure during cementing and fracturing, was found to be useful in refineries, chemical plants and mills. One new product was completely unrelated to the oil well service industry: the FreightMaster, a hydraulic, shock-absorbing coupler for rail cars, which reduced damage to goods shipped by rail.[34]

The diversification didn't stop the company from continuing to lead the industry in the development of oil field equipment. In 1960, Halliburton Company introduced a mechanical and electrical system for controlling the proportions and density of materials used for fracturing. The system was automatic and mounted on skids, so it was easy to use right at the well site. Halliburton also built an experimental fracturing truck equipped with a gas turbine engine. The truck showed promise when tested in the field, and it drew the interest of the industry when displayed that year at the Permian Basin Oil Show in Odessa, Texas.[35]

A Continuing Emphasis on Research

Research facilities were now vast, especially when compared to the small laboratory built

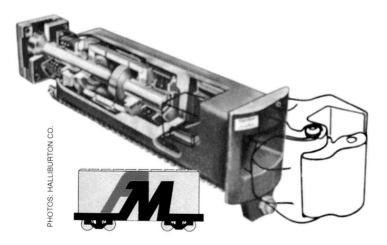

PHOTOS: HALLIBURTON CO.

Above: Logo of the Pressure Grouting Division, established in 1963, which introduced the mobile chemical pumping unit to perform grouting services in formerly inaccessible areas.

Center: One of the many products available from Halliburton in the 1960s: the Lo-Torq Valve.

Left: The FreightMaster Division developed products that made the bumpy and cargo-damaging ride of freight trains a little less rough. Pictured is FreightMaster's Cushioning Draft Gear and division logo.

HALLIBURTON CO.

some 30 years earlier over the garage in Duncan. In 1960, there were 413 employees at the Duncan Technical Center, and $4.8 million was spent on chemical and engineering research.[36]

Welex was particularly active. In 1959, Welex formed a division known as Welex Electronics Corporation. By 1960, the new division was operating profitably, doing research and manufacturing as a defense contractor. Its research was far ranging, branching into magnetic fields, radiation, and the firing and guidance systems for missiles. The division also built parts for communications, radar and air traffic control systems.[37]

Otis Engineering was also expanding, with top priority given to mechanical and electrical research and development. In 1961, Otis moved into a new facility so impressive that it was selected by *Factory Magazine* as one of the top 10 plants of 1963.[38]

One of the most notable events of 1961 was the company's decision to move its executive offices from Duncan to Dallas. Chairman Logan D. Campbell explained the move in a letter to employees. "The board of directors is of the opinion that we will be able to do a better job of building a bigger and better company by being farther removed from the day-to-day routine of the business."[39]

Another explanation appeared above the signatures of Campbell and Preach Meaders in the 1961 Annual Report. "The purpose of this move was to permit closer coordi-

nation of the diversified activities of the divisions and subsidiaries and to seek further investment opportunities."[40]

For the better part of the 20th century, Dallas had been a banking center, a big money town, first for cotton and then, after World War II, for oil. Extremely wealthy wildcatters such as H.L. Hunt lived in Dallas. The Mobil Oil Corporation was headquartered in Dallas; its flying horse logo atop the Magnolia Building was visible for miles as, appropriately enough, the most prominent feature of the downtown Dallas skyline. Dallas banks had long been heavily invested in oil. A Dallas Chamber of Commerce report of 1945 mentioned that "more oil production paper is handled by Dallas banks than (by banks) anywhere else in the oil belt."[41] The money in Dallas was in the hands of bankers and businessmen who themselves were likely to have started in the oil patch. The bankers and businessmen of Dallas enjoyed making a deal over a friendly bourbon and branch water. In fact, wheeling and dealing was the primary means of support in the offices of downtown Dallas, in the absence of any surrounding heavy industry. And the newest office building, the Southland Life Building, had become a prestigious, primary downtown location for such activity. Halliburton Company moved into the Southland Life Building in August 1961.[42]

One year later, however, the leaders of Halliburton would take a huge step outside the oil business. It would buy the engineering and construction giant Brown & Root.

HALLIBURTON CO.

Above: Artist's conception of the new corporate headquarters for Otis Engineering, under construction in Carrollton, Texas, in 1961.

Left: The executive offices of the Halliburton Company, established in 1961, at 3211 Southland Center in Dallas, Texas.

George and Herman Brown. George (left) was the suave businessman while Herman was the man in the field. "He wanted to run it. I got the business," George once said.

Mortgaged Mules & Romance

"If you make up your mind early enough in life where you want to go, kind of hitch your wagon to a star, you can take off, which my brother and I did. We mapped it out among ourselves how we were going to do it and went to work at it."

— George Brown, 1979[1]

BROWN & ROOT, A SMALL road-building company in Central Texas, grew out of another contractor's misfortune in 1914 to become the largest engineering and construction firm in the United States. Brown & Root would grow on the backs of worn-out mules, fueled by intense ambition and government contracts. Powered by the financial backing of a brother-in-law and the raw determination and dreams of two brothers, Brown & Root would expand across the United States and overseas to build huge highways, bridges, dams, military bases, underwater pipelines, a football stadium, and chemical and power plants. It would seek to burrow into the earth to learn the beginnings of history, design a space center and launch astronauts into space. But behind it all, Brown & Root is the story of two brothers who joined together to build. Herman Brown possessed the mules and the grit of years working in the rough world of road contracting, while his brother George, with a nose for business, had studied engineering, hoping it would allow him to see the world.

The brothers grew up in the Central Texas town of Belton. Herman, the elder of the two, was born November 10, 1892, and George was born 5½ years later, on May 12, 1898. Their parents were Riney Louis and Lucy Wilson (King) Brown, and the family boasted ancestors who had been judges and leaders in Texas. A great-grandfather, who had arrived in the Republic of Texas in 1836, became the first chief justice of the Supreme Court when Texas became a state in 1845. The brothers' grandfather was the first county judge of Lee County, a Texas county that he organized after his return from serving the Confederacy in the Civil War. The county was named after General Robert E. Lee.[2]

Riney Brown operated a dry goods store in the small Bell County town, which recorded a population of 3,700 in 1904.[3] A 1942 newspaper article described the Brown brothers' childhood as filled with daily chores. "Although the family lived in fair circumstances, the boys were not permitted to idle away their time, for, like most fathers of that generation Mr. Brown believed that work and experience was a great character builder."[4] The boys chopped and hauled wood for heating and cooking, greased the wagons and family surrey, fed the hogs and chickens, and cleaned and refilled the oil lamps.

After finishing high school in the nearby, larger town of Temple, Herman went to work there. He drove a grocery wagon for about a year,

---

George Brown as a boy, peddling magazines. Brown's parents did not believe in idleness.

earning $35 a month, before attending the University of Texas from 1911 to 1912. He then got a job with Bell County, working in the engineering department. His job was to check building materials, for which he was paid $2 a day. The only problem was that he couldn't work when it was raining, and "it seemed to the ambitious youth that it rained 'darned near' every day."[5] After about a year of this frustration, Herman got another job.

The work was as foreman for a road contractor, and it paid $75 a month. At least, that's how much it would have paid if the contractor, Carl Swinford, had been more successful. But Swinford was struggling to keep his business afloat, and paychecks were few and far between.

Some accounts state that Swinford finally went broke in 1914 and gave Herman his mortgaged mules and equipment in lieu of back pay. In a letter, Herman later recalled, "I had not been paid any salary for approximately two years, so I

Herman Brown entered the road-building business in about 1913 as a foreman working for a contractor in Central Texas.

1914: Herman Brown starts his contracting business with mortgaged, broken down mules.

1921: George Brown, working as a geologist, almost dies in a mine cave-in.

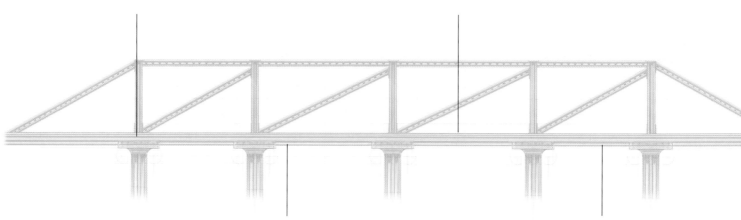

1919: Herman's brother-in-law, Dan Root, invests in the business, forming Brown & Root.

1922: George joins Brown & Root while he recuperates, adding his salesman's skills to his brother's venture.

was given part of his worn-out mule outfit from which to collect my back pay as, if, and when I had paid off the mortgage. Believe me, the paying of that debt with a three-fresno [a kind of road scraper] and plow outfit was something, but I struggled on, not only paying it off, but managing to buy additional teams on credit."[6]

Accounts also vary as to the number of mules and equipment Herman received. The 50th anniversary company publication put the number at 18 mules, while a 1942 newspaper account listed it as 14 horses and mules. Whatever the number, there is no dispute that the stock and equipment made a sorry lot. "Herman couldn't sell the stuff for enough to pay off the bank because it was almost worn out. So he kept it." He bought some more equipment on credit and went into business.[7]

Herman's first job was as a subcontractor working with a half-dozen other subcontractors to build some roads. Herman had been working for

BROWN & ROOT

about six months on the project when he ran into the contractor, a 1942 newspaper article recounted.

"The boss started looking over Herman's teams and equipment. His reaction was, 'My God, have I been paying you real money for that sort of worn-

A 1918 photograph of Dan Root, Herman's brother-in-law, in the Army, second man from the right.

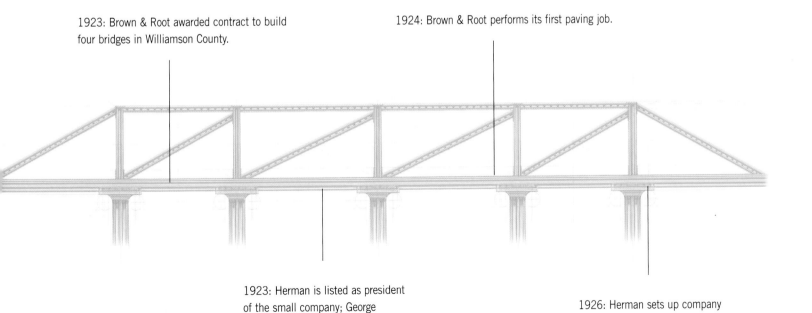

1923: Brown & Root awarded contract to build four bridges in Williamson County.

1924: Brown & Root performs its first paving job.

1923: Herman is listed as president of the small company; George becomes executive vice president.

1926: Herman sets up company headquarters in Austin.

out stuff!' But the young contractor kept on and after the job was finished, the boss was so sold on Brown's work that he offered to finance him or help him out otherwise."[8]

Grit and Mud

In those days, small contractors were known as gyppos, since they moved from job to job, often going broke, borrowing money, and still failing to meet payrolls.[9] Contracting was risky work, and if Herman were to fail, he would not be the first to do so. Herman got into all varieties of dirt work, building levees on rivers and railroad dumps, but few highways.[10]

Road contractors lived in camps, each with a mule corral, a cook tent, and sleeping tents for all the workers.[11] Mondays were spent bailing the building crew out of jail, where the men had landed after their weekend sprees. Tough ex-cowhands and oilfield roustabouts were among those who worked on the road-building crews and lived in tents next to the mule corrals.[12] Herman's brother, George, later described the contracting business as predicated on a simple formula. "All you have to do is bid low enough to get the job and be high enough to make a profit." Sounds easy, but as he quickly added, "Surety companies figure the average life of a contracting firm is from five to seven years."[13]

Herman was not the average contractor. He was blessed with outsized measures of determination and business sense, and he also happened to pick a good time to become a road builder. Henry Ford had introduced the Model T in 1908, and by 1916, Ford's revolutionary assembly line was churning out nearly 750,000 cars a year, at the remarkably affordable price of $360 each. For the first time, the new internal combustion engine vehicles could be purchased by Americans of average means. Automobile use was on the rise, and drivers wanted paved roads. In 1917, the Texas Highway Commission was formed, with state money available for building roads across the vast state.

Herman, who would die in 1962 with a fortune estimated at between $75 million and $100 million, described his first two road jobs as extremely modest. His first assignment with his own team was as a subcontractor in Henderson County, "where I cleared, graded and sand-clayed their roads on force account. From there, I moved over to Freestone County, where they were doing nothing more than grading their roads."[14] Herman had been worried that he wouldn't get the assignment because he looked so young. So, he "grew a moustache to make him look older than his 21 years, and talked the Freestone County commissioners into giving him his first contract."[15]

A Generous Brother-in-Law

In 1917, the young contractor married Margarett Root, a schoolteacher who taught his youngest brother, King. They were married in the Williamson County town of Taylor. For a time, the newlyweds lived in a tent as Herman built roads in the county.[16]

In 1919, Herman's brother-in-law, Dan Root, became an investor-partner in the contracting business, and Brown & Root was born. Dan Root was a bachelor farmer who lived in Williamson County. His involvement with Brown & Root was "really just a financer — never did have any actual management interest in the company."[17]

The infusion of $25,000 in new capital in the year the partnership was created meant that the company could expand.[18] In 1979, Brown & Root would list more than $1.5 billion

Center: George Brown after graduating from Temple High School in Central Texas in 1916.

worth of equipment. However, in 1919, inventory consisted of one combination buggy and saddle horse, one buckboard buggy, one saddle, 15 horses and mules, three fresnos (scoop-shaped road scrapers pulled by mules), one farm plow, one road plow, one four-mule grader and six two-horse wagons.

George Brown

Brown & Root, founded on a familial relationship, expanded three years later to create the team of George and Herman Brown. George Brown had graduated from Temple High School in 1916. He took the train from Temple to Houston, and enrolled in pre-med studies at the Rice Institute, later called Rice University, which had opened four years earlier. He attended Rice for two years, serving in the ROTC, then spent a couple of semesters at the University of Texas. In 1918, he joined the Marine Corps and served stateside during the final months of World War I.[19]

Following his military service, the young veteran enrolled in the Colorado School of Mines in 1919, graduating in 1922 with a degree in mining engineering. An inscription in the school's yearbook the year of his graduation aptly noted that George "gains his power through his ability to make friends."[20] It would be the same after college, when

Above: An early 1920 rock crusher, used in road building.

Below: Model T trucks haul rocks from a quarry to be used in construction.

his political and business connections helped secure contracts for Brown & Root.

George paid for his education by renting out two Model T Ford cars, which he got from his older brother, Louis, who operated a car rental service in Denver. Fellow students, who paid by the mile, could rent the cars for social activities or weekend trips. George lowered his operating costs by doing the mechanical work on the cars.[21]

George had gone into engineering in a search for adventure, not riches. "I never thought I'd make any real money as an engineer," he said years later. "What was important was the romance of engineering. Engineers were men

Center: Driving piling on a skid rig in an oil field in the late 1920s.

Below: A batch process in the early 1920s.

who went to far places, who built things all over the world."[22] After college, George set out on his first adventure, working in the Montana mines as a geologist for the Anaconda Copper Company.

Hoping to break into the engineering end of Anaconda, George was hired as a geologist, advising his mining superiors where to drill to find a new copper vein.[23] He went into the deserted mine early one morning, and found that workers had indeed found the vein. But at that moment, the mine collapsed. Falling rocks and debris fractured his skull and ribs, and broke his left arm. George managed to lie down on a 12-inch-wide beam as the floor fell away beneath him. He firmly pressed his head against a rock to stanch the bleeding, and waited several hours while workers frantically dug 2,200 feet below the surface to rescue him. George returned to Texas to recuperate, and Herman asked him to work on a temporary basis for Brown & Root.

The Brown Brothers

Weather, which so often ruined a road contracting business, provided an opportunity for Herman to diversify and bring George into the business. In 1922, Herman was awarded a contract to rebuild four Williamson County bridges that had been washed out in a flood. Setting piers for one of the bridges required dynamiting the rock bottom of the San Gabriel River, and Herman put George in charge of the job. "He had to do a lot of blasting under water to get the piers down, and I told him we'd been doing that

PHOTOS: BROWN & ROOT

in Montana," George recalled.[24] George later said that he "didn't know a thing about building a bridge, but I got it up."[25]

George and Herman found that they shared a burning desire for success. Their parents, fearing for George's safety in the mines, had pleaded with him not to return to Montana. But George had held out until Herman assured him that he was far too ambitious to want to remain a small road builder. Years later, George said those early dreams had fueled the rise of Brown & Root. "If you make up your mind early enough in life where you want to go, kind of hitch your wagon to a star, you can take off, which my brother and I did," he said in a 1979 interview. "We mapped it out among ourselves how we were going to do it and went to work at it."[26]

Although both were ambitious, the brothers were a contrast in mannerism and appearance. They had different responsibilities, adapted to their individual strengths. Herman ran the business in the field, while George was the sales-

man. To his workers, Herman was Mister Herman or The Boss, a burly, genial man with whom they shared a rapport. George, slimmer and with finer features, hobnobbed with business leaders and politicians.

Company publications described the brothers this way:

"Herman was the working man's man, while George was the smooth-talker, destined to walk and talk with presidents and royalty. Herman handled operations and George pursued business opportunities."[27]

Frank "Posh" Oltorf, who served as Brown & Root's representative in Washington after

Brown & Root paving the way for the automobiles rolling off assembly lines in the early 1920s.

BROWN & ROOT

World War II, described the Brown brothers as remarkable men who "had a complete devotion to each other."

"Their lives were so interwoven it is hard to tell where one started and the other began. The Brown partnership agreement was the most amazing thing I ever saw. Everything they owned, they owned together, fifty-fifty — except their homes and personal possessions like their wives' jewelry. If Herman bought a share of stock in his name, George would automatically own half of it. If George bought a farm, it would be half Herman's."[28]

Herman explained the reasoning behind the arrangement. "Brown & Root takes up so much time. If George were out doing something else, I might feel he's spending more time doing things for himself than for us, and if I were out, he might feel the same way. This way, always, anything we do is being done for both of us."[29]

But Oltorf said there was no doubt that Herman, as the older brother and founder of the firm, had the final say on Brown & Root's business dealings.

"I always felt George was the idea man. He could come up with ten very unusual ideas and Herman would shoot eight of them down as being ridiculous. He would then jump on the other ones and off the two would go. George had this tremendous imagination and would come up with tremendous ideas. Herman was very practical. George was very much at home in New York and Washington and with the presidents of the large corporations. Herman preferred the Austin and Houston business communities. But he could charm anyone. Both of them could. George was more diplomatic. Herman could be tough."[30]

Herman remained president of Brown & Root and George remained executive vice president until Herman's death in 1962. "He was the older one and I did everything he didn't want to do," George once said. "He wanted to run it. I got the business."[31]

Brown & Root workers prepare to go to work as a truck unloads road-building material.

BROWN & ROOT

BROWN & ROOT

Joe D. Hughes, a transportation company founded in 1896, provided Brown & Root with horses, mules and trucks in its early days. Brown & Root bought the company in 1942.

Outsmarting the Weather

An early strategy of the brothers was to take the weather into account when lining up work. Construction jobs in those days consisted of roads, streets, levees and railroad beds. George recalled that Brown & Root "took two jobs in West Texas, where there was no rainfall, for every job we took in East and South Texas, where there was a lot of rainfall. So we had a balance at the end of the year. We came up with a little profit."[32]

Williamson County was known for its black, sticky soil, and Herman recalled a dismal time in 1919 when heavy rains forced him to drive his mules to town to be fed. "The roads were so boggy that you couldn't haul feed out to the job," he said. "I didn't even make enough money to meet my payrolls."[33]

It was during this difficult time that the rains forced Herman to stop work and left him unable to buy feed for his mules. A merchant took pity and gave him the feed on credit. Years later, when

Herman learned the man had gone broke during the Great Depression and was living in poverty, a large check arrived in the old man's mailbox.[34]

This was possibly the same merchant that Oltorf recalled hearing about from Herman. He recalled that one time Herman showed him a letter written by an elderly man.

"Dear Mr. Brown:

I am not sure you will remember me, but back when you were building roads near Rogers, I had a feed store and I sold you feed on credit to feed your mules. I am in a low state of income, ill, and I am in a rest home. But I think about the old days and I hope this letter finds you well and prosperous."[35]

Not until after Herman's death years later did Oltorf learn the rest of the story. Herbert Frensley, who was treasurer of Brown & Root at the time, and would later become its president, was also shown the letter that day. "Brown said, 'Herbert, find out where this old man is and send him two hundred dollars a month for the rest of his life.'" Said Oltorf: "That was typical of Herman."[36]

In the early years of Brown & Root, Herman traveled 50,000 to 75,000 miles a year by automobile to inspect his scattered road construction sites. He would spend most of the day at one job, then climb into the back seat of his car to sleep while a driver took him to the next project. A third brother, unidentified, briefly worked for Brown & Root before returning to his job as a streetcar conductor. He told Herman to stop working 18-hour days. "You'll kill yourself," he said.[37]

By 1924, the company had graduated from dirt grading to its first hard-surface work. The paving was for some streets in San Marcos. Carl Burkhart Jr., who would retire from Brown &

Root 44 years later as senior vice president, went to work in San Marcos as a time-keeper and sign-up man for the property owners, earning $75 a month. He recalled that George had devised the company's first asphalt spreader, but the first batch was spoiled and had to be dumped in a ditch because the spreader was hooked up backward.[38]

Public works contracts in Texas tended to be small, and competition was fierce. When Brown & Root heard about a potential job, an estimator or engineer would be sent to the site to gather the information needed to make a bid. George later estimated that the company actually won perhaps 5 percent of the projects on which the company bid.[39]

As late as 1927, the average road construction contract was only $90,000, from which the contractor had to pay wages, buy feed for his

mules, and procure materials and equipment, bonding and insurance. Most of the time, the payment was not even in cash. Contractors were usually paid in paving notes, which were secured by municipal real estate and did not mature until five or 10 years after they were issued.[40]

In 1926, Herman set up company headquarters in Austin. That same year, George and his new wife, Alice Pratt Brown, moved to Houston, where George opened a branch office of Brown & Root. Alice Pratt had met her future husband in Georgetown, where she had graduated from Southwestern University. Her aunt, with whom she lived, "could not be enthusiastic about a suitor who always came to call for her beautiful niece in a construction truck. She was sure that George Brown had no promising future."[41] Despite this disapproval, the young couple married. Their first home was a boarding house outside Houston, where George was building a bridge.[42]

Houston, the city where George first went to college, was booming. Its population had more than doubled between 1920 and 1930, and with 292,352 residents, it was the largest city

---

A Brown & Root worker, E.L. Lawrence, in front of the cook shack at a municipal paving job in Beeville, Texas, in 1927. Many workers depended on the company for food in hard times.

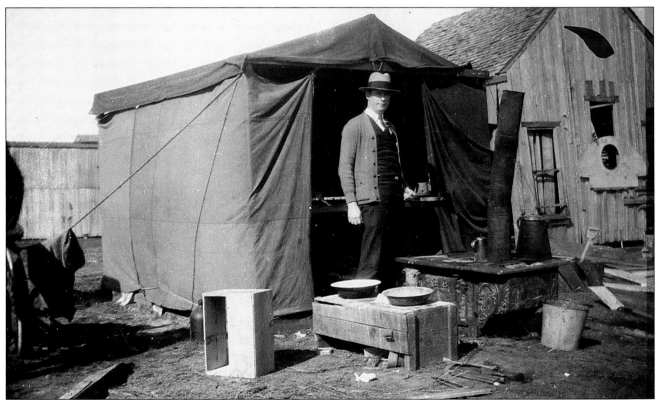

BROWN & ROOT

A road gang hard at work on the 1927 Beeville road paving project in Texas.

in Texas.[43] It was a logical location for a branch office. Houston's port provided a source of contracts, and the city was in the midst of significant street construction. Streets were more complicated than roads, since utilities needed to be installed and drainage provided during the concrete work.

Dan Root, the silent partner of Brown & Root, died March 10, 1929, of colon cancer. George acquired Dan Root's interest in the business from his heirs. Even though Dan Root had passed away, and his family was not involved in the company, the Browns decided not to change its name. George said the name of Brown & Root was retained because there was "good will in the name and we saw no reason to change it."[44]

Brown & Root was incorporated in June 1929. The company had capital stock of $200,000. Herman paid in $155,000; his wife, $30,000; George, $10,000; and W.A. Woolsey, $5,000. The three Browns made up the board of directors of the company, which listed net assets of $223,096.02.[45]

Brown & Root's incorporation occurred just a few months before the Great Depression hit the country. In the thirties, Brown & Root became so desperate for work that it accepted garbage-hauling contracts in order to stay in business. But the lessons learned during those troubled years established the foundation for Brown & Root's amazing success. The thirties marked Brown & Root's entry into the heavy construction and power industries, with construction of the huge Marshall Ford Dam near Austin. The company had never before built a dam, but then again, George had never built a bridge before he did the San Gabriel project.

BROWN & ROOT

The completed Marshall Ford Dam, later renamed Mansfield Dam. The project would lift Brown & Root from a struggling contractor to eventual world-class status.

CHAPTER SIX

From Desperation to Dam-Building

"Atop the already completed portion of the dam, men move about on skeleton-like frame 'catwalks,' looking like big brown bugs crawling up and down. Near one end of the massive masonry structure an unseen man, in a toy-like room perched on a steel scaffold, guides huge buckets of concrete, each weighing several hundred pounds, along a steel cable to the opposite side of the dam, where the contents are dropped with exact precision, each adding its bit to the completion of this piece of master work."

— *Houston Chronicle,* 1941[1]

EVEN BEFORE THE Great Depression began, hard times had already taken root in Texas. In the 1920s, municipalities found themselves unable to pay debts or finance new construction jobs. George and Herman Brown held thousands of dollars in municipal paving notes, which were in effect municipal bonds that matured in five to 10 years.[2]

Brown & Root's banker warned the brothers to sell the notes at a discount fearing that they would become worthless and Brown & Root would be left with nothing. But the thought of selling the notes was unbearable to Herman. Those pieces of paper represented years of sweat and struggle for him and his men, toiling in the harsh Texas weather. For years, Herman refused to listen to the advice, waiting until it was almost too late. By the end of the decade, however, he could see that the economy was getting even worse, and Herman reluctantly agreed to let his brother sell off the notes.

A mere three months before the stock market crashed, George took the paving notes to Chicago and sold them at a discount. "It was a good thing we sold," he later said. "Another month or two, and we wouldn't have been able to."[3] The sale meant that the company could survive the Great Depression. "We had money in the bank, and we survived and could keep the key men on the payroll, which most contractors could not," George recalled.[4] With construction at a halt, the proceeds from the sale of the notes became the company's lifeblood. "We lived off that paper in 1930 and 1931 and 1932 — for years, really, during the Depression," George said.[5]

The Depression grew worse, and it became obvious to many that prosperity wasn't around the corner. At age 16, Bill Morrow was one of many young people who left home during the Great Depression, taking to the road in a desperate search for work. Morrow wound up at a Brown & Root camp in east Texas, near the Louisiana state line. The crew there could not offer him a job because there simply wasn't enough work to go around. But the men invited him to share their meals. With no place else to go, Morrow kept hanging around the camp. Finally, his big break came. He was made corral boss in charge of the mules. Morrow became a loyal employee of Brown & Root, where he remained for many years. "What made Brown & Root great was Mister Herman Brown," he told a magazine writer in 1982.[6]

A Brown & Root worker uses a road grader to spread dirt in Callahan County, Texas, in 1939.

Morrow and other employees were confident that Brown & Root would survive the Depression. But there were struggles. One time, just as a crew was finishing a job near El Paso, Herman informed his workers that another job had fallen through, even though Herman had bid low. "We built a fence around the equipment and left it for a while," Morrow said.[7]

During this slow period, Morrow and his fellow workers in West Texas kept busy by using Brown & Root's heavy equipment to build earthen water tanks for ranch livestock. This work was done through contracts between the workers themselves and the ranchers, without involvement from Brown & Root.

Brown & Root offered job security at a time when many workers were routinely laid off between projects. Employees worked under annual contracts, so they didn't need to protect their jobs by joining unions. In order to keep employees on the payroll during hard times, Brown & Root sometimes bid so low that it lost money on projects. Herman figured that at least the company was maintaining a cash flow and keeping people away from soup lines.

Company literature describes Brown and Root as financially sound during the Great Depression, though hurt by the scarcity of construction jobs. The company won other jobs not related to road construction, including a contract to haul garbage for the City of Houston. The company also expanded geographically, building a board road for Humble Oil and Refining Company in Roanoke, Louisiana, in 1934.

The Browns learned a lesson from the economic crisis. Herman vowed that he would never again put all his eggs in one basket. Brown & Root began a strategy of diversification.[8]

Emerging from the Depression

The event that pulled Brown & Root out of the Depression and into its future as a diversified corporate giant was construction of the huge Mansfield Dam project on the Colorado River. The river runs near the New Mexico state line, over the steep area above Austin, known locally as the Hill Country, and into the Gulf of Mexico. The crookedly flowing 800-mile-long river fed fertile areas of the state but also caused tremendous destruction to people living in its rich bottom lands.

1929: Herman Brown relents just in time to allow George to sell off notes to save the company.

1936: George and Herman Brown win the contract to build the Marshall Ford Dam, Brown & Root's big break.

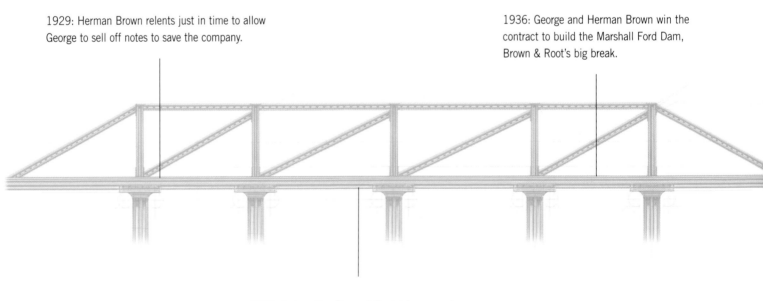

1934: A struggling Brown & Root takes a road job for Humble Oil, later known as Exxon.

PHOTOS: BROWN & ROOT

Desperate for work, Brown & Root expanded into Roanoke, Louisiana to build a board road, used to cover boggy ground with a stable surface, for Humble Oil in 1934. Humble Oil would later be known as Exxon.

Inset: Brown & Root employee Dave Bratton stands on a board road under construction in Louisiana.

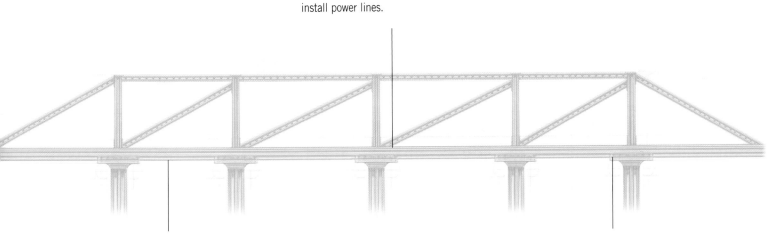

1938: Brown & Root wins contract to install power lines.

1937: Because of a legal technicality, the dam project almost sinks Brown & Root. Lyndon Johnson intervenes.

1942: Construction of the dam is completed. Brown & Root poised for bigger and better projects.

"Each year, angry floods would rush down, overflowing great expanses, causing property losses of millions of dollars, and taking the lives of hundreds of residents. ... The loss over a period of years, just before the flood control movement began, was set at $4 million annually. In 1915 and 1935 alone the loss was estimated at more than $50 million."[9]

The Lower Colorado River Authority (LCRA) was created by the Texas legislature to harness the river by building a series of dams. The Mansfield Dam, 18 miles upriver from Austin, would be the largest and most important. When it was completed, it was the fifth largest dam in the world, for a short time.[10] The dam project was originally called Marshall Ford, but was later named the Mansfield Dam, after Congressman Joseph Mansfield, chairman of the House Rivers and Harbors Committee. The project's initial dams, called Buchanan and Roy Inks, had been fully funded and nearly completed in early 1937. Construction of the Mansfield Dam was expected to cost $10 million, funded by a grant from the federal Department of Interior's Bureau of Reclamation. Enough money was available under an initial $5 million appropriation to the LCRA to request bids and begin construction.[11]

A Brown & Root drilling and blasting crew at a rock quarry in Callahan County, Texas, collecting building material for the company's projects.

Brown & Root had cleared the reservoir at the Buchanan site, but had no experience in actual dam construction. Nonetheless, the company assumed two-thirds responsibility in a joint venture with McKenzie Construction Company of San Antonio. Their joint bid of $5.78 million compared favorably to a bid of $5.9 million by Utah Construction Company of Salt Lake City and one of $7.3 million by W.E. Callahan Construction Company of Dallas.[12] The contract, awarded in December 1936, called for constructing the dam in two stages. The first stage, known as the low dam, would be 190 feet high, with a reservoir capacity of about 600,000 acre-feet. The second stage, the high dam, would increase storage capacity to more than three million acre-feet.[13] The dam would stand 27 stories high and would be a mile wide when completed four years later. It would require two million tons of concrete and one million tons of dirt fill.

Early in 1937, Brown & Root began preliminary work at the site. Since it was an out-of-the-way stretch of the river, roads had to be widened and improved, and an 11-mile railroad spur had to be constructed.[14] The camp for workers had to be built, and heavy equipment had to be secured. At a groundbreaking ceremony on February 19, 1937, Secretary of the Interior Harold Ickes made a surprise announcement — the second phase of the dam project would be 265 feet, instead of 190 feet, and would cost $20 million instead of $10 million.[15]

Even though Congress had not yet authorized funding for the project, the Brown brothers were confident that Texas Congressman J.P. Buchanan, chairman of the House Appropriations Committee, would get the project approved during the 1937 session of Congress. The brothers borrowed heavily to buy the equipment needed for the huge job, as Robert A. Caro explained in the first volume of his Lyndon Johnson biography, *The Path to Power.*

"So much larger was the dam than any previous Brown & Root project that the company would have to purchase $1,500,000 worth of heavy construction equipment, including one particularly expensive item — a cableway consisting of two steel towers erected on either side of the river, with, hung between them, huge cables along which ran a trolley from which buckets filled with concrete mixed on the cliffs could be lowered to the men pouring it into the foundations — for which they might never again have a use. 'We had to put in a million and a half dollars before we could get a penny back,' George Brown recalls."[16]

Caro wrote that the Browns would not recoup any of this huge investment from the first $5 million appropriation. The brothers' estimated profit from the appropriation would be $1 million, which was already eaten up by the equipment

purchase. It would not be until the second $5 million appropriation that they would be able to cover the remaining $500,000 cost of equipment and clear an overall profit of $1.5 million.

It was, Caro wrote, "an amount double all the profit they had made in twenty previous years in the construction business."[17]

With all of the tools and equipment purchased, the Brown brothers eagerly waited for the go-ahead to begin the company's biggest project to date. But an unexpected technicality threw the entire dam project into jeopardy. The United States Comptroller's Office discovered that the land

did not belong to the federal government. It was owned by the LCRA.

The 1903 federal act that created the Bureau of Reclamation prohibited the use of federal funds for construction on nonfederal

Above: A Brown & Root employee operates a Victoria sand and gravel drill in February 1939.

Inset: Workers lug many tons of rock, blasted from quarries, for the Marshall Ford Dam project. This photo is from 1939.

lands. But under Texas law, the LCRA could not deed the land to the federal government or anyone else. State law ran up against federal regulations, with Brown & Root stuck somewhere in between.

Former state Senator Alvin Wirtz, who was legal representative for both Brown & Root and the LCRA, feared the Comptroller General would not approve the second appropriation, even if Congress authorized it, unless the land problem was resolved.[18]

George said he would never forget the day when he and Herman learned the federal government did not have title to the land. Brown & Root had already built the cableway and purchased the equipment. "[The cableway] cost several hundred thousands of dollars, which we owed the banks. And we had to set up a quarry for the stone, and build a conveyor belt from the quarry to the dam site. ... We had put in a million and a half dollars."[19]

But Wirtz came up with a bold solution to the legal problems.

"[It] called for a parlay of Buchanan's tremendous power, President Roosevelt's blessing of the Marshall Ford project, and the belief that the

LOWER COLORADO RIVER AUTHORITY

Above: The symbol of power. A 1940s brochure for the Lower Colorado River Authority after completion of the dam.

Left: The Marshall Ford project, later renamed Mansfield Dam, under construction in 1938. The project was a joint effort between Brown & Root and McKenzie Construction Company of San Antonio.

Above and below: Photos from 1941 of the almost completed dam, the biggest in a series of three to control and harness the Colorado River.

George met with the young congressman (and future president) to talk about the appropriation problems with the dam. "I went to Washington to talk to Mr. Johnson and see if I could be helpful in any way to get this appropriation booster, which I knew he, by the nature of being in his district, would be for," George recalled in a 1968 interview.[22] Johnson pushed for passage of Wirtz's bill, and secured the second $5 million appropriation for the dam.[23] Johnson also worked for the additional $17 million appropriation to build the dam to its final height.

The Browns and Johnson, who had also worked in a road gang once, became lifelong friends. The Browns would become heavy contributors to Johnson's future campaigns.

The LCRA began generating electricity at Marshall Ford on January 27, 1941. Less than a month later, the LCRA Board of Directors voted to name the structure after Congressman Mansfield, who had just celebrated his 80th birthday.[24] A 1941 newspaper article painted a vivid portrait of 500 men working on the massive dam.

"Atop the already completed portion of the dam, men move about on skeleton-like frame 'catwalks,' looking like big brown bugs crawling up and down. Near one end of the massive

Comptroller General's Office would be happy for any excuse to get off the hook. ... They needed congressional passage of a bill not only specifically authorizing the project but also validating the contract with Brown & Root."[20]

With Buchanan's backing, the bill was scheduled for routine approval by the House Rivers and Harbors Committee, which was chaired by Congressman Mansfield. But Buchanan died suddenly on February 22, 1937, only days after the groundbreaking ceremony at the dam site. Lyndon B. Johnson, the 28-year-old state director of the National Youth Administration, entered the congressional race to replace the powerful Buchanan. Wirtz, who had befriended Johnson years earlier, advised Johnson to position himself as Roosevelt's man in Texas.[21] The advice apparently worked, because Johnson won the April 1937 election.

BROWN & ROOT

masonry structure an unseen man, in a toy-like room perched on a steel scaffold, guides huge buckets of concrete, each weighing several hundred pounds, along a steel cable to the opposite side of the dam, where the contents are dropped with exact precision, each adding its bit to the completion of this piece of master work.

"The three 25,000-pound turbines can be seen resting in their nests of solid concrete. Within these are stored the machinery which converts the water rushing through into electrical power. ... An aged man serenely goes his way, picking up any stray pieces of waste matter and dropping it in a small basket, while around him other men move quickly and quietly to their tasks of keeping the great power projecting plant in operation."[25]

Construction of the dam was completed in May 1942. The dam's foundation width is 228 feet, its average thickness 125 feet, and it has more than three miles of inspection tunnels in its interior. It created Lake Travis, 65 miles long and 8.5 miles wide, containing about 652 billion gallons of water.[26]

The dam meant that residents could look upon the Colorado River as "one of the most valuable servants in the entire state" instead of one of the most destructive, according to a 1941 newspaper article.[27]

The Mansfield Dam was Brown & Root's steppingstone into million-dollar projects and politics. While the company earned a profit of $1 million on the original $10 million contract, its profit on the subsequent contract, the one that increased the total cost of the dam to $27 million, is unknown. However, out of a single $5 million appropriation for the higher dam, George wrote Congressman Johnson that the company's profit was about $2 million. Brown described it as a "nice bit of work."[28]

The Browns continued their warm relationship with Johnson, exchanging Christmas gifts, letters and visits. The relationship would become important to the future of both parties.

Building Power Lines

In 1938, while the dam was still under construction, Brown & Root won the contract to construct power lines in the rural, impoverished Hill Country. The federal Rural Electrification Administration loaned $1.8 million to the

The Mansfield Dam was a watershed moment for Brown & Root. The dam's builders gathered for a reunion in 1974, where George Brown spoke to the assembly.

Pedernales Electric Co-operative, a corporation formed to purchase electricity created by the LCRA dams. The loan funded 1,830 miles of electric lines, bringing power to 2,892 Hill Country families.[29]

Many of the 300 men toiling on the power line project could not afford the $5 deposit required to get electricity before they started on the project. But the job paid well enough so that those who managed to save their money could get electricity.

The work was particularly grueling because the 35-foot-tall pine electric poles had to be sunk in rock. Brown & Root's mechanical hole-digger broke, so workers had no choice but to dig every hole by hand. The sweaty, dirty work took on an efficient rhythm. As some workers hacked paths through the cedar, other men would begin digging a hole by pounding the end of a crowbar into the limestone. "After the hole reached a depth of six inches, half a stick of dynamite was exploded in it, to loosen the rock below, but that, too, had to be dug by hand." Other workers set the poles, attached the insulators, and then strung the wires.[30]

In the early 1940s, the Brown brothers entered a new phase as the United States readied for war. The brothers had gone from being road builders to hydroelectric dam builders. They would create a separate company, called Brown Shipbuilding, to construct ships for use in World War II.

This expansion would not have been possible without the dam project. "That's when we first developed our nucleus of engineers and why we would be so good in shipbuilding," George said in a 1980 interview. "Up to then, we'd been dirt contractors, but we went from making roads to paving to dams to building power plants."[3]

Corpus Christi Naval Air Station, built by the Brown brothers in just nine months, helped launch Brown & Root into shipbuilding.

CHAPTER SEVEN

Texas Wonder Boys

"If a man can stand on his head in a bell hole and weld a high-pressure oil field pipe, he can weld a ship. We've got plenty of good mechanics in Texas. They can be adapted to shipbuilding."

— L.T. Bolin, Brownship general manager, 1945[1]

WORK ON THE Mansfield Dam was completed just months before the United States entered World War II. With the frenzied construction of naval bases and training stations, the nation had already begun to gear up for war. Herman's appetite for big projects continued after the dam contract was finished, and he wanted Brown & Root to be part of the military construction. "His car still roared endlessly back and forth across Texas as he pushed his projects and searched out new work," wrote Robert Caro, a Lyndon B. Johnson biographer. Johnson, a close friend of the Brown brothers, would sometimes send telegrams to two or three towns at once to locate the restless Herman.[2]

Brown & Root, in a joint venture with W.S. Bellows Construction Company of Houston, had bid in 1939 on a proposed base in San Juan, Puerto Rico, but the bid went to another company. "While both firms had 'extensive construction experience,' they had no experience whatsoever in the type of construction necessary to build a naval air base," Navy officials stated.[3]

In 1940, Brown & Root bid on the construction of the Corpus Christi Naval Air Station on the Gulf of Mexico at Flour Bluff, an area of sand dunes, scrub oaks and scattered tourist cabins. The contract for the base was on a cost-plus fixed-fee basis, meaning that it was not competitively bid, but was instead awarded through negotiations. Brown & Root was the only firm with which serious negotiations were held.[4]

Brown & Root's two partner companies in the Corpus Christi project were Bellows, and Columbia Construction Company, headed by industrialist Henry Kaiser.

In a 1969 interview, George Brown said that Lyndon B. Johnson, a member of the Naval Affairs Committee at the time, was helpful in getting the base project. But George said the company secured the job because of its reputation. "We got in on the basis that we could and would perform it quicker and cheaper than any one set of contractors."[5]

On June 13, 1940, President Roosevelt signed the contract. The price was fixed at $23.4 million for the base, with the contractors to be paid an additional $1.2 million.[6] Appropriations for the 2,050-acre base increased as the project progressed, and it was eventually completed at a cost of $100 million. Speed in building the base was of the utmost importance because President Franklin Roosevelt feared an invasion of the United States, George said.

The coveted Army-Navy "E" Award, which Brown & Root won five times. The "E" stands for "excellence."

BROWN & ROOT

"Roosevelt was convinced when Hitler overran France in early 1940 that he would try to invade us through Mexico. FDR thought there ought to be a naval training station built in Texas at once. ... We put everything we had to it and built it in about a third less time than he and the Navy thought we could do it in."[7]

A mere nine months after the contract was signed, the base held opening ceremonies. In a

Naval training aircraft at the Matagorda Island Bombing and Gunnery Range in 1943, built by Brown & Root.

1940: Brown & Root wins bid to build the Corpus Christi Naval Air Station.

1941: The Brown brothers create the Brown Shipbuilding Company, nicknamed Brownship, to build warships.

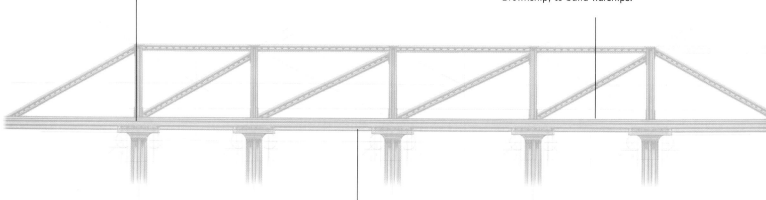

1941: Just nine months after the project officially began, the air station is completed.

ceremony on March 12, 1941, Secretary of the Navy Frank Knox dedicated the station to a "peace of justice and righteousness."[8] The base would train more than 40,000 naval fliers during World War II, with the first class graduating in November 1941, just one month before Pearl Harbor.

Brown Shipbuilding Company

The Brown brothers' next major venture earned them the title of Texas Wonder Boys. They set up a new company, Brown Shipbuilding Company in mid-1941, after taking over a contract from a local shipbuilding firm, which was about a year behind in producing four submarine chasers.[9] George credited Texas Congressman Albert Thomas, a friend from his Rice University days, with giving the Brown brothers the opportunity to take over the contract. "The Bureau of Ships, through the advice of Albert Thomas, asked me to come and talk to them," Brown recalled in a 1968 interview. "Although we had never built a ship, we did know how to organize people, and we did have some good electrical engineers, and electrical mechanics and craftsmen from the Marshall Ford

The Brown brothers in 1942. The business-savvy George is on the left and Herman, known as "Mr. Herman" to his men, is on the right.

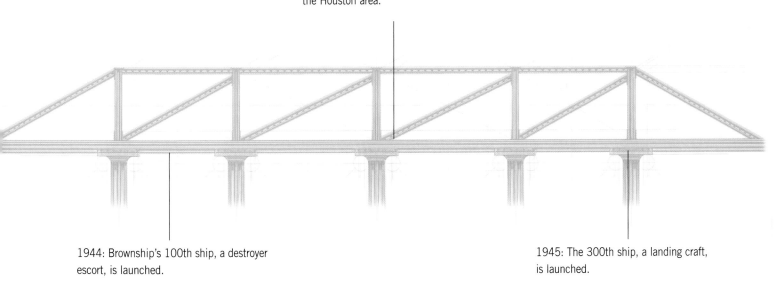

1944: Brownship installs first dry dock in the Houston area.

1944: Brownship's 100th ship, a destroyer escort, is launched.

1945: The 300th ship, a landing craft, is launched.

days."[10] The shipbuilding company was nicknamed Brownship by its workers.

The Navy's lump sum contract would pay $640,000 per vessel. "We had no idea whether that price was high enough to make a profit or not, but the best we could figure, we could at least break even," George said.[11] Herman recalled, during a 1942 interview, that the brothers had to decide quickly. "I talked it over with George, and he looked at it this way: 'If a geologist can build a bridge, then an ordinary general contractor can certainly build ships.' So the deal was made."[12]

The contract led to other warship contracts, and Brownship completed $357 million worth of work for the Navy during World War II.[13] The venture, financed out of the brothers' own pockets, was incorporated separately from Brown & Root in May 1944. By the time the war ended, the company had constructed 359 destroyer escorts and other vessels for the Navy. With the launching of the shipbuilding venture, the brothers also moved Brown & Root's main office from Austin to Houston.[14]

The Browns invested $2 million before even launching their first ship.[15] The brothers constructed their shipyard at Greens Bayou, about 15 miles south of Houston, in a place where the bayou empties into the Houston Ship Channel.

According to an account in the shipyard's weekly newspaper, L.T. Bolin, general superin-

Above: The hastily constructed Brown Shipbuilding Company, which built more than 350 ships during World War II. Work on the shipyard started before the deed to the land was even transferred to the Browns.

Below: The destroyer escort U.S.S. *Moore*, built by Brownship on Dec. 21, 1942. The ship was named for a seaman killed on the battleship U.S.S. *Arizona*, sunk at Pearl Harbor a year earlier.

PHOTOS: BROWN & ROOT

BROWN & ROOT

L.T. Bolin, manager of the Brown Shipbuilding Company. Bolin picked the site for Brownship while eating lunch one day in Greens Bayou, 15 miles south of Houston.

tendent of the Houston district for the Browns, discovered the location after borrowing a motor boat and traveling down the channel. Bolin chose a small peninsula, with 300 feet fronting the channel's deep water and 5,000 feet on the shallower, curving bayou. He ate a picnic lunch in a nearby meadow as he assessed the land. "True, the bayou was shallow. But it could be dredged. Part of the land was a clay hill. It could be carved down. Part was a swamp. It could be filled. The whole area was a forest. The trees could be cut. Bolin bought it."[16]

Wartime Ingenuity

Speed was critical, so workers didn't wait for the final purchase agreement. They knocked down the first tree on the property while lawyers were still drawing up the deed to the 156-acre tract.

Because material was needed for the war effort, ingenuity was necessary to quickly obtain tools and machinery. An abandoned sawmill 40 miles away was purchased, torn down, and reassembled into a warehouse and machine shop. Secondhand machinery, including a lathe in Seattle and a plate roller on the East Coast, was collected wherever it could be found. Workers ripped up the rails from an abandoned line to extend a nearby railway to the Brown shipyard.[17]

No cranes were available at first, so workers carried the steel by hand. The keel plates for the first subchasers were shaped with a hand-operated press, while heating and shrinking were done with a hand torch and a bucket of water.[18] The closest paved road was three miles away, and the nearest passable road a mile and a half distant. When it rained, workers parked their cars, pulled off their shoes, and waded to work. Worker Sally Goodin recalled cleaning her feet off in a wash basin before sitting down to her job at the switchboard.[19]

Bolin, who found the shipyard site and became Brown Shipbuilding's general manager, had a can-do attitude. After learning that long-established shipyards had already hired all the experienced shipbuilders Bolin said, "If a man can stand on his head in a bell hole and weld a high-pressure oil field pipe, he can weld a ship. We've got plenty of good mechanics in Texas. They can be adapted to shipbuilding."[20]

Workers came from all over the Southwest and from all different backgrounds. They included waitresses, housewives, office workers, students, architects, engineers and doctors. Classes trained them as welders, shipwrights, boilermakers, carpenters and clerks.[21]

Employee Albert Sheppard was hired in 1942 to design the shipbuilding facilities. After the work was done, Chief Engineer M.P. Anderson asked him to stay to build ships. "My reply was that I didn't know much about it. He answered,

'Neither do I, we can learn together.' So we became shipbuilders."[22]

Quicksand and Banana Peels

A crisis at the shipyard in January 1942 threatened the fledgling shipyard's first two ship hulls. As workers dredged Greens Bayou, they hit a stretch of quicksand. The foundation holding up the nearly complete hulls began a slow, relentless slide into the bayou. Workers were frantically pulled off Brown & Root construction jobs all over South Texas and loaned to Brownship to drive piling to shore up the bank. Herman surveyed the predicament. As he "stood on the bank, he could see almost a million dollars slipping into the murky waters of the bayou. He turned to Bolin and said: 'Do the best you can. This is just one of the risks you have to expect in the contracting business.' But the piling was driven in time."[23]

Six months after the yard opened, the first submarine chaser was launched. The PC-565 was the first naval combat ship to be launched with bananas as skids, a practice previously used only in merchant ship launching.[24] Bananas were used to grease the slipways when more traditional lubricants were not available. By August 1944,

41 ships, including a dry dock section, had mashed 38,800 pounds of bananas that had been carefully placed by hand. In 1944, the shipyard newspaper duly noted that 16,000 bananas, costing a total of $143.60, greased the launch of a dry dock section.[25]

A newspaper account of the February 27, 1942, champagne-christened launch proclaimed, "a veritable greyhound of the seas, the subchaser PC-565, Friday noon slipped sidewise down the banana-greased ways into Greens Bayou, and Uncle Sam was just a tiny bit better-prepared to deal with his ruthless enemies."[26]

At the launching of PC-565, a reporter asked George Brown what he had been thinking as his first boat slid toward the water. "George grinned and answered, 'I was praying she wouldn't turn wrong side up!' "[27] He needn't have worried. PC-565 was the first patrol chaser from any shipyard to sink a German U-boat.[28]

The U.S. Navy needed more subchasers. A contract in early 1942 called for a medium-sized

With commonly used lubricants in short supply, banana peels were often used to slide ships sideways into the water. The skids are visible on the left.

BROWN & ROOT

PHOTOS: BROWN & ROOT

fleet of destroyer escorts at $3.3 million each. The workforce at the expanding shipyard would grow from nearly 500 employees in late 1941 to about 10,000 workers, just one year later. Brown Shipbuilding reached peak employment of 23,000 in October 1943.[29]

The Brownship Community

Brownship grew into a community, complete with its own band, social clubs and newspaper. The paper provided information on shipyard news and sports, rides and bus schedules, places to rent, and the deaths and marriages of workers and their relatives. The paper exhorted residents to conserve gas and other items for the war effort. Workers were informed that by prohibiting the manufacture of manicure tools, such as nail files and clippers, the War Production Board saved 1,815 tons of steel a year, enough to make more than 170 155mm guns. They learned that a single 9-foot by 12-foot rug provided enough jute to make 32 sand bags.[30]

Ships built at Brownship were lauded for their successes in battles and mourned when sunk. A 1944 article lamented the "heroic death of the destroyer escort U.S.S. *Samuel B. Roberts*,

which was built by men and women of Brownship and went down on October 25 in the great naval battle in the Philippines. ... She died game, charging an overwhelmingly superior force of Japanese warships."[31]

Above: A partially completed destroyer escort slides into the channel at Brownship. The superstructure and armaments are missing.

Below: An aerial photograph of Brownship during World War II.

PHOTOS: BROWN & ROOT

Launchings in the early days were festive, flag-bedecked events with bunting, bands, and a sponsor to christen every ship with a bottle of champagne. At the second launching, in March 1942, the name of 13-year-old Ruby Joyce Halfin was drawn from a bowl containing the names of workers' daughters. She christened PC-566 by breaking a bunting-wrapped champagne bottle against the steel prow. More than 1,500 people attended the launching, and the company presented the young girl with a watch. Workers were treated to a dance at the country club that night. "The most popular dancer was the ship's sponsor. Ruby Joyce wore the evening gown which the men at the yards had taken up a collection to buy for her. It was pink and pretty as Cinderella's ball gown."[32]

Above: Herman Brown's first airplane, a Douglas DC-3, purchased in 1942.

Right: Herman, second from left, and George, second from far right, holding up the Army-Navy "E" For Excellence honor flag, awarded to Brownship for excellence in shipbuilding.

On December 21, 1942, 10 months after its first ship hit the water, Brown Shipbuilding was awarded the coveted Army-Navy "E" flag for excellence in its work. The presentation at the shipyard came on a particularly busy day, in which Brownship launched two destroyer escorts and five invasion boats. A crowd of 31,000 was in attendance as Navy Secretary Frank Knox told the Brown brothers and their workers that "you have given us a miracle of production."[33] The shipyard would receive four stars, each signifying a six-month renewal of the "E" flag excellence award, to add to its pennant.

The Brown brothers were written up in *Time* magazine in early 1943. The article dubbed them Texas Wonder Boys and described their shipyard

as one of the most remarkable in the United States, with "low-cost mass production of small naval vessels in one-third Navy-schedule time. Its management: dapper, energetic Herman Brown, 50, and fast-thinking, early-rising George Brown, 44, a pair of six-foot brothers who were construction contractors only 18 months ago."[34] The article went on to note that the "infant company's backlog is now over $300 million — more orders on hand than giant 38-year-old Bethlehem Steel had three years ago."[35]

However, workers completed the shipyard's first destroyer escort in May 1943, nearly five months behind schedule. The shipyard newspaper explained that "any yard's first ship is a tough ship, and the DE was a new type designed for anti-submarine and other convoy problems peculiar to World War II. ... But the long months of struggling with the first DEs were not in vain. Suddenly, almost magically, the workers 'caught on,' " and began to cut down production time, with the 24th destroyer escort delivered on schedule and the 55th one completed 70 days before contract time.[36] On average, workers would take 98 days to complete a destroyer escort.

Brownship launched its 100th ship, a destroyer escort, in February 1944. Workers were not idled by the launch, as the vessel slid into the water during the Saturday noon lunch period. The shipyard paper said that the 100 ships, placed bow to stern, would stretch 4½ miles and that 168 million pounds of steel had gone into the fleet.[37]

At the time of the 100th launch, work began on another type of ship. The landing ship-medium was faster than larger invasion ships. It would have a length of slightly more than 200 feet and a 34-foot width. The vessels, carrying battle tanks, would be used for the initial assault on enemy beachheads. Brown Shipbuilding was named the leading shipyard to construct the newly designed ships and provide specifications to other yards.[38] Brownship also constructed a small number of patrol frigates and rocket-firing boats.

Also in February 1944, two years after the first launch, Brown Shipbuilding installed the first Navy dry dock ever located in the Houston area. The structure passed its initial test by lifting a 1,300-ton destroyer escort out of

the water. Its introduction meant that ships could now leave the shipyard ready for combat. Previously, they had to be drydocked elsewhere for finishing touches, such as painting and adjustments.[39] One year later, more than 10,000 Brownship workers and their families watched the launch of a landing ship-medium, the 300th ship to slip down the banana-lubricated ways.[40]

Germany surrendered in May 1945. Five days later, five destroyer escorts built by Brown Shipbuilding received a Presidential Unit Citation for their work in sweeping the seas of enemy subs and keeping supply lines open. In June, a Brownship patrol frigate sunk a German submarine in the last battle in the Atlantic Ocean. Japan surrendered in August. A few weeks later, Brownship completed its first peacetime repair job by painting and refurbishing a freighter. By that time, Brownship had launched 355 vessels and repaired or converted 90 other ships.[41]

For cleanup purposes after the war ended, the shipyard built four naval salvage ships, flat-bottomed vessels with two protruding arms, from which cables would be lowered to lift sunken ships that were blocking harbors.[42]

Taking Stock of Brown & Root

While Brown Shipbuilding was busy constructing ships, Brown & Root took steps in December 1942 to increase its capital stock from $700,000 to $1 million. Herman and George each paid in $146,528.55, and Brownship general manager L.T. Bolin, listed simply as a stockholder, made up the difference of $6,942.90. In a financial statement, Brown &

Above: While Brownship built ships, Brown & Root went on to construct other wartime necessities, such as this ammunition depot in McAlester, Oklahoma.

Left: A destroyer escort is decorated in preparation for launch.

BROWN & ROOT

Root listed total assets of $4.7 million and liabilities of $2.5 million. Net profit for the six-month period ended June 30, 1942, was $157,732.21.[43]

Brown & Root was growing, and its owners' shipbuilding enterprise had become the stuff of legends. However, Brown & Root came under IRS scrutiny in the 1940s for alleged contributions to Lyndon Johnson's failed 1941 U.S. Senate campaign. Agents, in examining company books, grew to suspect that Brown & Root had deducted hundreds of thousands of dollars in bonuses and attorneys' fees that actually were disguised campaign contributions, which were not tax deductible.[44] The IRS submitted a final report showing tax deficiencies of $1.1 million and a penalty of $550,000, and Brown & Root ultimately paid a settlement of $372,000.[45] The tax case did not come to light until the 1950s, and by then, the growing company was stretching out globally with its construction projects and reaching beneath the seas for oil.

Brown & Root employees work inside the 1,500-foot diversion tunnel dug through solid rock as part of the construction of the Fena River Dam in Guam.

CHAPTER EIGHT

The World Arena

"'Say,' said the man, 'I know who you are. You're the fellow who built Rice Stadium.' Herman ... neither confirmed nor denied it.'"

— George Fuermann, 1951[1]

WITH WORLD WAR II over, the Brown brothers sought new ventures for their shipyard and engineers. There was no longer any need to build warships and ordnance depots, so they joined in rebuilding war-ravaged areas and converting warships and materials to peacetime use.

Brown & Root's first overseas work came in 1946 when the company participated in reconstruction of the military base on Guam. Developing the huge U.S. military base on the Pacific island would take 11 years and cost $290 million under a contract by the Navy Department Bureau of Yards and Docks. Airfields, roads, utilities, water supply and distribution systems, warehouses, office buildings, shops and communications facilities were all part of the massive project. At one point, workers built a water diversion tunnel, 1,500 feet long and 12 feet in diameter, through solid basalt rock. Guam would become an important base for American bombers during the Vietnam War.

Other construction work included several small U.S. Navy bases in the Micronesian Islands and a Marine base at Tsingtao, China. Company literature tagged the mammoth project as "both the beginning of Brown & Root's worldwide operations and the culmination of a transition of the company from a heavy construction contractor in Texas to a major international engineering and construction firm."[2]

In assessing their wartime workers and facilities, the brothers found that "the equipment that was assembled to build ships was ideal for the construction of process plants. They also found that the mechanics and engineers who were highly skilled in the construction of ships that could cross the Atlantic or Pacific were capable of engineering and fabricating pressure vessels, bubble towers, pipe networks and other components of process plants."[3]

Big Inch and Little Inch

In 1946, Brown & Root created a new petroleum and chemical division, with 1,800 people, at the old Brown Shipbuilding site near Houston. An engineering department was formally established, which employed almost 100 engineers who had worked for the shipyard. M.P. Anderson would be its chief engineer for the next 22 years.

The company's first major engineering contract was to build a $10 million chemical plant for

Elephants were necessary to handle logs at the Bhumiphol Dam site in Thailand in 1962.

Diamond Alkali on the Houston Ship Channel near Pasadena, Texas, outside Houston. The project took about 24 months to complete and required the work of 65 engineers and draftsmen.[4] It was a good project to break into engineering with, as Brown & Root already had some familiarity with the chemical industry, having begun construction of the $35 million Cactus Ordnance Works at Dumas, Texas, near the end of World War II.

Later, Brown & Root won contracts to design gasoline plants, including a project for Shell Oil at No Trees, Texas. The need for gasoline plants had been created after the war, when the Texas legislature enacted legislation forbidding gas flaring on oil wells. For years, gas flaring was a common practice. Companies that lacked equipment to transport the natural gas simply burned it on the spot.

Herman and George had turned their acquisition sights on the Big Inch and Little Inch pipelines, built during the war for defense purposes. The enormous pipelines pumped crude oil and petroleum products 3,000 miles from Gulf Coast oil fields to East Coast cities. The brothers believed that converting the oil lines to gas lines

would be less expensive and time-consuming than building new gas lines. They had their engineers on Greens Bayou study the possibility. When the engineers produced a supporting plan, the brothers convinced three other investors of the merits of the project. In 1947, the group founded the Texas Eastern Transmission Company, which successfully bid $143 million, or 98 percent of cost, to buy the pipelines from the government. A magazine writer noted, "the presentation of that check awed a lot of newsmen, but not George Brown. He thought it was a fair price."[5]

The pipelines were a financial boon for the Browns and fellow investors. Texas Eastern made a profit in its first full year of operation in 1950, despite the payment of principal and interest on the huge bond issue floated to start the company.[6] Texas Eastern, with George as chairman of the board, relied upon Brown & Root for much of its engineering and construction work. Between 1947 and 1984, Brown & Root completed $1.3 billion in work for Texas Eastern, including at least 88 major pipeline and compressor station jobs.[7]

Brown & Root also bought military surplus items, including several ships from the U.S. Navy.

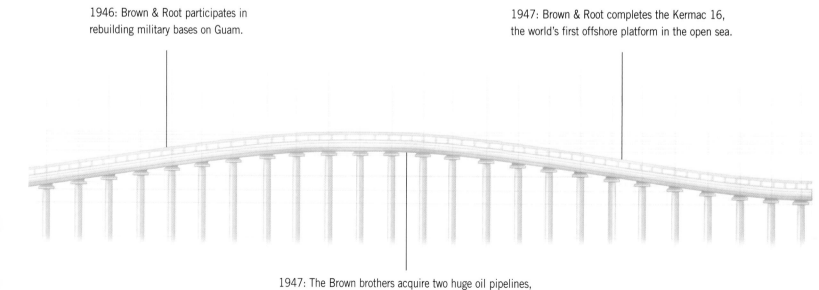

1946: Brown & Root participates in rebuilding military bases on Guam.

1947: Brown & Root completes the Kermac 16, the world's first offshore platform in the open sea.

1947: The Brown brothers acquire two huge oil pipelines, running from the Gulf Coast to East Coast cities.

BROWN & ROOT

Texas Eastern officials deliver a check for $143,027,000 to the federal government in 1947 as final payment for the purchase of the War Emergency Pipelines. From left are: Harvey Gibson, president of Manufacturers Trust Company; George Brown, chairman of Texas Eastern; R.H. Hargrove, president of Texas Eastern; and War Assets Administrator R.M. Littlejohn.

1950: Rice Stadium is completed, at cost by Brown & Root, in time for the first home game, September 30.

1961: Brown & Root wins the contract to design and construct the NASA Manned Spacecraft Center in Houston.

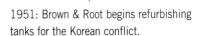

1951: Brown & Root begins refurbishing tanks for the Korean conflict.

1954: The world's longest bridge, across Lake Pontchartrain in Louisiana, is started by Brown & Root and two other construction companies.

The ships were converted into derrick barges for offshore work. The first derrick barge was the *Herman B.*, which had a fixed gantry crane for heavy loads and a smaller revolving crawler crane for lighter loads. In the late 1940s, Brown & Root charged $154 an hour for the use of the *Herman B.* Another converted military surplus freight barge was named for longtime employee, L.T. Bolin.

Frank Motley, who had joined Brown & Root in the early 1930s, recalled that in the days after World War II, a common belief was that offshore work had no future. "When we first went offshore with those two barges, the general opinion in the marine industry was that offshore work would never amount to much," Motley said. "There was no weather warning system, no way of communicating from the barge to the people on shore, and marine-minded people didn't think there was any way to anchor the equipment."[8] That early doubt may sound ridiculous from today's vantage point but "with those first rigs, 15- to 20-foot seas could put you out of business." Motley, who had designed the industry's first pipeline-burying machine in the 1930s, said a ramp and barge system for laying pipe grew out of his "experience with losing the pipe so many times."[9]

Motley's pipe-laying system was introduced in 1951 after he came up with the idea of attaching a ramp to the Herman B. Previously, all submarine pipelines had been laid by the time-consuming flotation method: pipelines were floated into position by barrels and then sunk. With the new system, the pipeline could slope to the ocean floor. Using the ramp, a 10-inch diameter concrete-coated line was laid at a distance of 10 miles, in depths ranging from 14 to 30 feet. The work was done at an average of 3,500 feet per day, far more than what could be done by flotation.[10]

Kermac 16

In 1947, Brown and Root completed the design and construction of the world's first offshore platform that was out of sight of land. Offshore platforms previously had never been in more than about five feet of water and never in the open sea.[11] The platform, called Kermac 16 and built for Kerr-McGee, was located 10 miles off the Louisiana coast in 20 feet of water in the Gulf of Mexico. It cost only $230,000 to build the platform, which was 38 by 71 feet, with a 16-pile jacket.

The *Herman B*, purchased by Brown & Root from the U.S. military after World War II and converted into a derrick barge for offshore work.

BROWN & ROOT

Above: Workers drive piling in 1947 for the Kerr-McGee platform in the Gulf of Mexico.

Below: The Bull Shoals Dam, under construction in 1950 in Arkansas.

Ferdinand Hauber, a civil engineer for Brown & Root, designed the first-of-a-kind platform. His thoughts upon getting the assignment: "How am I going to build this thing?"[12] The platform had to withstand hurricane-force wind and waves, but he had no comparable data on how strong to make the pilings, welds and jacket. Desperate for any information at all, he used data about the jetties, gates and walls of the Panama Canal, which had been built to withstand hurricanes. Kermac 16, with a loading factor of 2,000 pounds per square foot, could withstand winds as fierce as 125 miles per hour, even though it did not have guiding wires. The platform, supported by 16 steel pilings, each 24 inches in diameter, penetrated an average of 104 feet into the ocean floor.[13]

The offshore drilling experiment paid off in November 1947 when Kermac 16 struck oil. Over the next 37 years, until it was shut down in 1984, the well brought in 1.4 million barrels of oil and 307 million cubic feet of natural gas. By that time, Brown & Root had designed and built several billions of dollars worth of offshore facilities around the world.[14] But that well was the first, and a plaque near Morgan City, Louisiana, commemorates it.

By 1947, Brown & Root could look back on a history of various jobs, including paving, bridges, oil field work, dams and military construction, that added up to about $1 billion. Contracts during the late 1940s included a $3 million dock for the U.S. Navy at Orange, Texas; a $6 million paper manufacturing plant expansion for the Southland Paper Company at Lufkin, Texas; and work in association with other companies or individuals, the $7 million Granby Dam in Colorado and the $40 million Bull Shoals Dam in northern Arkansas.[15]

The Bull Shoals Dam

The Bull Shoals Dam on the White River was built by a Brown & Root-sponsored joint venture called Ozark Dam Constructors. The joint venture later would be awarded the contract for the dam's powerhouse and switchyard. Work on the dam would include a seven-mile-long rubber conveyor belt that transported crushed rock for concrete from a quarry site to the batch plant. The

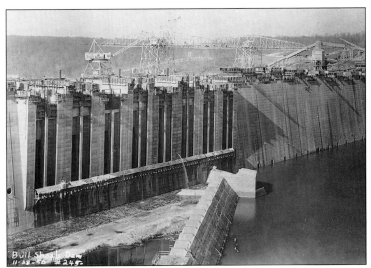

PHOTOS: BROWN & ROOT

BROWN & ROOT

project required a mass concrete cooling method to prevent stress buildup and subsequent cracks. At Bull Shoals, Brown & Root introduced an inundation cooling technique in which heat, created by the concrete when it hydrates, is held to 50 to 65 degrees Fahrenheit.

Progress on the Bull Shoals Dam screeched to a halt in 1948, however, when union men organized a strike. The strike naturally drew the personal attention of Herman, said longtime employee Lloyd Dooley.

"On the 2,000-man job, only 80 people kept working. Herman spent two weeks of the strike at the site helping to keep up morale. ... Herman's presence showed his loyalty to the workers, and they defeated the union vote."[16]

In 1949, Ozark Dam Constructors signed a labor agreement with the International

Cranes from a 180-foot high trestle poured in 2.1 million cubic feet of yards of concrete to build the Bull Shoals Dam.

Association of Machinists, specifically stating union membership was not required. In July 1952, President Harry S. Truman would dedicate the hydroelectric dam as a symbol of "the progress that has come to the South" from his administration.[17]

In December 1948, Brown & Root increased its capital stock from $1 million to $2.5 million. The 15,000 additional shares, worth $100 each, were distributed as a stock dividend, in the amount of $732,600 each to Herman and George, and $34,800 to L.T. Bolin.[18] A scant six years later, in 1954, Brown & Root doubled its capital stock to $5 million.[19]

Suite 8-F

Although Brown & Root's headquarters moved to Houston during the war, Herman continued to live in Austin until 1948. Corporate offices in Austin were located downtown, in the Brown Building. When Herman moved to Houston, he bought a house next door to George in the exclusive River Oaks section. Before the move, Herman used to travel to Houston for a few days in the middle of the week, and then return to Austin for the weekend.[20]

While in Houston, Herman stayed in Suite 8-F of the downtown Lamar Hotel. The two-bedroom suite, decorated by the wives of the Brown brothers, served as a social and political gathering spot for businessmen and power brokers, as well as a place where Lyndon Johnson often stayed. In her book on early Houston, Marguerite Johnston discussed the importance of that suite.

BROWN & ROOT

"From 8-F would come plans for a quail shoot in West Texas or the annual trip to the Kentucky Derby. But also from 8-F came the decision on which candidates they would back, a multi-million-dollar deal on a pipeline, the purchase of land for a future airport to be sold back to the city at cost when the time came, and ultimately, the placement of NASA's Manned Spacecraft Center."[21]

Frank Oltorf, Brown & Root's representative in Washington for many years, described 8-F as a place for Herman's friends and cronies to talk politics and business. "He liked to know what people were thinking and keep his ear to the ground," Oltorf said. "Brown & Root closed every day at 5:15, and various friends would come up to 8-F for a social hour."[22]

The Browns owned a 450-acre dairy farm in Middleburg, Virginia, which they had purchased after World War II. Huntland, as it was called, was a place to stay, and to entertain friends, when the brothers were in Washington. In 1955, Lyndon Johnson, who was then a senator, had a heart attack while visiting Huntland. George called a local doctor, and Johnson was taken by ambulance to Bethesda Naval Hospital in Washington. Oltorf accompanied Johnson to the hospital.

Post-War Tanks and Other Projects

In 1949, Brown & Root once again got involved in dam building. This time, the company was contracted to build not one, but two dams on the Colorado River for the Lower Colorado River Authority. These structures, the Granite Shoals and Marble Falls dams, were built upriver from the Mansfield Dam, Brown & Root's first venture into dam building. The Granite Shoals Dam, which created Lake Granite Shoals, would later be named the Alvin J. Wirtz Dam after the LCRA's first general counsel. Wirtz had helped to iron out legal difficulties that threatened the Mansfield Dam project, a catastrophe that might have put Brown & Root out of business. Lake Granite Shoals would be renamed Lake Lyndon B. Johnson in 1965. The Marble Falls Dam, constructed for hydroelectricity, would also undergo

BROWN & ROOT

Center: The actual key to Suite 8-F, a two-bedroom suite in the Lamar Hotel in Houston. Prominent socialites and power brokers often gathered here, including Lyndon B. Johnson.

Above: A 1951 photograph of the Granite Shoals Dam on the Colorado River in Texas. The 110-foot-high dam was later renamed Alvin Wirtz Dam and its lake named after President Lyndon Johnson.

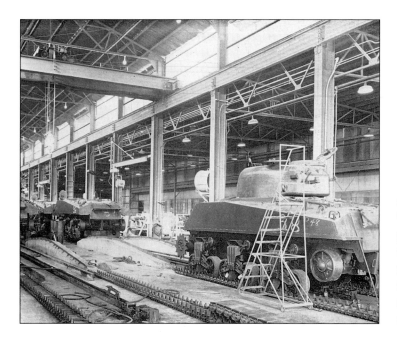

"[Some have] holes burned through their turrets by enemy rockets. Others have paint scarred by rifle and machine gun fire. The white insides of tanks are deep crimson in spots where soldiers were wounded or killed during tank battles in World War II. ... The only thing that identifies them as army tanks are the white stars on the sides, and the faded, rusted-over khaki color."[26]

The article recounted the reconditioning and assembly work at two company locations. "First step in readying a tank for action is to give it a good bath. Live steam is used to scour the tank inside and out." The engines were removed and parts were cleaned and replaced, if necessary. The shell of the tank was then sand-blasted, repaired, repainted and placed on the assembly line.

"The monster of war begins to take shape again. Finally the tracks are fitted, and the smooth, massive unit moves out the door, its engine drowning all sounds, a proud driver grinning from his port. Before the tank is ready for

Above: Brown & Root refurbished battle-scarred tanks from World War II for use in the Korean War.

Below: The tank refurbishing plant in Houston. Old tanks are parked at the left and repaired tanks are parked at the right, inside the circular testing track.

a name change, becoming the Max Starcke Dam in honor of the LCRA's second general manager.[23]

During the 1950s, the Korean War, football, and construction work in other countries led to more Brown & Root projects. In 1950, Brown & Root de Mexico was formed. Its first projects were to build a road in Guajacas and a pipeline in Tuxpan. The following year, the company opened an office in Canada, near Edmonton in the Alberta province. It served as a base for the company during construction of a $50 million petrochemical and synthetic fiber plant for Celanese of Canada. In 1952, Brown & Root expanded to Venezuela, where it began a series of gas injection plants on Lake Maracaibo for various clients.

Brown & Root employees were reconditioning old World War II tanks and manufacturing hulls and turrets for new tanks. In 1951, Brown & Root won a $5 million contract to recondition 1,500 World War II tanks. The company was also constructing a $4 million tank manufacturing plant.[24] Brown & Root would eventually complete $55 million worth of tank work during the early 1950s.[25]

A 1951 newspaper article described the meticulous work that was required to repair the battered war machines. Many of the grimy machines were missing tracks or were incapable of running.

Rice Stadium under construction. The Brown brothers swore to have the 70,000-seat stadium up by the next home game on September 30, 1950.

action, it is run 17 miles by Brown & Root drivers and another 10 miles by army ordnance experts. It has to take a bath in 36 inches of water to see if it has any leaks."[27]

Like the Brownship workers during World War II, the tank refurbishers had a patriotic stake in their finished products. "Many of the machinists, painters, gun experts are World War II tank unit men, and they take special pride in doing a good job on the tanks, because they know what it means to operate in a dependable vehicle. Finally the new-looking tank is shipped, either to a training command or overseas, months ahead of the time it would take to build a new model. A tanker veteran may say 'looks like my old tank,' and he may be right."

Brown & Root on the Gridiron

Brown & Root took on a peacetime project with sentimental value when it built, at cost, a 70,000-seat stadium for George's beloved alma mater, Rice University. Constructing the $2.5 million stadium at cost saved the university $250,000.[28]

The stadium meant a lot to fans because in the late 1940s and early 1950s, Rice football was the only game in town. "There was no professional competition to the Southwest Conference until 1950; the University of Houston at the time was strictly minor league; and the 30-year-old stadium the Owls were playing in was just too small to handle the crowds."[29]

The Rice Stadium project added to the legend of the Browns and their company. The brothers were described in a 1950 newspaper article as avid football fans, who,"by flying in the Brown & Root plane, often see two games on the same day." Herman would root for the University of Texas and George would root for Rice.[30]

At the end of the 1949 season, Brown builders started on the stadium, promising to complete it by the next home game on September 30. To meet the deadline, employees worked 16- and 18-hour days, seven days a week, from

January through September. As if the workers didn't have enough of a challenge, union pickets were set up to disrupt the work.

"But loyal Brown & Root employees crossed the lines and kept laying the huge foundation. Still, it appeared for a time that the stadium would never be ready in time for the game, when a reporter cornered Herman Brown and asked him about it. What would he do if the stadium were not finished by game day, the reporter asked. 'Well, it's a night game, isn't it?' snapped Herman Brown."[31]

Legend has it that wheelbarrows of dirt were still being carted off the field when Rice kicked off to Santa Clara. The Owls went on to win 24-6.

When the stadium was completed, the field was 26 feet below ground level, allowing for easy access to all seats. The sunken field was protected from sub-surface water by a dam that the company built 40 feet below the playing surface.[32] George, a Rice trustee since 1943, was named chairman of the school in 1950. Twenty years after the stadium was built, Brown & Root did the excavation and paving needed to install Astroturf.

Although company publications bragged about Rice Stadium, the Browns themselves did not. "Compared with the Browns, [the famously reclusive] Greta Garbo is a wild, arm-waving publicity hound," commented George Fuermann in his 1951 book on Houston's movers and shakers. Herman, he wrote, "really keynoted the brothers' thinking one day when he seriously allowed that he could not decide which kind of publicity was worse — good or bad."[33]

In one wonderful anecdote, a young couple was thumbing a ride on a downtown Houston street in 1950 when a chauffeur-driven limousine slowed to pick them up.

"Their host, they found, was Herman Brown, and in the car also were several others they did not meet. 'Say,' said the man, 'I know who you are. You're the fellow who built Rice Stadium.' Herman ... neither confirmed nor denied it, but the couple was obviously impressed and they thanked Brown profusely when they got out.

They would have been additionally impressed had they known that in the car also was Allan Shivers, governor of Texas. The Browns, though courteous men, would never make a show of being with a governor or anybody else who was important."[34]

National Causes

Brown & Root, which prided itself on its open shop, had battled unions on the legislative front several times. "By 1947 Brown & Root was so powerful in Texas, it led a many-aspected campaign against unions which made Texas one of the most anti-union states in the Union and the only major industrial state that has a law prohibiting workers from voting to be all-union," wrote Lyndon B. Johnson biographer Ronnie Dugger.[35]

In 1950, the company also battled unions in the courtroom. Brown & Root sued the American Federation of Labor, the national building crafts, and local unions and trade councils in Houston, Austin and Beaumont. The sweeping lawsuit charged that union men had picketed Brown & Root job sites as part of a conspiracy to force the company to become a closed shop. The judge in the case ruled for Brown & Root, and forbade 56 local unions and their councils from picketing Brown & Root, placing its name on any unfair list, or conspiring to force a closed shop on the company. Labor, which accused Brown & Root of discriminating against employees for union activity and refusing to deal with unions, appealed and the case finally was settled by agreement.[36]

In early 1951, President Harry S. Truman wrote George to ask him to be a part of a newly created commission to study the nation's supply problems, "in view of your extensive knowledge of the United States economy and your well-known concern for the public interest." George joined four others on the President's Materials Policy Commission, also known as the Paley Commission since it was headed by Columbia Broadcasting System Chairman William S. Paley. The commission worked for 18 months, giving Truman a five-volume report on metals, petroleum and other resources in June 1952. Recommendations included the elimination of tariffs on important raw and processed materials, government-supported research to improve exploration methods and changes in tax laws to encourage conservation.[37]

A 1952 company advertisement, quoting a newspaper article, noted that in 1951, Brown & Root led Texas contractors in construction contracts. Of $1.1 billion in contracts throughout the state, Brown & Root was estimated to have won nearly $200 million in business, including a $73 million contract to build a plant for Lone Star Steel Company near Daingerfield.[38] A year later, Brown & Root landed its first $100 million job, to design and build a polyethylene plant for Union Carbide in Seadrift, Texas. When the facility was complete, Brown & Root was hired to maintain it.

While still involved in the military rebuilding work on Guam, Brown & Root began construction and management of NATO bases in France and Air Force and Navy bases in Spain. In 1953, naval officials announced that Brown & Root was one of three companies chosen to build five Air Force bases, a Navy base, and several aircraft warning stations in Spain. The other two companies were Raymond International and Walsh Construction Company. At one point, the three companies had to lay a 470-mile pipeline to provide fuel for the Spanish bases. The entire thing had to be placed underground to protect it from bombing. The total project employed 20,000 Spaniards and 4,000 Americans and cost $360 million.[39]

George Brown, far left, was asked by President Truman, seated on left, to join a committee studying the nation's material supply problems. George would serve four presidents during his life.

BROWN & ROOT

Back in the United States, Brown & Root in 1953 was continuing its involvement in the pulp and paper industry. In December of that year, Brown & Root joined with Valite Corporation, an affiliate of Valentine Sugars, to form the Valentine Pulp and Paper Company. The new company built a paper mill in Lockport, Louisiana, that initially produced 50 tons of finished paper products daily. The plant in south Louisiana's sugar belt "was the first in the world to use both the pith and the fiber of the sugar cane in the manufacture of paper." In its first three years in production, more than $10 million worth of paper was sold.[40]

Valentine Pulp and Paper merged with Brown & Root in late 1958.[41]

The Longest Bridge in the World

In 1954, Brown & Root joined with Raymond International and T.L. James and Company to form Prestressed Concrete, a joint venture that constructed the world's longest bridge across Lake Pontchartrain in Louisiana.

Conventional highway equipment could not be used to build the 24-mile bridge. Derrick barges were relied on to set and drive pilings, and then position and attach the precast deck sections. The precast spans, piles and beams for the bridge were manufactured at a precast plant built specifically for the project.

At the site, whirly cranes lifted the concrete piles from the cargo barge and placed them in pile-driving

Below: The fuel storage tunnel at the El Ferrol Naval Base in 1958.

Inset: The 470-mile underground pipeline provided fuel for bases throughout Spain.

MAP ADAPTED FROM *NEW YORK TIMES*, 1956

BROWN & ROOT

Above: This 1968 photograph shows the twin spans of the Lake Pontchartrain Causeway; the original span was built for two-way traffic a dozen years earlier.

Inset: The Escambia Bay Bridge near Pensacola, Florida, is a 13,597-foot-long dual bridge built by Brown & Root.

PHOTOS: BROWN & ROOT

templates. With the templates holding the piles in place, the supporting piles were driven into the lake bed by other cranes. Caps were carefully positioned on top to line and grade, and a reinforcing cage, which would be encased in concrete, was used to securely attach the caps to the piles, as well as support the huge precast deck sections. Derrick barges then set the deck sections in place on the 126,055-foot-long bridge.[42]

Prestressed's work did not end there. It constructed a section of Interstate 10 through Louisiana's marshlands. More than a decade after the first bridge was built, the same joint venture constructed a parallel causeway across the lake — at even less cost.[43] The cost reduction was made

possible by the development of more efficient construction methods. Prestressed also built the Escambia Bay Bridge near Pensacola, Florida, and seven miles of twin-trestle bridges across Alabama's Mobile Bay and the Tensaw River.

Offshore Platforms

Back in Houston, Brown & Root was busy offshore. In 1956, the company installed the first offshore platform in depths of 100 feet, progressing to 200 feet and then 300 feet and deeper. In 1957, the derrick barge *L.T. Bolin* assisted in the laying of several pipelines in Lake Maracaibo in Venezuela, including a 40-inch diameter line for the Creole Petroleum Corporation.[44]

Brown & Root knew enough about precast concrete to know it could build the world's longest bridge — the 24-mile-long Lake Pontchartrain Causeway — for a lot less money than with poured-in-place. On this basis the company won the contract not only to design and build the first bridge in 1956, but also its companion bridge in 1967.

GREEN/BROWN & ROOT

In 1959, Brown & Root built the largest self-contained platform the world had ever seen, capable of drilling 40 wells at a depth of 70 feet.[45] The company also laid pipe in greater depths than ever before, and had developed the technique for "floating" drilling. Floating vessels proved valuable for marine drilling because they permitted greater mobility and allowed for drilling at almost any water depth. Using a large barge, Brown & Root had drilled hundreds of test holes in the bottom of the Gulf of Mexico to determine the factors needed in the design of stationary drilling and production platforms. The company used barges to drill 32 offshore core holes for Texas Gulf, Inc.

International Ventures

Toward the end of the decade, Brown & Root went into both Australia and Thailand for the first time to build dams. In 1958, the company won a contract for construction of the Tantangara Dam and Tunnel for the Snowy Mountains Hydroelectric Authority. Also that year, Brown & Root began construction of the Bhumiphol Dam in Thailand. When completed in 1963, the high-arch dam was 504 feet high and 1,500 feet long. The dam was located in a mountainous jungle region of northern Thailand that was accessible only by rugged dirt roads. The major source of equipment and supplies was 12,000 miles away by ship. Bangkok, the nearest big city, was 385 miles away. At the peak of construction, 60 American employees and 4,000 Thais worked on the project.[46] To make life more pleasant in the remote camp, workers planted trees and shrubs and opened a school house. Some of the American workers bought spider monkeys and young ocelots as pets, and golf enthusiasts journeyed to an air strip a few miles away to hit balls.[47]

As the 1950s ended, the Browns expressed pride in their organization but warned against overconfidence. "We must approach 1960 with additional vigor and determination. Money will be tight for new construction, and the competition for what business there

Right: The concrete for the 504-foot-high Bhumiphol Dam, Thailand, shown here in this 1962 photograph, was deposited from a steel trestle using three whirley-type cranes on gantries.

Inset: Elephants comprised the log-handling equipment at the Bhumiphol Dam site. Elephants removed teakwood logs from the reservoir to prevent blocking the water diversion tunnels.

PHOTOS: BROWN & ROOT

is will be even greater. The companies who are able to reduce overhead and find a better way to do the job will survive."[48]

Through the 1960s, there seemed to be no limits to what Brown & Root could achieve. The company participated in the space program that represented the nation's future and prepared to bore deep into the earth to learn about the distant past. Amid these exciting times, the aging Brown brothers were preparing to sell

the company that Herman had literally raised out of the mud.

President John F. Kennedy promised to put a man on the moon by the end of the decade. In 1961, the National Aeronautics and Space Administration announced plans to build a spacecraft center somewhere in the continental United States. Many cities clamored for the chance to host the project, but political clout and a creative real estate swap landed the center in Houston. George Brown said Texas Congressman Albert Thomas, chairman of the House appropriations subcommittee that controlled NASA funds, played a key role in locating the center in Houston. "Everybody wanted it, and he couldn't get it for Houston ... unless we got some land," George said. "So, knowing about this big ranch the Humble Oil company had, I went to the head of the Humble company and he agreed to give a thousand acres." Humble Oil, now known as Exxon, donated a 1,000-acre tract of cow pastures and rice fields to Rice University. Rice then gave the land, plus 600 adjoining acres it bought from Humble, to NASA.[49]

NASA named Brown & Root as the architect-engineer for the $200 million Manned Spacecraft Center, now known as the Johnson Space Center. With a $2.3 million contract to design a complex that would resemble a large campus, Brown & Root lined up architectural and engineering experts from other firms, including master planners Charles Luckman Associates of Los Angeles, to help design the office buildings and laboratories. Design contracts for the more exotic facilities, such as the mission control center and environmental test facility, went to other firms.[50]

Company officials described the space project as similar to a joint venture, with Brown & Root providing all management functions. About 200 men worked on it, including 120 Brown & Root workers. About half of the 80 employees who did not work for Brown & Root were architects. Four months into the work, with the job about two-thirds completed, NASA cut the project's building budget from $24.5 million to $18 million. Company officials said the Brown brothers gave their personal word to Vice President Lyndon B. Johnson that the firm would meet all schedules. Brown & Root project manager

William M. Rice said employees worked 16- to 18-hour days on the redesign. "We never missed a deadline and the Browns have maintained their reputation for getting things done," Rice proudly stated in a 1962 interview.[51]

Gary Morris, senior vice president of Shared Services, explained that meeting deadlines and honoring contracts have always been historical imperatives for the company.

"When Brown & Root says they will get it done, they will get it done. [Customers] know that once the contract is signed, we live by our contract. ... Brown & Root tries to state its intentions: we're to do this, and we have done it."[52]

Within a single year, all 25 of the initial buildings for the space center, as well as the master plan infrastructure, had been designed. It was more than a million square feet. "When you're talking about designing 25 buildings, that's not much time," Brown & Root architect Albert Sheppard said in a 1980 interview. "Normally, you do a building in six months. But we were working simultaneously on all of them, and when you're doing this, the master plan is also going simultaneously."[53]

Brown & Root returned to the space center in 1963 to design the Thermochemical Test Facility, which tested pyrotechnic, propulsion and electrical power systems. That same year, Brown & Root formed a joint venture with Northrop Corporation called BRN, responsible for the start-up, operation and maintenance of the

BROWN & ROOT

A model of the drilling platform designed by Brown & Root for Project Mohole.

various labs within the center. Company workers were involved in everything from testing laboratory environments for safety to training astronauts in using the survival equipment necessary for rescue missions. Some even went through crew training so they could be available as substitute test crew members.[54]

Project Mohole

Space was not the only frontier that Brown & Root helped to explore. In 1960, the National Science Foundation began ambitious plans to drill through the earth's crust to pierce the mantle, many miles down. Scientists hoped to develop an accurate profile of the earth, and learn how it evolved over millions of years. Princeton University geologist Harry H. Hess, one of the scientists to first advance the idea of drilling into the mantle, considered pure scientific curiosity the main reason for the project, explaining, "Every school child wants to know what is inside the earth."[55]

The project was called Project Mohole, in honor of Andrija Mohorovicic, who had discovered the seismic discontinuity between the earth's crust and the harder, thicker mantle below. The mantle lies 18 to 30 miles below the earth's land surfaces but only three to six miles below the ocean bottom. In 1962, after two years of preliminary drilling, the National Science Foundation awarded Brown & Root the contract for Phase II, the actual penetration of the mantle. The site chosen was 170 miles northeast of Honolulu in the Pacific Ocean, where the crust was thinnest. The site was in 14,000 feet of water, and from there, 21,000 feet from the crust to the mantle. The deepest drill on record was 25,000 feet on land.[56]

The project would never come to fruition but it would create new technology that would benefit the offshore industry. The drilling would require a stable floating structure, a way to keep it in position, and at least three years to drill. Brown & Root designed a self-propelled, semi-submersible drilling platform, which would serve as the prototype for all subsequent semi-submersibles. It was 279 feet long, 234 feet wide and 23 feet high. Other companies also contributed newly designed equipment. Honeywell Inc. developed a dynamic positioning system that was the forerunner for today's system to keep the platform on location. It combines sonar, radar and computers to control the platform's electrically powered underwater propulsion units. Dresser Inc. developed the turbo corer, which was essentially a downhole-motor supply torque to the drill bit. It minimized drill pipe rotation and thus wear and tear on the riser pipe.[57]

Controversy over the project's cost and opposition to selection of Brown & Root plagued Project Mohole. Bidders complained that the company was not the first choice in three evaluations for the $1.2 million contract to proceed with preliminary design and engineering studies. However, a National Science Foundation spokesman said Brown & Root got the contract because it had wide experience in project man-

agement and an enviable record in design and management. The spokesman said the foundation also wanted to prevent the other applicants, which just happened to be oil companies, from reaping a competitive advantage from the Mohole drilling.[58] Herman said one of the big problems on a project like Mohole was that "you'll find a lot of experts will develop overnight in something no one has ever done before, and we're running into that here."[59]

But it would be the ever-rising costs that would scuttle the project. A company publication would say that Mohole funds were cut off to help fund the Vietnam War. Expected costs for Mohole, dubbed "Project Rathole" by critics, had jumped from $20 million or so in 1959 when it was first conceived to $127 million in 1966.[60] In any case, Congress voted 108-58 to reject the 1967 appropriation of $19.7 million to continue the project. Brown & Root company officials characterized the lost effort as "a tragic regression in our nation's scientific advancement."[61] A Senate report estimated the total cost of the aborted project at $36.6 million — $25 million already expended and $11.6 million to close out the contract with Brown & Root.[62]

In 1962, not long after the start of Project Mohole, Brown & Root would undergo a dramatic, but largely invisible, change of ownership.

ADVERTISING

Innovation, reliability and versatility are the hallmarks of the Halliburton Company and its subsidiaries.

The Giants Join Forces

"Halliburton management told Brown & Root, 'You can continue to run your operation because we know the oil field service business. You know the engineering construction business.'"

— John P. "Jack" Harbin, 1995[1]

BY 1962, THE SUN literally never set on Halliburton. The small Texas well-cementing company had become a mammoth international conglomerate. Its employees operated on every continent except Antarctica, and was recognized for this unusual global scope with an E-For-Export flag for its achievements in foreign trade. Revenues topped $195 million. But the biggest news of the year was Halliburton's acquisition of the engineering and construction giant, Brown & Root.

Herman and George Brown had been searching for a suitable buyer for Brown & Root ever since 68-year-old Herman underwent heart surgery in 1960. "It became apparent to Herman and me that we couldn't live forever, and that the company had gotten so large that death taxes would curtail operations pretty badly," George recalled. In early 1962, the brothers quietly turned over all their Brown & Root stock to the Brown Foundation, a charitable organization founded in July 1951 by the Browns and their wives.[2]

By that time, Brown & Root had generated revenues of about $250 million annually for the previous five years.[3] With a payroll of more than 25,000 employees and $4 billion in work, it had sent workers around the world.[4] Senior Vice President and Regional Manager Stephen Zander commented in 1996 that the company had never shied away from difficult or dangerous assignments.

"Things like Project Mohole, pipeline work and offshore platforms, we didn't have any doubt we could do it. No matter what the challenge was, I think, then and now, you'll find that the Brown & Root people believe they can handle virtually any challenge."[5]

The Brown brothers wanted to sell Brown & Root to a corporation that reflected their business practices, philosophy and history: an enterprise grown by work-roughened hands that knew how to make money. George took the initiative with Halliburton, he later explained. "We began to look around to see a service company that we thought had the same concepts of operation and treatment of employees and of free enterprise that we had, and I approached the officers of Halliburton."[6]

The original deal fell through. Though the reason is unclear, it appears likely that Herman was ultimately reluctant to sell off the company that he had struggled so hard to build. More than 30 years earlier, it had been Herman who had

---

Herman Brown, who built his company up from worn-out mules, died five days following his 70th birthday.

resisted his banker's pleas to sell off municipal paving notes — which represented years of work — at a discount at a time when municipalities were going bankrupt. George had been the one to sell the notes and save the company. "The deal was called off," recalled Jack P. Harbin, who was vice president of finance of Halliburton while the deal was under negotiation, and CEO from 1972 to 1983. He explained what happened next.

"When I was [in Argentina], Herman Brown died. George said, 'Let's get this deal back on.' I came back, and I negotiated with George. ... We made the deal. They did not want to sell to a competitor. They did not want to sell to a company that had unions. They wanted somebody who would agree to let the management run the engineering construction operations. They chose Halliburton because we met the criteria."[7]

Herman had died November 15, 1962, just five days after his 70th birthday. Working a full day on the day of his death, he had flown to Austin on business, then returned to Houston for a luncheon meeting with the directors of an affiliated company. After a brief rest, he worked in his office until 6 p.m. before attending a business reception at a downtown private club, where he suffered a fatal heart attack.

A commemorative company publication mourned his death. "'Mr. Herman' to many an old-timer was Brown & Root, and his passing shocked the company from top to bottom as nothing had ever done before," noted one article.[8] "Herman Brown, who built a construction empire from a team of mortgaged mules, died ... within reach of a dream to explore space and the depths of the earth," commented the *Houston Press*.[9]

In remarks published the day of his passing, Herman discussed the business philosophy that had made his company so successful. "Keep up with the new things," he advised, "or you'll be obsolete yourself before you know it. Anybody can do the easy things. Look for the harder jobs if you want to keep ahead."[10]

More than 1,300 people overflowed the large stone Gothic church for Herman's funeral. Among those attending were Congressman Albert Thomas, governor-elect John Connally and Vice President Lyndon Johnson, who described Herman as "a builder ... of his community, his country, and his world."[11] In February 1963, the Texas House of Representatives honored Herman and his wife, Margarett, who died only two months later, with a resolution that described Herman as a "tycoon" and a "master builder, a giant who made the earth shrink."[12]

In the days following Herman's death, George was elected president of Brown & Root. L.T. Bolin, the former number three man at the company, assumed George's position as executive vice president. Bolin continued as chairman of the company's operating committee, which consisted of the company's six vice presidents. The committee, which included future Brown & Root presidents Herbert J. Frensley and Foster Parker, met every Monday to discuss company business. Company spokesman Brown Booth, a nephew of Herman and George, said in a 1962 interview that the brothers had not wanted a formal board of directors. "The Browns can do what they want to, take any risks they want to, and move as fast as they want to without having to answer to a board of directors."[13]

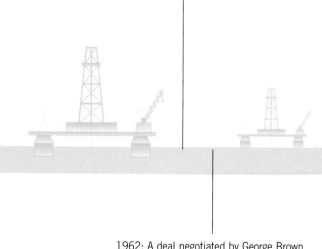

1960: After Herman's heart surgery, the Browns begin looking for buyer for Brown & Root.

1962: A deal negotiated by George Brown and Halliburton executives falls through.

HALLIBURTON CO.

Herbert Frensley, future president of Brown & Root, shown soon after the purchase by the Halliburton Company.

November 1962: Herman Brown dies. Deal with Halliburton back on track.

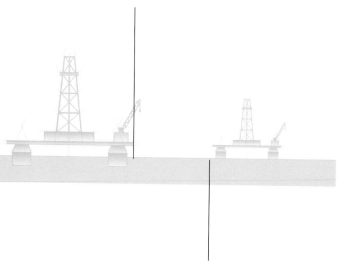

December 1962: Halliburton purchases Brown & Root.

One month after Herman's death, in December 1962, Dallas-based Halliburton acquired Brown & Root. The two companies shared many similarities. Both were engaged in research and engineering projects around the globe. Both were industry leaders involved in some of the most exciting and challenging projects of the times. Both were started by men of courage and determination, unafraid to risk everything they owned. Herman Brown had started Brown & Root in 1919 with mortgaged mules, the very same year that Erle Halliburton borrowed mules to start his well cementing business.

Former CEO Jack Harbin said Halliburton was interested in Brown & Root because it welcomed the chance to invest in the marine construction business, which was booming. Halliburton Company paid $36.7 million for the

95 percent interest in Brown & Root that was owned by the Brown Foundation. George was elected to Halliburton's board of directors. The purchase included Brown & Root's subsidiaries: Southwestern Pipe, Inc.; the trucking company, Joe D. Hughes, Inc.; and Highlands Insurance Company. As each subsidiary had its own management, Halliburton Company had, in effect, become a holding company. Primarily because of the acquisition, Halliburton's net revenue in 1963 increased 76 percent, to $344,553,382.[14]

A Diversified Whole

Even though it was now a part of Halliburton, Brown & Root operated much as it had under the Brown brothers. Halliburton's philosophy was to leave successful subsidiaries alone. It was a philosophy that had worked with Otis and Welex, and it was one that Halliburton intended to continue with Brown & Root, as Harbin explained.

> *"Halliburton management told Brown & Root, 'You can continue to run your operation because we know the oil field service business. You know the engineering construction business.'"*[15]

Thousands of Brown & Root employees had been worried about what would happen after "Mr. Herman" passed on. Halliburton's hands-off policy generated a collective sigh of relief. Brown & Root Senior Vice President Gary Montgomery, who got his first full-time job at Brown & Root in 1961 after working several summers there, recalled the atmosphere at Brown & Root. "There were probably two schools of thought: one is the fear of the unknown and the other is at least now we know what might happen after Mr. Herman Brown dies."[16] Workers had no reason to worry because Brown & Root's management and philosophy remained the same, explained Thomas Cruikshank, who joined Halliburton in 1969 and was chairman and CEO from 1989 to 1995.

> *"Halliburton and Brown & Root had totally different cultures. Our philosophy at Halliburton was that when we acquired something, we wanted it with 'stand-alone' management. We were very proud of the fact that we didn't go in and take over, we just bought and let them have free range to grow. With Brown & Root, every year its income was higher compared to the year before. ...*
> *For years people*

As a lasting memorial to Mr. Herman Brown, the Directors of Brown & Root, Inc. have established the Herman Brown Memorial Fund at Southwestern University in Georgetown, Texas, with their initial personal contributions totaling ten thousand dollars.

Any of our employees and friends who would like to make a memorial contribution to this fund in remembrance of Mr. Herman Brown may send their check directly to Southwestern University.

BROWN & ROOT

who knew that there was a connection thought that Brown & Root had bought Halliburton rather than the other way around."[17]

The purchase of Brown & Root gave Halliburton Company a world-respected engineering and construction asset, one of the biggest in the world. Dale Jones, who joined Halliburton in 1965 as an intern and is now vice chairman of Halliburton, said Brown & Root brought to Halliburton "the reputation to build and manage big projects, especially in the oil and gas industry."

"It can manage the laying of pipeline and the setting up of the facilities. The name 'Halliburton' doesn't bring that sort of thing to mind for our

HOUSTON CHRONICLE

customers, but the Brown & Root name does. Now if you want to talk about downhole technology or well site technology, Halliburton's the name that pops up."[18]

The acquisition was not without the difficulties that are inevitable when two dynamic and independent organizations, each with its own history and loyalties, are brought into close proximity, Jones noted. He said Brown & Root officials wanted limited contact and control by Halliburton.

"Jack Harbin was the primary contact, and his involvement was not always welcome at other than the highest levels. Relations between Brown & Root and Halliburton could have been better."[19]

Despite the friction, the acquisition provided each company with the combined benefits of resources and research. A 1962 *Time* magazine article described the mutual benefits of the sale.

"The Brown Foundation will be able to diversify its investments, and George Brown will stay on as President of Brown & Root. For Halliburton, the purchase is primarily a way of hedging its bets: Said Halliburton Vice President John Harbin: 'The oil industry in general is troubled with excess production and capacity, and we see no immediate hope of things improving. We're trying to develop a cushion, and all we would like is for Brown & Root to keep going as well as it is now.'"[20]

Of mutual interest to both Brown & Root and Halliburton was the rapidly growing field of oil exploration beneath the seas. The services and products of previous acquisitions, such as

Opposite: A special company publication included this memorial announcement for Herman Brown.

Left: More than 1,300 people came to mourn the passing of Herman Brown, affectionately known as Mr. Herman by his workers.

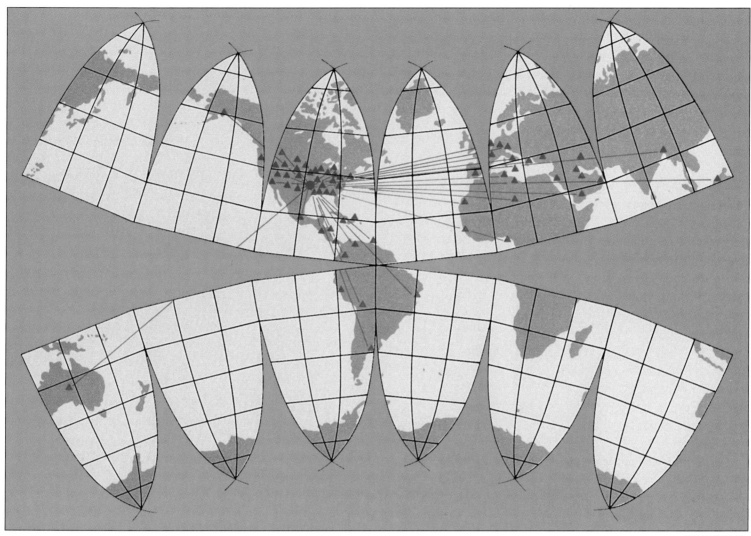

Otis Engineering, provided new tools for this exciting new challenge. Otis had developed, for example, a system that used pumps to operate tools from remote sites. Halliburton also provided a deep reservoir of cash available to Brown & Root. Two years following the acquisition, Brown & Root would expand its marine fleet at a cost of $100 million.[21]

In spite of its size, Halliburton kept a low profile, especially compared to Brown & Root. Halliburton could be a mystery even to some of its own employees, commented Susan Keith, vice president-secretary and corporate counsel, who joined Halliburton after graduating from law school in 1975.

"Even when I was first hired, for the first few months I couldn't figure out what it was that Halliburton did. Brown & Root is sort of simple. Everybody knows about engineering and construction companies, but I had not a clue as to what oil field services meant."[22]

Above: The ever-growing World of Halliburton was spread over 45 nations and in 32 states, as shown in this Halliburton map.

Left: 1963 Halliburton Annual Report.

In its 1963 Annual Report, President Preach Meaders took pains to remind employees and stockholders that Halliburton continued to focus on its original mission to provide complete oil well service to customers, despite its recent acquisitions.

"It should be carefully noted that concerted emphasis is still given to oil field services which continue to be extremely important to your company and, in addition, similar emphasis is being given to the expanded scope of activities in order to strengthen the company and provide additional earnings."[23]

After the merger, Halliburton's revenues in 1963 skyrocketed from $195.6 million to $344.6 million, representing increased earnings of 22 percent, from $15.8 million to $19.3 million. The company had a combined workforce of 16,600 employees, working from 250 locations in 32 states and 140 locations in 45 foreign countries.[24]

Construction News

FEBRUARY 1975

To Highlands Fabricators, in association
with the Man of the Year award, in recognition of the
successful completion and launch of the world's
largest steel jacket for installation in the BP Forties Field,
at a depth greater than previously attempted

BROWN & ROOT

The venerable British trade magazine *Construction News* praised Brown & Root's joint venture to build Highland One.
The Man of the Year Award was presented to a British petroleum manager.

New Frontiers

"You kept going into these new frontiers and deeper and deeper water, more severe climates and higher waves. There were technical break-throughs that helped create a new industry. A lot of those things look pretty routine now, but I tell you there were some real gut-wrenching times when it started."

— Tommy Knight, 1996[1]

I N SEPTEMBER 1963, George Brown stepped down as president of Brown & Root to become chairman and chief executive officer of the organization. Although the company was owned by Halliburton, George maintained control over major corporate changes. He offered the presidency to longtime Brown & Root manager L.T. Bolin, who turned it down, electing instead to become senior executive vice president. Bolin would reach the mandatory retirement age of 65 in three years. He thought it better, for the sake of continuity, to give the job to Vice President Herbert Frensley, who would not reach retirement age until 1975.[2] Frensley, an Oklahoma native and certified public accountant, had joined Brown Shipbuilding in 1942 as an administrative assistant and moved on to Brown & Root after World War II.

After George left the presidency, he became more involved in public service. In 1965, President Lyndon B. Johnson appointed George and 11 other men to a special presidential committee that studied United States trade relations with Eastern Europe and the Soviet Union. George did not see as much of his old friend during Johnson's busy years as president. But during a 1967 visit, George, in a 1977 interview, recalled how he became one of the first people to learn that Johnson would not seek re-election.

"We went swimming, just the two of us, in the pool in the White House, and he told me, 'you don't believe me, but I am not going to run.' I said, 'I don't believe you. It's in your bones and in your mind. You couldn't quit if you wanted to.' He said, 'I'm going to.'"[3]

Vietnam

In 1965, Brown & Root reached another milestone in its history with the construction of the Phan Rang Air Base in Vietnam. Brown & Root was part of a four–company combine called RMK–BRJ, sponsored by Morrison–Knudsen Company Inc. The other two companies were Raymond International and J.A. Jones. This venture became the largest civilian contractor of the war, with a peak workforce of 52,000. Projects included airfields, harbor facilities, roads, bridges, hospitals and a fuel storage and distribution system.

Brown & Root supervised the construction of Phan Rang Air Base, one of the largest projects built by the consortium. But the General

Sharon Gillean, daughter of receptionist Louise Gillean, holds up a copy of the service pin awarded to employees with two years of service.

BROWN & ROOT

Phan Rang Air Force Base, built by Brown & Root in Vietnam.

1963: George Brown steps down as president
of Brown & Root.

1966: The Trading Bay Monopod oil platform
is built by Brown & Root.

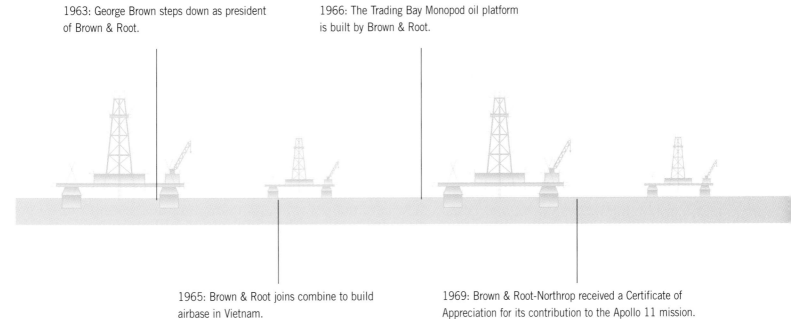

1965: Brown & Root joins combine to build
airbase in Vietnam.

1969: Brown & Root-Northrop received a Certificate of
Appreciation for its contribution to the Apollo 11 mission.

Accounting Office, an independent government agency responsible for auditing government expenditures, delivered a critical report on the joint venture that said, in part, that "normal management controls were virtually abandoned." The report claimed that RMK–BRJ lost accounting controls of $120 million, and the company's security controls were so lax that millions of dollars worth of equipment had been stolen.[4]

Deeper into Offshore Work

Brown & Root had been involved in offshore work as early as 1936, when workers laid a wooden platform and piping for Humble Oil (later known as Exxon) in Galveston Bay, Texas. Thirty-three years later, Brown & Root laid the first marine pipeline in the rugged waters of the North Sea for British Petroleum Development Ltd. The pipe was 45 miles long and 16 inches in diameter. Tommy Knight, former president and CEO of Brown & Root, said the financial and personal risks involved in building oil platforms grew quickly.

"You kept going into these new frontiers and deeper and deeper water, more severe climates and higher waves. There were technical breakthroughs that helped to create a new industry. A lot of those things look pretty routine now, but I tell you there were some real gut-wrenching times when it started. You designed platforms, and you had $100 million on the line. You'd dump one of those things in the ocean and you didn't know for sure if it was going to come back up. We installed a platform in the North Sea where we had explosive bolts to separate two pieces of it, like in a lunar module. If every one of those things didn't work right, you had a $100 million monument laying there on the bottom of the North Sea. That's the reason why I'm so gray."[5]

Thad "Bo" Smith III, who is today president of Brown & Root Services, remembered going into the North Sea when he was in his late 20s. Before this assignment, Smith had been in the waters off Kuwait, where he helped lay the world's first 48-inch, 10-mile-long offshore pipeline. A typical day for Smith meant working the midnight-to-noon shift, living on the barges,

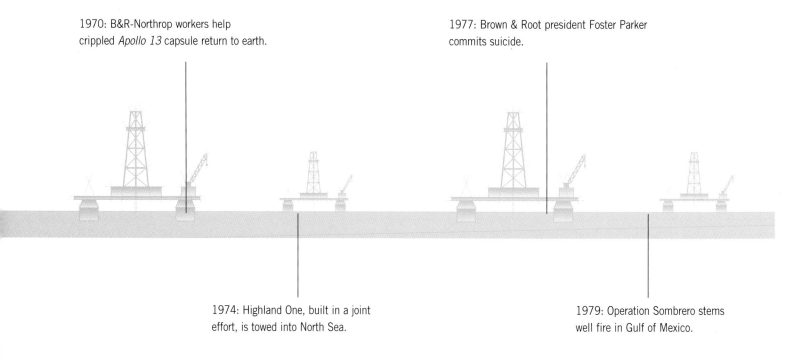

1970: B&R-Northrop workers help crippled *Apollo 13* capsule return to earth.

1977: Brown & Root president Foster Parker commits suicide.

1974: Highland One, built in a joint effort, is towed into North Sea.

1979: Operation Sombrero stems well fire in Gulf of Mexico.

ice, which often moved in tidal currents as fast as eight knots. Dubbed the Trading Bay Monopod, the 5,000-ton platform could withstand temperatures as low as minus 40 degrees.[7] The platform was placed in the Cook Inlet, about 60 miles southwest of Anchorage.

Brown & Root continued to expand its presence in Alaska, especially after British Petroleum discovered oil in Prudhoe Bay on Alaska's North Slope in the late 1960s. The big problem was building the gathering and processing facilities on this icy plain 250 miles north of the Arctic Circle. Temperatures in the region were minus 70 degrees Fahrenheit, with wind chill factors of minus 125 degrees. In 1969, British Petroleum awarded design of the first production facility installed on the North Slope to Brown & Root. The facility, designed as modular components, would be prefabricated in the warm Houston cli-

Left: The barge *L.E. Minor* lays a 48-inch pipe in the Persian Gulf, near Kuwait.

Below: Brown & Root designed and installed the first ice-resistant "monopod" offshore drilling platform in Cook's Inlet, Alaska.

and working in freezing weather with seas that rose between 20 and 40 feet.

"I'll never forget standing and looking down the hallways of the barge. You could see that barge rolling and moving, which was a pretty good sign because if it didn't flex, it would probably have broken. For a young guy like myself, it was a great challenge because we were far away from home and given a lot of responsibility. I was hooked. I just fell in love."[6]

In 1966, Brown & Root opened an office in Anchorage, Alaska, to support the design and installation of a first-of-a-kind offshore drilling platform for Union Oil. The platform's single-post construction offered minimum resistance to pack

PHOTOS: BROWN & ROOT

mate, barged to Alaska and placed on pre-installed pipe foundations.[8]

The Moon Walk

In 1969, *Engineering News-Record* ranked Brown & Root, with orders of $1.7 billion, as the largest engineering and construction firm in the United States. Of Brown & Root's revenues of $669 million, industrial construction accounted for 33 percent and marine operations for 32 percent. Bechtel Corporation of San Francisco was second, the ranking that Brown & Root had held for the previous two years.[9]

A greater source of pride than the ranking was the company's involvement in the first moon landing. On July 20, 1969, astronauts Edwin "Buzz" Aldrin and Neil Armstrong became the first human beings to walk on the moon. Their spacecraft, *Apollo 11*, had been controlled from the space center that Brown & Root had engineered and built in Houston. Following the historic event, George sent a telegram to the director of the Johnson Space Center with his congratulations for the "most dramatic achievement in history of man. I am supremely proud of our participation through Brown & Root-Northrop in this incredible mission."[10] Brown & Root-Northrop, which built and maintained the center's testing chambers, received a Certificate of Appreciation for its contribution to the success of the Apollo 11 mission.

"Houston, we have a problem ..."

The excitement and perils of space would continue for Brown & Root. Its joint venture project, B&R-Northrop, played a critical role in the April 1970 safe return of astronauts Jim Lovell, Fred Haise and John Swigert aboard the crippled *Apollo 13*. For its help, B&R-Northrop received the Medal of Freedom certificate from President Richard M. Nixon.

Two days into the mission, an exploding oxygen tank on the spacecraft caused a rapid loss of electrical power. The astronauts were forced to abort the moon landing, and their very survival was thrown into doubt. The astronauts crammed into the lunar module, which served as

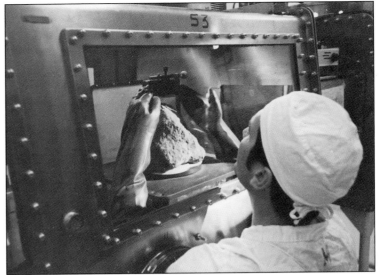

BROWN & ROOT

A B&R-Northrop lab technician prepares to photograph a lunar rock collected during the Apollo 14 moon mission.

a lifeboat. Meanwhile, ground control in Houston feverishly worked to return the crew home as the world anxiously watched on television. The most immediate threat was from carbon dioxide, which reached life-threatening levels because the lunar module was designed for two, not three, astronauts.

B&R-Northrop's Test Support Group worked with the Crew Systems Division of the Johnson Space Center to test an adapter for the removal of carbon dioxide from the lunar module. The adapter, designed by the Crew Systems Division, made it possible for the crew to use the command module's carbon dioxide removal system. It consisted of a liquid cooling-and-ventililation garment storage bag, adhesive tape, and the toe cut from a liquid-cooled garment sock. Hurried testing in a simulation chamber showed the converted system would remove the necessary amount of carbon dioxide, and the *Apollo 13* crew was given step-by-step instructions on building the adapter. The system enabled the astronauts to remain in the lunar module until just before their safe splashdown. The carbon dioxide crisis and its ingenious makeshift solution were highlighted in the popular 1995 movie *Apollo 13*.[11]

Offshore Expansion

In 1971, Brown & Root opened offices in Singapore and Norway to support offshore oil and gas development within those regions. Also that year, the company began the design of four platforms that would be installed in 400 feet of water in British Petroleum's Forties Field in the North Sea.

The jackets and decks of the platforms would be six to eight times more massive than their forerunners.[12] The sheer size of the components for the platforms prompted the need for a fabrication yard to build and launch the mammoth structures. Highland One, a 475–foot–tall jacket, would have a total floating weight of 33,850 tons and contain more steel than the Eiffel Tower. One and a half times the size of the Statue of Liberty, it was designed to withstand wave heights of more than 94 feet and wind gusts up to 131 miles an hour.[13]

The design was so new that educated guesses had to be made about what sort of violent conditions the platforms would have to withstand. In 1969, Dr. Jay Weidler, today senior vice president

Above: On August 14, 1974, Queen Elizabeth paid a royal visit to Highland One, Brown & Root's award-winning joint project.

Below: The jacket for Highland One was built for British Petroleum.

PHOTOS: BROWN & ROOT

of Brown & Root Energy Services, said he was recruited to write a computer program that would predict how the jackets would react in the water after they were winched off the barge. "We had some situations where jackets would stick to the bottom or hit the bottom, and we had some situations where they would roll and do things they weren't supposed to do."[14]

Brown & Root joined with George Wimpey & Co. to form Highlands Fabricators, which later became wholly owned by Brown & Root. Its fabrication yard at Nigg Bay, Scotland, takes up 150 acres and has one of the world's largest graving docks — a hole that measures 1,000 feet by 600 feet with a depth of 50 feet.[15]

Two 11,000–horsepower tugs pulled Highland One to the North Sea in August 1974. The huge jacket, still bearing a Christmas tree and a Scottish flag, was sunk to the bottom of the ocean and pinned into place. Each successful phase of the huge undertaking had been marked with grins of relief, and workers had worn hardhat decals saying, "Not to Worry." But a Brown & Root publication noted that after the successful placement, "one of the largest sighs of relief came from the insurance brokers."

"The jacket and flotation tanks were insured by Lloyd's of London for 50 million pounds. 'When they towed that platform out into the sea, it was the largest sum of money that has ever been on the end of a piece of string,' said one of the brokers. ... It also was being placed in one of the most hazardous stretches of water in the world.'"[16]

Bo Smith, president of Brown & Root Services, recalled just how dangerous areas like the North Sea can be.

BROWN & ROOT

"One of the things you learn is to respect the sea. One night we were picking up anchors and ... one of the deck crew had gotten washed off into the North Sea in the middle of the night. Captain Whitey Adams ... knew the best way to pick him up was to follow the waves and kept positioning that boat. When he caught that wave just right, the guy got washed up back on the tugboat."[17]

Highland One took 30 months to complete. In the days before the launching, Queen Elizabeth and members of the royal family visited the site. A completion party drew more than 12,000 people who listened to bagpipe music and feasted on a menu of soused herring, salmon, venison, salads, strawberries and raspberries, and drank more than 30,000 pints of beer. Christine Pearson, a secretary and the first female employee at the yard, christened the Highland One with a 40-ounce bottle of Glenmorangie, a "locally brewed malt whiskey better known for sipping than for smashing," according to a B&R publication.[18]

Brown & Root also designed and built the Sunda Straits Fabrication Yard in Indonesia, and in 1973, added the Labuan Fabrication Yard in Malaysia. The Labuan yard was built off the coast of Borneo, near the island of Labuan in the South China Sea. The area had a swashbuckling but deadly history. Many of those buried near the yard in an old British naval cemetery had reportedly been slain by fierce pirates in the 19th century. It was also the scene of World War II battles.

New Directions

As the offshore industry expanded, Brown & Root finished up its joint-venture work in Vietnam and in space. The company's eight-year liaison as Brown & Root–Northrop ended in 1972 when Northrop Services, Inc., acquired all assets of the joint venture that had supplied technical support for NASA at Houston and also at the Goddard Space Flight Center at Greenbelt, Maryland. That same year, Brown & Root completed its work as part of the RMK–BRJ joint ven-

Highland One in operation in the perilous North Sea.

Incorporating the world's largest graving dock, the Highlands Fabricators Ltd. yard in Nigg, Scotland, was originally designed and built by Brown & Root in the early 1970s. It was designed to accommodate the fabrication of the massive offshore jackets for British Petroleum's Forties Field development in the North Sea.

ture for the U.S. Navy Facilities Engineering Command in Vietnam.

Divisive debate and demonstrations over Vietnam continued, and Brown & Root became a target of anti-war sentiment. In October 1973, when George Brown accepted a Distinguished Alumnus award from the University of Texas at Austin, several hundred people demonstrated outside and several protestors were taken into custody. His reception at Rice University was also marred by protest. A magazine article noted that "for a number of years he could not appear on the Rice campus without a student group protesting Brown & Root's work in Vietnam, particularly the 'Tiger cages' built to imprison Viet Cong prisoners."[19]

In 1973, Brown & Root returned to the number one ranking for the second time in its history as the nation's largest engineering-construction firm with contracts of $5.3 billion. Brown & Root had remained among the top four companies for years. The number one ranking by *Engineering News-Record* would be awarded to the company again in 1976 and 1977. In 1976, Brown & Root recorded $5.2 billion in contracts. The following year, however, orders fell to $4.7 billion, although the company's ranking did not.[20]

Above: Vice President G.A. Dobelman was among six who perished in a plane crash in 1976.

Below: Foster Parker, president of Brown & Root from 1974 until his death in 1977.

The decline in revenue was mirrored in the orders of other top companies. *Engineering News-Record* attributed it primarily to "weak domestic markets and stronger competition for apparently fewer jobs abroad." The magazine noted that more than three-fourths of Brown & Root's contracts were for work in the United States, with more than $600 million in design-construction contracts.[21]

Brownbuilders continued to relish their ingenuity and perseverance in difficult situations. In the early 1970s, they used cold weather to their advantage in building the 1,745-foot-long Fort Vermilion Bridge over Peace River in Alberta, Canada. With wind-chill temperatures plunging to minus 80 degrees, workers installed several of the huge concrete piers for the bridge using the iced-over river as a construction platform. The ice

PHOTOS: BROWN & ROOT

was five to seven feet thick. The bridge, which replaced a ferry used for river crossings, was completed in 1974.[22]

The years of 1974 and 1975 were marked by executive changes. Foster Parker was named president in July 1974. Parker, a business administration graduate of the University of Texas, had joined Brown & Root in 1956 as controller. He became a vice president only a couple of years later. The Texas native had previously worked for Arthur Andersen & Company of Houston and the Houston Oil Company.

Herbert Frensley, CEO of Brown & Root when Parker became president, was named vice chairman after he stepped down. Frensley retired in January 1975. The same month, George Brown retired as board chairman but continued as a director on the Halliburton board. For the first time, a Brown brother was not directly overseeing Brown & Root.

The next two years would be marked by consecutive tragedies — a plane crash in 1976 that killed four Brown & Root executives, and the suicide a year later of Foster Parker. On January 4, 1976, the chartered plane carrying two pilots and six Brown & Root executives crashed as it attempted to land at Anchorage International Airport. The plane was returning from Deadhorse, Alaska, on the North Slope where the executives had been reviewing the progress of company projects.

Both pilots died in the crash, as did G.A. Dobelman, senior group vice president; Warren T. Moore, president, and Wolf Pabst, vice president, of the Brown & Root subsidiary, Alaska Constructors; and Vic H. Abadie Jr., manager of engineering for the company's San Francisco office. Two other company officers were injured but survived the crash. They were Charles L. Buck Jr., vice president and project director in San Francisco, and W. Bernard Pieper, senior vice president and chief engineer. Pieper, who would become Brown & Root's president 13 years later, vividly recalled the crash.

"It was a really bad day, snow was all around, miserable weather up there. We crashed when we were landing in Anchorage. We hit the ground about 1½ miles short of the runway. There were eight of us on the plane, six were

Following the death of Parker, Thomas Feehan became president in 1977.

killed. ... I stayed conscious pretty well the whole time. Charlie Buck began to get his sense back. We got to talking, and I finally got my seat belt unfastened. I was so disoriented I didn't realize that I was hanging upside down. Charlie, pinned under some chairs and suitcases, found a window broken out."[23]

Suffering from internal injuries, Pieper managed to crawl out of the plane, walk to a nearby road and wave down a passing truck. "The last thing I really remember is that they were sticking a needle into my stomach to see whether I was bleeding or not. ... I remember the doctor coming up later in intensive care and the doctor saying, 'You are going to live.'" Pieper spent more than a week in the hospital recovering from his injuries.

Then, on January 23, 1977, Parker committed suicide at the age of 58 for reasons that remain unclear. Thomas J. Feehan, who had started at Brown & Root in 1947, became the company's fifth president and its chief executive

IN 1977, A BIBLICALLY INSPIRED office wag composed a brief history of Brown & Root. The inter-office memo was reprinted in the *Houston Business Journal* on Aug. 30, 1982, as part of a three-part series on the engineering-construction company:

In the beginning Brown owned several mules and a few wagons.

And the earth was without form, and void; and darkness was upon the face of the deep. And the Spirit of Brown moved upon the face of the earth.

And Brown said, "Let there be roads;" and there were roads.

And Brown saw the roads, that they were good; and Brown divided the roads from the remainder.

And Brown called the roads Highways, and the remainder he called For Future Consideration. And a growth in activity marked the end of the first period.

And Brown said, "Let there be capital in the midst of the business, and let it come from my Wife's Brother."

And Brown received the capital, and bought more mules and equipment, and muchly progressed in his workload; and it was so.

And Brown called the business Brown & Root. And the joining of his Brother marked the end of the second period.

And Brown said, "Let the waters under the heaven become spanned, and let the dry land be linked;" and it was so.

And Brown called the links between dry land Bridges; and the water below called he Profit; and Brown saw that it was good.

And Brown said, "Let the business bring forth culverts, and dams, and even water and sewage plants after their kind;" and it was so.

Let There Be Roads

And the business did bring forth culverts, dams and even water, and sewage plants after their kind; and Brown saw that it was good.

And the Marshall Ford Dam marked the end of the third period.

And Brown said, "Let there be ships on the waters of the oceans to help our fighting men; and let them reveal our prowess and our skills, and our engineering ingenuity;

And let them be of the U.S. Navy on the waters of the oceans to spread the cause of freedom;" and it was so.

And Brown made 359 fighting vessels; greater ones, and lesser ones; he made middle classes also.

And Brown set them on the waters of the oceans to give muscle to the Navy, and to spread the cause of freedom; and the business won an "E" for Excellence because even the Navy saw that it was good.

And the end of the war marked the end of the fourth period.

And Brown said, "Let the scattered departments bring forth abundantly the engineering creatures and the technicians that draw upon the board."

And Brown created a central engineering department, and it included every engineering creature after its kind, and every drafting creature after its kind; and Brown saw that it was good.

And Brown urged them, saying, "Be fruitful and produce and changeover the 'Big Inch' and 'Little Inch' oil lines to the transmission of natural gas.

And the establishment of the Petroleum and Chemical Division marked the end of the fifth period. And Brown said, "Let the business expand off-shore and bring forth overwater gas compressors after their kind, and offshore drilling platforms after their kind," and it was so.

And Brown constructed overwater gas compressors after their kind, and off-shore drilling platforms after their kind; and Brown saw that it was good.

And Brown said, "Let us lay marine pipelines of the largest diameters conceivable; and let them carry oil to our energy starving nation."

So Brown laid marine pipelines, of large diameter, he did lay them.

And Brown saw everything he had done, and behold it was very good. And his departure and the succession of his Brother marked the end of the sixth period.

Thus the earth was filled with construction, including both land and sea.

And in the seventh period you would think the new Brown would have rested, but, lo, he maintained the Manned Space Craft Center so that even the planets in the sky were not untouched by Him.

And the return of men from the moon marked the end of the seventh period.

And now Brown looks ever outward, continually and inexhaustibly expanding the boundaries of engineering-construction knowledge.[1]

officer. Feehan, a chemical engineering graduate from Tulane University, had joined Brown & Root as a process and project engineer, becoming a vice president in 1968, senior vice president in 1970 and group vice president two years later. A magazine article noted that Halliburton's choice of Feehan also ended the last, visible trace of influence by the company's founders. "Even after the acquisition by Halliburton, George Brown was calling the shots as to who would run the company, for both Frensley and Parker were Brown's men. This time around, as related by Feehan, the choice was announced when Halliburton men arrived at the Brown & Root offices and called a meeting."[24] Feehan would guide the company for the next six years.

But Brown & Root's problems in the 1970s were not over. In December 1978, in federal court in New Orleans, Brown & Root pleaded no contest to charges of conspiring to fix prices for marine construction in the Gulf of Mexico with J. Ray McDermott & Company of New Orleans. The accusations covered a 16-year period prior to 1977. Brown & Root paid $1 million in fines. Six top executives of the companies also pleaded no contest to charges of conspiracy and wire and mail fraud. They were fined and given suspended jail sentences.[25] Brown & Root also paid some $90 million to settle associated civil claims, including lawsuits by the biggest names in the oil industry.[26]

John P. Harbin, chairman and chief executive officer of Halliburton at the time, described the antitrust case as an embarrassment, but said the company was not permanently damaged by it. "We're still doing business with these big customers, and our records don't show any guilt," he said in a 1980 newspaper interview. "There are three sides to everything — ours, theirs, and the government's."[27]

The Islamic Revolution

The Iranian Imperial Army wanted to build a naval base at Chahbahar on the Gulf of Oman and enlarge another base at Bandar Abbas. The project at Chahbahar, a small fishing village in southeastern Iran, was a $3 billion effort that "would have encompassed the widest range of

Equipment to build the naval base at Chahbahar in Iran is off-loaded in late 1977.

shipyard facilities ever assembled in a single project."[28] In 1975, Brown & Root established an office in Tehran.

Two years later, Brown & Root was awarded two contracts totaling $800 million with the government of Iran for the design, engineering and construction at the two sites.[29] But in February 1979, when design work was nearly complete, the Ayatollah Khomeini overthrew the Shah of Iran, and the U.S. State Department notified American firms to evacuate their workers. Brown & Root used its own barges and supply boats to withdraw 114 employees from the country to waiting naval vessels. Meanwhile, pro-Khomeini students in Iran stormed the American embassy, an incident that led to the Iranian hostage crisis. Brown & Root later sued the government of Iran in an attempt to recover millions of dollars in vendor and sub-contractor claims.[30] The abrupt end of the Iran project also forced Halliburton to write

off $23 million in 1979, creating a 28-cent reduction in earnings per share.[31]

In addition to the Iranian crisis, 1979 was made difficult because of the escalating cost of fuel, which meant higher costs to operate vehicles and equipment for both Halliburton and Brown & Root. For example, Brown & Root's work on the Tennessee-Tombigbee Waterway for the U.S. Army Corps of Engineers was under a fixed-fee contract, and higher gas prices meant less profit.

Brown & Root's London office had grown rapidly between 1977 and 1979 because of the North Sea oil reserves activity, and in 1979 Brown & Root, for the fourth time that decade, emerged as the largest engineering-construction firm based in the United States. Contracts reached $6.5 billion that year.[32]

A Diversity of Projects

Brown & Root had continued to grow during the tumultuous years, despite embarrassments, tragedies and a changing oil market. Rapidly growing Brown & Root employed 40,000 in 1975, 65,000 in 1977 and 80,000 in 1979.[33]

Not all of Brown & Root's work was overseas or underwater. A small sampling of its projects during the late 1970s included a major expansion of Cyprus Bagdad's copper–producing facilities west of Prescott, Arizona; construction of a grass-roots facility for production of reinforcing fibers for Owens–Corning Fiberglass at Amarillo, Texas; and engineering and construction of an assembly plant for Peterbilt trucks near Denton, Texas, for PACCAR, Inc.

For Cyprus, Brown & Root increased the copper mining company's production capacity nearly sevenfold by installing new equipment that could process 40,000 tons of raw ore per day. Brown & Root completed the project in 1977, four months ahead of schedule and 10 percent below budget estimates, a feat that was even more amazing since more than half of the peak workforce of 975 consisted of area residents with little or no previous construction experience.[34]

Also, in 1977, Brown & Root completed a joint venture contract for the construction of the Eisenhower Tunnel at Loveland Pass,

Colorado. The 8,000-foot tunnel through the Rocky Mountains became a part of Interstate Highway 70. That same year, Brown & Root constructed five power plants that delivered a total of 3,200 megawatts.[35]

In 1979, Brown & Root began work on a joint venture project on the Tennessee-Tombigbee Waterway in Mississippi and Alabama that would make the Tombigbee River navigable to Mobile, Alabama. As for marine construction, by 1979, Brown & Root had laid 8,000 miles of submarine pipelines. In 1978, Brown & Root bought the SEMAC 1, a 487-foot-long semisubmersible barge capable of laying pipe in 1,200 feet of water, and containing living quarters for 362 people.

In a 1980 interview, Halliburton and Brown & Root officials assessed both their union and their individuality. Halliburton's John Harbin described Brown & Root as "full of rugged individualists," while George Brown expressed no surprise at Halliburton's success, pointing out that its stock went up "25 times in 16 years, mostly due to Brown & Root. We had the manpower, we had great

engineers, and all the potential was there."[36] Feehan, whose opinion was correct at the time, noted that Brown & Root had never ceased to grow. "There have been some saw-teeth on the curve, but it's always been a steady curve upward," he said. However, 1979 was "a hard year, and we're not accustomed to having a down year," he reflected.

The 1970s, however, would end with a bang for Brown & Root. The company helped stem a huge oil well blowout in the Gulf of Mexico. Petroleos Mexicanos, or Pemex, was drilling in the summer of 1979 in the Bay of Campeche, just off Mexico's southeastern coast, when its I Ixtoc well blew. A plume of oil and gas spewed from the wellhead upward, burning like a torch where it broke the water's surface 164 feet above the wellhead, spewing 30,000 barrels of oil a day into the Gulf and polluting beaches as far away as Texas.[37]

In the early 1970s, Brown & Root workers expanded Owens-Corning's Waxahachie plant in north-central Texas, shown here in 1978.

BROWN & ROOT

Thousands of pounds of cable and thousands of feet of drill pipe fell onto the seabed around the wellhead. The tangled debris cut off access to the wellhead and made any quick solution impossible. Pemex quickly called in international well control and environmental specialists to help and put them under the direction of legendary wild well fighter Red Adair, a former Otis Engineering employee. Workers began drilling two relief wells to intercept I Ixtoc, but those efforts were expected to take months and concerns about the growing environmental threat were mounting.

Brown & Root had been working with Pemex since 1976. In fact, over a three–year period, Brown & Root had engineered and constructed drilling and production facilities that took Pemex from producing 200,000 barrels of oil a day to 2.5 million.[38] Jay Weidler was Brown & Root's

chief marine engineer, and employees in Brown & Root's Mexico City offices called him to see if the company could help in some way.

Since Adair was in charge of controlling the well, Weidler devised a plan to provide interim relief that became known as Operation Sombrero. The plan was to channel as much of the oil and gas as possible into an inverted funnel, separate the oil and water, flare the gas, and offload the crude onto oil tankers. After a successful model test in Houston, Brown & Root received the go–ahead from Pemex.

In the Gulf of Mexico, oil and gas spewed from the wellhead at 120 mph, damaging the oil platform, which was towed from the scene. The wellhead continued to shoot burning liquid through the water.

PHOTOS: BROWN & ROOT

The 310–ton inverted funnel, with a 40–foot diameter, was barged to I Ixtoc and coaxed into position. Weidler said the sombrero was attached to a gate–like frame that held it about 10 feet from the top of the wellhead. "The velocity of the fluid got up to be about 110 feet per second, so you've got a tremendous force over a diverging area as the cone [spray] works its way to the surface. What we basically did was to put [the funnel] on two hinges and swing it over on top of this thing."[39]

The sombrero, in place from October through December, substantially reduced I Ixtoc's spill as Pemex hurried to complete its relief wells. I Ixtoc was shut off on March 12, 1980, and plugged 10 days later.

Brown & Root took great pride in its role in battling the disaster. A company publication noted that "Operation Sombrero was a spontaneous initiative, a long shot that Weidler readily admits Brown & Root wasn't sure would work. That the effort paid off

Above: Brown & Root devised a 310-ton inverted funnel, called the sombrero, which was barged into place with its frame.

Below: Close-up of the funnel in position.

wasn't what mattered. What mattered was that the company thought it could help, felt a responsibility to try, and acted on it."[40]

The success didn't help Brown & Root financially. The company would soon wrestle with new problems in the decade of the 1980s as it came to terms with a weakening economy. Earnings from worldwide marine operations had declined in 1978, and again in 1979, to $90.9 million, compared to a record $217.5 million in 1977. Brown & Root's industrial, or land-based, projects also experienced steep declines, to $48.1 million in 1980, compared to $112.8 million in 1978, as the company headed toward a period of downsizing and reassessment.[41]

Arkansas has a brighter future, thanks to Brown & Root.

Within weeks of getting the job to build a coal-fired power plant for Arkansas Power & Light Company, Brownbuilders in Arkansas began carving a road and an eight-mile rail spur from the nearest railroad line.

Construction of the White Bluff Power Plant included twin 815-megawatt units, each capable of generating enough energy to power the city of Little Rock on an extremely hot day. A 98-story stack, one of the tallest in the South, and a 400-ton receiving hopper were also part of the project.

Brown & Root installed special vibration-absorbent pedestals on which two 1-million pound turbine generators were placed. For future maintenance of the generators, a 100-ton crane was built into the ceiling.

In total, Brown & Root spent five years completing the White Bluff Power Plant. The workforce peaked with 2,100 Brownbuilders and contractors.

Let us show you how we can help brighten the future of your area.

Brown & Root, Inc.
And Associated Companies
A Halliburton Company
P.O. Box 3, Houston, Texas 77001
An Equal Opportunity Employer

Nuclear power plants held great promise in the early 1980s, and Brown & Root stayed at the forefront of the industry, as shown in this advertisement of 1982.

CHAPTER ELEVEN

Bouncing Back from Economic Decline

"When oil prices went to $15 a barrel, the world collapsed."

— T. Louis Austin, 1988[1]

THE GREAT DEPRESSION had been tough for Brown & Root, but the 1980s would mark the first time the company would take a huge step backward. The recession would lead Brown & Root by the mid-1980s to slash its workforce by three-fourths as the number of contracts plummeted. As a consequence, the company began a process of renewal that included the strategic acquisition of key firms. As in the 1970s, three different presidents, including the first one ever hired from outside the company, would be at Brown & Root's helm. George Brown would not see the vast changes in the company that he and his brother had nurtured through both the lean and plentiful years, as he would die in 1983.

The decade began with promise. Brown & Root, for the sixth time in its history, was number one among the nation's top engineering-construction firms, with $10.7 billion in sales in 1981. But the rankings in the *Engineering News-Record* showed Brown & Root just narrowly edging past Fluor's $10.6 billion in sales. Brown & Root, with 65,000 employees, and offices and projects in 27 foreign countries, garnered new international contract awards totaling $2.6 billion in 1981, a 172 percent increase from the previous year. The increased overseas activity made up for a 12 percent decline in domestic contract awards.[2]

Brown & Root opened a new office in each of the first three years of the 1980s. In 1980, it established an engineering office in Mobile, Alabama, so it could be near the petrochemical work in the southeastern United States. A year later, the company added another engineering office in Kuala Lumpur, Malaysia, and the following year, an office was opened in Caracas, Venezuela, to handle petroleum, chemical, and oil-related work. Recruiting experienced workers for these far-flung sites was often a challenge, said B.K. Chin, who joined Brown & Root in 1974 after graduating from Singapore University. Chin, who took over the entire engineering section for the Far East in 1985, commented on some of the difficulties of overseas operations.

"In Houston, there are more experienced resources available, so if you need to have more experienced people, you can recruit them locally. In Singapore or the Far East, you have to plan longer and train those resources yourself."[3]

George Brown, photographed in 1981 following his retirement as chairman of Brown & Root.

BROWN & ROOT

The Great Man-Made River Project, begun in 1980 and still ongoing, is a $20 billion effort to pipe water from underneath Libya's desert to its coastal cities.

The Great Man-Made River Project

The largest desert in the world, the Sahara, is the least likely place a person would turn to for water. But underneath thousands of miles of sun-scorched sand lies a vast network of underground aquifers containing enough fresh water to supply Libya with millions of gallons a day. The challenge for Brown & Root's United Kingdom subsidiary was to get this water to the cities and agricultural fields.[4] The solution was a system of pipelines connecting the southern desert regions with Libya's coastal cities. Two key recommendations, which made the pipeline economically feasible and won Brown & Root the contract, were the use of a gravity-based hydraulic system to minimize the need for pumping stations and energy, and the installation of specially designed, 14-foot-diameter, prestressed concrete pipe.[5]

The $20 billion-plus Great Man-Made River Project was designed to be completed in five phases. Some 2,000 pieces of equipment, including heavy crawler cranes, bulldozers, excavators, trucks and buses, were used.[6] The first phase, located in eastern Libya, involved two parallel pipelines extending 1,160 miles from water wells

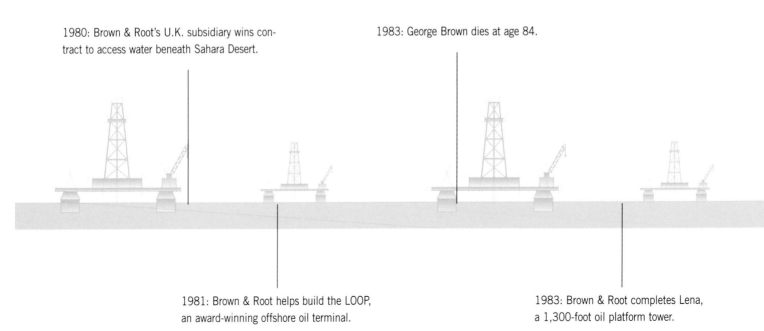

1980: Brown & Root's U.K. subsidiary wins contract to access water beneath Sahara Desert.

1983: George Brown dies at age 84.

1981: Brown & Root helps build the LOOP, an award-winning offshore oil terminal.

1983: Brown & Root completes Lena, a 1,300-foot oil platform tower.

500 miles inland to Sirt and Benghazi. This stretch to the populous northern coastal area was about the distance from New York City to Kansas City. The 230 wells had an average depth of 1,500 feet and accessed aquifers as old as 38,000 years. Phase I alone required 245,000 pipe sections, each more than 24 feet long. To meet the rigorous completion schedule, a section of pipe had to be laid every six minutes, 24 hours a day, for four years.[7] Each piece of the stub was about 20 feet long, weighing about 75 tons, noted Gary Montgomery, senior vice president and director of Brown & Root. "That's about the weight of an M1A1 tank."[8]

Phase II was designed to transport another 530 million gallons daily. Subsequent phases would increase the Phase I capacity to nearly one billion gallons a day, link the Phase I and II systems, and finally, connect the Phase I system to Tobruk. In addition to pipelines, the project required reservoirs, small villages for support and maintenance, concrete pipe plants and a 75-megawatt power plant with substations. More than 1,100 miles of road were constructed just for Phase I.[9]

BROWN & ROOT

The first phase of the Great Man-Made River Project was completed in 1995.

"Do It Right the First Time"

In 1981, Brown & Root introduced a quality improvement process and long-term strategic planning program. The goals of these programs were to encourage open communication, teamwork, market research and continuous improvement. The quality improvement program, taught

1985: South Texas Nuclear Project Lawsuit settled for $750 million.

1986: Brown & Root wins the Queen's Award for Technological Achievement.

1986: Hard times hit Brown & Root, workforce is reduced by thousands.

1989: Revenue growth returns to Brown & Root, the largest single revenue-producer for Halliburton.

in-house to managers and supervisors, emphasized a "do it right the first time" philosophy.[10] In a review more than a decade later, a company publication noted that the programs did away with turf battles and fostered cooperation among business units. In addition, "adversarial contractor/client relationships were replaced with partnering alliances and team-building efforts."[11]

Randy Harl, current president of Brown & Root Industrial Services, said working closely with clients has always proven beneficial and challenging, and remains part of the company's mission. "The challenge is always to figure out systems that allow people to understand what you are trying to do and get that feedback to the right places so you can change something."[12]

The efforts paid off when the National Society of Professional Engineers designated the Louisiana Offshore Oil Port, or LOOP, as one of 1981's top 10 engineering accomplishments. Brown & Root was one of the principal firms that provided engineering design on the structure, often called the Superport. The offshore oil-receiving terminal was the nation's first deepwater port able to handle crude oil from supertankers too large to enter conventional U.S. ports. Designed to move 1.4 million barrels of oil a day into America's pipeline system, it greatly slashed work time by eliminating the need for smaller tankers to transfer oil from supertankers to inland ports.[13]

George Brown's Death

Although George Brown was no longer directly involved in Brown & Root, he remained a director of Halliburton, as well as Texas Eastern Corporation, until his death at age 84 on January 22, 1983. In his last years, he devoted much of his time to philanthropic work. A Texas Senate resolution, praising his generosity, noted that the Brown Foundation had given $170 million to such entities as the Museum of Fine Arts in Houston, Rice University and Southwestern

University, which George's wife, Alice, and his sister-in-law Margarett Brown had attended.[14]

Lady Bird Johnson, whose husband had died 10 years earlier, described George as "one of the most creative, wide-ranging minds I ever knew. He retained a youthful search for knowledge. ... All of our family loved him."[15] More than 1,000 people attended George's funeral, mourning as his mahogany coffin, topped with a bouquet of yellow roses, was carried from the church. In his honor, the city of Houston would name its $104.9 million red, white and blue exhibition and meeting center, which opened in 1987, the George R. Brown Convention Center.

The Louisiana Offshore Oil Port, or LOOP, which Brown & Root helped to construct.

The Recession

An economic downturn began to have increasing impact on many American companies. In early 1982, a company publication noted that Brown & Root continued to turn a profit, though other companies were not doing as well. "No one needs to tell you that we are in a recession, that competition is getting tougher, and that many of our clients are simply not financing expansions or new grassroots facilities, and that some are even canceling projects that were scheduled to begin in 1982."[16]

Six months after George Brown's death, Brown & Root was in the midst of management changes that would, in effect, return it to the structure built by the Brown brothers. Thomas J. Feehan, who had been the company's president and CEO since 1977, became chairman of the board, where he would concentrate on developing new construction prospects. Brown & Root's new President and CEO, T. Louis Austin Jr., was given the task of making sure the projects got built. "We are going back to the method and philosophy we had years ago," Feehan said. "In the old days we had George Brown as our number one salesman, and his brother Herman Brown ran the company."[17] The chairman of the board position had been vacant since George's

retirement in 1974. Not having someone like him to drum up business had become a critical problem in the previous year and a half. With all the multimillion- and billion-dollar projects that began in the late 1970s and early 1980s, companies like Brown & Root had not needed to devote much time to seeking new work. But the dream days of clients knocking on builders' doors with huge projects were past. W. Bernard Pieper, senior executive vice president for operations and a future Brown & Root president, said at the time: "The megabuck projects aren't there now. So, we are trying to get more of the smaller jobs."[18]

Austin had a background similar to that of George Brown. Both men had earned a mining engineering degree, and both had received the engineering profession's most prestigious award, the John Fritz Medal, an honor they shared with such inventors as Thomas Edison and Orville Wright.[19] Austin, a Tennessee native and World War II Navy officer, had retired in early 1983 as chairman and director of Texas Utilities Company of Dallas, a holding company of three Texas investor-owned electric utilities. The 64-year-old Austin began working for Brown & Root in August 1983, expecting to remain at the company for no more than four or five years, but remaining for seven.[20]

Austin believed that economic realities had changed forever and companies needed to cut costs to remain competitive. "We saw a heyday in the 60s and 70s in the economic situation of the world that, in my opinion, is never coming back again," he said.

"We were overbuilding and overspending to the point that now we have got to get lean. If we're going to do any business, we have to be lean. Everybody has got to understand that. The other side of the coin is that, when we reach the point that the company prospers, then the employees will prosper as well."[21]

The clients had also changed over the years, and the company's top executives needed to be more involved in contract negotiations. In the past, the private sector purchased most services, but now most of Brown & Root's work was for the public sector. Overseas, most of the company's

clients were government ministries for petroleum or trade. It took a lot of time to negotiate with those agencies. For example, it took three years for Brown & Root to work out the details of a joint venture with the People's Republic of China.[22]

Reorganization

Brown & Root reorganized and scaled back its workforce to meet the new economic challenge, while still expanding geographically. It now employed 40,500 people, a big drop from 66,500 workers just a year before. Larry Pope, president of Brown & Root Petroleum & Chemicals, said the shift overseas was necessary because "the market projection in the U.S. was flat." Pope joined Brown & Root in 1987, but the trend was well under way before that time. "The construction industry was going to slow down considerably from the early 80s. ... There had to be a switch in strategy."[23] With the construction

The South Texas Nuclear Project, under construction in 1979.

business sluggish, competition grew more fierce. Jack Browder, vice president of Business Development, said competition became particularly tough after Ronald Reagan became president. Browder, who joined Brown & Root in 1973, said Brown & Root used to have an advantage over many competitors because it was an open shop. With Reagan in the White House, that scenario changed.

"The [Reagan] administration became very pro-business, which encouraged a lot of other competitors to get into the non-union construction business. At that point our game completely changed because our competitors were upstart construction companies who didn't have some of the infrastructure costs that we had, as opposed

to a competitor being a union contractor who was substantially more expensive than we were."[24]

Brown & Root cut overhead by consolidating some activities and aligning its operations into business units along industry lines.[25] The corporate organization oversaw the operations as a whole.[26]

South Texas Nuclear Project Lawsuit

Brown & Root would also settle a massive lawsuit by the owners of the South Texas Nuclear Project. Brown & Root had started construction of the $5.5 billion two–reactor nuclear plant near Bay City in late 1975. In September 1981, Houston Lighting & Power Company and its three partners replaced Brown & Root as the project's designer, engineer and project manager. Brown & Root later quit as the builder, and in a lawsuit, the utilities company sought $6.3 billion in damages for alleged mismanagement by Brown & Root.[27] In 1985, Brown & Root settled the lawsuit for $750 million. The cash settlement, negotiated by Austin with the project's owners, would put "an end to the rumor that the settlement would be the end of Brown & Root."[28] Former CEO W. Bernard Pieper commented that Brown & Root decided to settle, but did not believe the amount was warranted.

"Those of us in the organization thought that was outrageous. We felt that it wasn't the best nuclear plant in the world, but it was a long way from the worst."[29]

What was deemed acceptable changed following the accident at the Three Mile Island Nuclear Power Plant. Nuclear plant construction has halted for Brown & Root, as well as for the entire industry, said Peter Arrowsmith, senior vice president of Brown & Root Environmental. Arrowsmith headed Nuclear Utility Services, a company used by Brown & Root in its last nuclear plant project. Brown & Root owned 10 percent of NUS until it was purchased entirely by Halliburton Company in 1980.

"The nuclear dream has been overtaken by scare tactics on the part of environmentalists in one sense, and secondly, it has been decimated by the price of gas to the place where a brand

new gas plant can produce electricity at half the cost of a nuclear plant. The plants were delayed and delayed by the environmentalists so that interest on construction just kept piling up. A plant that was originally supposed to cost $2 billion wound up costing $10 billion. You can't beat the price of a gas plant. ... The safety record of nuclear plants has been very good, but every time somebody gets their courage up to even think about buying a new plant, something like Chernobyl happens. As a matter of fact, there was a buy about to happen about the time of Chernobyl, and of course, it was canceled.[30]

The Bottom Falls Out

More difficulties loomed as the company came to grips with an economic downturn fueled by weak oil prices and high interest rates. "When oil prices went to $15 a barrel, the world collapsed," Austin said in a 1988 interview. "We cut $36 million out of our 1986 budget and thought we'd be in good shape." But the market for oil-related construction was worse than estimated and Brown & Root "lost $6 million in the first month of 1986, $6 million in the second month and about $6 million in the third."[31] New offshore contracts became almost non-existent, but the company still had to pay for its marine equipment. Emil Zerr, who recently retired as executive vice president of operations for Brown & Root, said expensive equipment sat idle, draining money from the company's reserves.

"We had a big marine engineering construction business going, and then when the bottom fell out on the oil prices, everybody stopped drilling, and here we were, stuck with this big fleet of vessels to service that particular part of the industry. We were still paying for that equipment but had no place to use it."[32]

Austin, in a 1990 interview, recalled that it was a critical crossroads for Brown & Root. "We had to retire a lot of good people," he said. "The choice was whether to retire a few or lose the whole company. Our work backlog couldn't support the overhead."[33] Indeed, the workforce that could handle $6 billion worth of work now had

BROWN & ROOT

Brown & Root briefly closed its Alief offices during the 1980s recession. The offices are located southwest of Houston.

contract awards of only about $1.5 billion.[34] As a result, Brown & Root's workforce dropped to 20,000 by the mid-1980s. Wages were frozen and salaried personnel were required to work a 45-hour week for 40 hours of pay. Some complained the layoffs had gutted the company. "They let some very good people go that you cannot replace at any moment," said one former employee, who recalled the close kinship of earlier days.[35] Brown & Root, which had begun the decade with contract awards of $10.7 billion, would have $3 billion worth of new contracts in 1987, making it the eighth largest U.S. contractor.[36]

Austin put Brown & Root through a restructuring to improve internal relations and efficiency. Senior Vice President Charlie Buck recalled that during boom times, "business was so good that each division operated like a separate company."[37] For example, Buck said, the various units would not want their engineers to work for another section, which meant that at times, one division would have too much manpower while another would have too little. To overcome the fiefdoms and allow quick transfer of engineers among units, Senior Vice President Gary M. Montgomery restructured the

company's central engineering group.[38] The head of each industry group would report to central engineering rather than to another layer of senior management. W. Bernard Pieper noted that instead of six layers of management between a senior project manager and Austin, there were now only two or three. Each Brown & Root unit became responsible for its own bottom line.[39]

In short order, an industry magazine noted that "Austin's strategy has paid off." In 1987, for the first time in two years, the company was in the black, with earnings of about $5 million after taxes.[40] In 1988, Brown & Root, like other engineering firms, hired additional workers as industrial construction picked up. The company, which had mothballed its huge engineering complex southwest of Houston during the layoffs, reopened it in 1988. The 600,000-square-foot building had been designed to accommodate 2,200 workers when it was built in 1978.[41]

Offshore and Overseas Projects

Brown & Root had experienced challenging times, but continued to delve into its areas of expertise. Projects during the 1980s included the construction of an offshore platform taller than the Empire State Building, a food-processing plant and a military base in the Indian Ocean. In 1983, it completed a green field carbon graphite mill for Airco, Inc., a subsidiary of the London-based BOC Group, near Ridgeville, South Carolina.

The Airco mill took shape on 90 acres of undeveloped land near a place known as Four Hole Swamp, a low-lying area that had served as a hiding place for American soldiers during the Revolutionary War. Brownbuilders would complete the job, which included project management, engineering, procurement and construction, in 24 months. During the peak of construction, 810 workers were employed, erecting 5,300 tons of structural steel, moving more than 700,000 cubic yards of dirt, constructing more than a mile of conveyor systems, and installing enough wire to stretch from Charleston to Knoxville, Tennessee.[42] The plant would manufacture graphite electrodes for use in steel industry furnaces.

In 1984, Brown & Root designed and built the company's largest lump sum engineering-procurement-construction project to date, a new $520 million pulp mill for Leaf River in New Augusta, Mississippi. A year later, Brown & Root completed its first foray into food processing with the design and construction of a NutraSweet plant at Augusta, Georgia, for G.D. Searle & Company. Back in Houston in 1988, the company put the finishing touches on an award-winning design of a complex interchange on Interstate Highway 10.

Overseas, in construction reminiscent of its past work in Guam and Spain, Brown & Root participated in a $475 million joint venture to expand existing military facilities on the remote island of Diego Garcia. The base, completed in 1986, was for the U.S. Navy and Air Force. The joint-venture company, RBRM, also included Raymond International Builders, Inc., and Mowlem International, PLC. The initial phase

BROWN & ROOT

Brownbuilders shown working on the carbon graphite mill for Airco Inc., in South Carolina, in this 1983 photograph.

BROWN & ROOT

of the project called for the building of an aircraft apron and taxiway, deep-water wharf, personnel housing, a power plant and other support facilities.[43]

In offshore work, the company constructed and installed the world's first guyed tower in 1,000 feet of water for Exxon in 1983. The 1,078-foot-tall guyed tower was anchored to the seabed of the Gulf of Mexico, off Louisiana, with 20 five-inch-thick guy lines. Specifically designed for deep water, the platform, known as Lena, reduced structural fatigue by moving with the waves instead of resisting the motion of the water. Among the benefits, Lena cost less than conventional towers consisting of more structural steel.

The primary challenge for Brown & Root had been installing the tower. Exxon believed that an end launch would put too much pressure on the tower, but no one had done a side launch of such a huge structure. To ensure an even launch, Brown & Root designed a holdback system with explosive bolts like those used by NASA in rocket launches.[44] With the decks and drilling rig added after its successful installation, the tower loomed about 1,300 feet high, 50 feet taller than the Empire State Building. Its two acres of platform deck space could hold drilling and production equipment, as well as living quarters for up to 140 people.[45] James Jacobi, vice president and chief engineer of Brown & Root, began his career at the company in 1976 in marine engineering. He said marine technology never stands still. "It keeps stretching," he commented. "It's been, I believe, very innovative compared to some of the other industries."[46]

Another compliant structure designed for North Sea installation was the world's first tension leg platform (TLP), built for Conoco U.K. Brown & Root's contract, in association with Vickers Offshore Limited, required a unique design that allowed the economic extraction of oil from depths of more than 1,000 feet of water.[47] The TLP was essentially a floating platform tied to the seabed with four sets of tethers. It could be hooked up and commissioned onshore to minimize offshore con-

A dramatic illustration of the guyed tower built for Exxon. The jacket and deck stood about 50 feet taller than the Empire State Building.

struction costs, and it also could be moved from one location to another.

For their innovative work, both Brown & Root and Vickers would receive the coveted Queen's Award for Technological Achievement in 1986.[48]

To further reduce costs, Brown & Root designed platforms that were easier to hook up in deep waters. The result was its patented HIDECK system, an integrated deck that was completely equipped onshore and barged to a preinstalled jacket. It could be hooked up in one-tenth of the time of traditional decks. The first HIDECK was successfully installed for Phillips Petroleum in 1983 in the North Sea.[49]

In 1987, Devonport Management Limited, a United Kingdom consortium in which Brown & Root had 30 percent ownership, won a seven-year contract to operate and maintain the Royal Navy's Devonport Royal Dockyard at Plymouth, England. The consortium would manage all design, procurement, construction, installation, and commissioning activities for the 300-year-old dockyard. Admiral Horatio Nelson, who won a decisive naval engagement at Trafalgar in 1805 against the French and Spanish, had once set sail from the site, which now included nuclear submarines.[50]

That same year, Brown & Root's London office would become the first major engineering firm certified for BS 5750, the British equivalent of ISO 9000, an international certification program based on the firm's quality assurance program. Brown & Root's Singapore office and later its U.S.-based operations would also become certified under the standards, which include a requirement for a written quality assurance manual.

Two years later, in Aberdeen, Scotland, Brown & Root, in a joint venture with SMIT,

established Rockwater, the world's largest diving company, as subsea oil production systems became scaled-down alternatives to platform production. Rockwater, equipped with semi-submersible diving support vessels and hyperbaric welding and subsea trenching equipment, could offer clients integrated design, construction and maintenance services.[51]

To complete work on schedule, Brown & Root divers often had to remain pressurized for 30 to 40 days at a time, which meant they lived in the pressure chambers. The divers usually got along, but Brown & Root's Bo Smith recalled an instance when two of them had a bit of a spat.

"One of the divers had just found out the other diver was running around with his wife, and they were threatening to kill each other. I got both of them on the phone and said, 'Let me explain something. If I have to bring y'all

Above: Brownbuilders work on the massive Lena guyed tower, built for Exxon.

Right: The sun sets over the Gulf of Mexico, and the lights come on aboard the derrick barge *Atlas 1*, involved in building Lena.

PHOTOS: BROWN & ROOT

*back to the surface and shut the operation,
y'all will never work again in the North Sea for
Brown & Root. I don't care about your personal life, but this is very lucrative for both us and
y'all and by God, we're going to finish this project.' We didn't have any more problems."[52]*

In other international ventures, Brown &
Root joined with Det Norske Veritas in Oslo and
Stavanger, Norway, to form Veritec, an engineer-
ing and project management company. Also,
Brown & Root and Saipem of Italy would create
an offshore pipeline construction company called
European Marine Contractors Limited. The EMC

Above: A 1983 photograph of the first HIDECK, which was installed
in the North Sea for Phillips Petroleum.

Inset: A model of the Phillips platform, which included the
HIDECK system, capable of holding 650,000 barrels of
oil in three tanks.

would prove to be extremely successful in years to come, laying the longest and second longest pipelines off Norway and the South China Sea, respectively in the 1990s.

A Diversification Strategy

In the late 1980s, Brown & Root acquired and created several companies as part of its diversification and niche marketing efforts. In 1986, the company formed Brown & Root Services Corporation (BRSC) to pursue government operations and maintenance work. Early contracts provided services to the city of Houston, NASA's Johnson Space Center, and the U.S. Navy and U.S. Army.[53] BRSC would also get an emergency contract to repair damages from Hurricane Hugo at Shaw Air Force Base in Sumter, South Carolina.[54]

In 1987, Brown & Root acquired Howard Humphreys, a worldwide civil consultancy firm headquartered in Leatherhead, England. Howard Humphreys had expertise in water, dams, roads, bridges and tunneling. Two years later, Brown & Root acquired CF Braun in Alhambra, California, a world leader in process engineering. As of early 1990, Brown & Root could count more than 100 companies as subsidiaries or affiliates throughout the world.[55]

Halliburton announced in late December 1988 that W. Bernard Pieper, senior executive vice president of operations, would be promoted to president and chief operating officer of Brown & Root. Pieper, a Beeville, Texas, native and Rice University graduate, had joined Brown & Root as an engineer in 1957.

On January 1, 1989, Austin would move up to chairman, while still retaining his title of chief executive officer. Austin had pulled Brown & Root through the rocky years of settling the South Texas Nuclear Project lawsuit and the anguish of cutting the workforce to help the company weather the recession.

John Redmon, president of Brown & Root Power & Manufacturing, said Austin "changed the whole focus of the company. He said, 'Boys, we've got to hang in or Halliburton will get rid of us.' We got smaller and everybody banded together."[56]

Profitability had improved and the employee count had swelled to about 35,000 worldwide. In 1989, Brown & Root would generate revenues of about $2.7 billion to make it the largest single revenue–producing segment of Halliburton.[57]

The other segments of Halliburton faced similar challenges during the economic turmoil of the 1980s.

A late 1970s oil well in Wyoming. Reliance on foreign oil would lead to several "oil shocks" in the 1970s.

Limitless Opportunity

"Offshore supply bases, the ability to load vessels and supply material and products from the coast in Scotland, none of that was in place and had to be built from five or six different locations. ... It was existing technology being applied to new conditions."

— Ken LeSuer, 1996[1]

AFTER THE ACQUISITION of Brown & Root, Halliburton began to grow at an astounding rate, not slowing until the 1980s recession. In 1963, President John F. Kennedy awarded Halliburton the E-for-Export flag, a commendation in recognition of superior achievement in foreign trade.[2]

Halliburton's New Headquarters

By 1964, Halliburton had outgrown the original site in Duncan where the company had been founded. The organization consolidated all 39 of its buildings into new facilities constructed by Brown & Root. The East Plant was located about a mile from where Erle Halliburton had established Howco's first yard. With 11.4 acres under one roof, the massive structure had plenty of room for a machine shop, a welding shop, a tools and small parts assembly and pump shop, a truck shop and tank fabrication shop, a raw material warehouse and metal cutting department, a heat-treating and plating machine shop, a floating equipment warehouse, an inspection department, and a mezzanine for offices. Five auxiliary buildings housed a paint shop, a sand blast and vat shop, an equipment test shop, a welding gas storage facility and a 300,000-gallon water storage tank and pump house.[3]

On December 6, 1964, Halliburton celebrated its 40th anniversary with the opening of this mammoth new facility. Oklahoma Governor Henry Bellmon proclaimed the occasion "a great day for Oklahoma as well as for Duncan," and more than 13,000 people streamed through during the all-day open house. So enormous was the plant that it took about 90 minutes for a visitor to cover the length of the tour.[4]

In 1967, services that formed the core of Halliburton, such as fracturing, cementing and logging, were brought under the Halliburton Services Division. Edwin Paramore, the man who began his career at Halliburton holding the business end of a wash hose in 1937, was named president and chief executive officer of the new division.[5]

In 1968 Halliburton Services completed its 500,000th hydraulic fracturing job on a well just east of Duncan. The innovative Hydrofrac process added over eight billion barrels of oil to North American reserves since the introduction of the process.[6]

Halliburton services such as drill stem testing were consolidated under the Halliburton Services Division.

The 1970s Oil Boom

The steady growth of Halliburton in the 1960s paled in comparison to the spectacular expansion of the 1970s, as work began on some of the richest oil fields ever discovered. Several fields were located under the frigid North Sea, off Scotland and Norway, and another was in the arid Middle East. But no location was too dangerous or too remote for Halliburton crews, who traveled the world to provide oil field service.

The excavation of oil under the North Sea presented incredible technological challenges for Halliburton, said Ken LeSuer, president and CEO of Halliburton Energy Services.

"Offshore supply bases, the ability to load vessels and supply material and products from the coast in Scotland, none of that was in place and had to be built from five or six different locations. ... It was existing technology being applied to new conditions. Then we had the big sophisticated semi-submersible vessels that were coming into the North Sea; that was also fairly new to the company."[7]

Although oil was plentiful in the North Sea, the supply wasn't enough to satisfy the world's growing appetite for fuel. The reserves in the Middle East, however, could. By the mid-1960s, the Arab nations comprising the Organization of Petroleum Exporting Countries (OPEC) collectively produced and sold more oil than all other nations in the world combined.

In October 1973, Arab nations attacked Israel in the Yom Kippur War. OPEC slashed oil supplies to countries supplying fuel and war munitions to Israel.[8] Almost overnight, oil prices skyrocketed from $2.95 a barrel to $11.65, and soon climbed to more than $40 a barrel. Lines at gas pumps grew and economies faltered as oil companies struggled to make up the shortfall through increased oil exploration and drilling. As a result, Halliburton's revenues shot up 20 percent to $470 million by 1974.[9] Marion Cracraft, corporate communications manager for Halliburton, remembered the unprecedented growth that Halliburton experienced, during this tumultuous time and into the early 1980s.

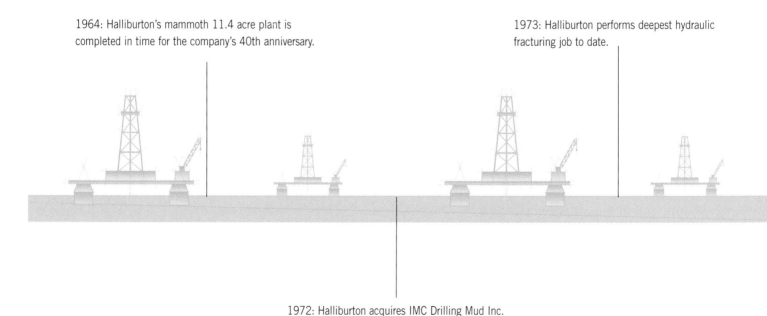

1964: Halliburton's mammoth 11.4 acre plant is completed in time for the company's 40th anniversary.

1973: Halliburton performs deepest hydraulic fracturing job to date.

1972: Halliburton acquires IMC Drilling Mud Inc.

AP/WIDE WORLD PHOTOS

Gas lines wrapped themselves around corners following the oil embargo in 1973.

1976: The Halliburton Energy Institute
is established.

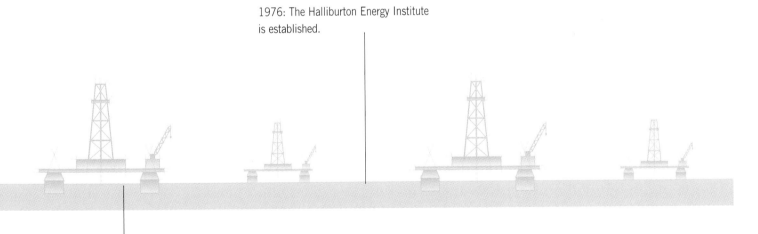

1974: Halliburton revenues shoot
up 20 percent.

"The industry was quite concerned that, if oil prices went to $100 a barrel — and they were over $40 at the time and seemingly climbing to the stars — that we simply would not have the trained people or the equipment to meet the need for all the drilling." [10]

Guy T. Marcus, vice president of investor relations for Halliburton Company, said the changing price of oil also affected the company's stock.

"There's been a sentiment that as oil and natural gas prices rise Halliburton should prosper more because our customers have more discretionary income to reinvest in their business." [11]

Changing of the Guard

In 1970, Senior Vice President W.D. Owsley, one of the company's most influential men, was preparing to retire. Owsley had worked for Halliburton since the late 1920s and was responsible for introducing the Super-Cementer, the first portable high-pressure cementing and acidizing pump. He also led the company into the enormously profitable area of hydraulic fracturing in 1949. Owsley's book, *Drilling Practices*, written in 1937, was still a standard text for the oil industry in 1970.

Another member of the old guard, Halliburton CEO Preach Meaders, retired in 1972. Meaders' rise was similar to that of many corporate officers. He began working for Howco as a truck driver in 1928, and was noticed early on by Erle Halliburton. He became president and director in 1953, CEO in 1962 and chairman of the board in 1972. When Meaders became chairman of the board, Jack Harbin became chief executive officer, and Ed Paramore became president and chief operating officer.

The technological leaders of Halliburton during this period helped chart the course of Halliburton Services through the fast-changing industry. Dwight Smith, an "industry guru for cementing" according to Dale Jones, and A.B. Waters, a master of fracturing, developed better oil field methods to meet the challenges around the world. [12]

Though Halliburton was changing, much remained the same. The company still attracted rugged adventurers who were willing to put their hearts into their work. Greg Loyacano Sr., vice president of sales and marketing, joined Halliburton Company in 1971 as a petroleum engineer. His first cementing job was in Harvey, Louisiana.

"I learned how to rig the truck up and do all of those details that you learn as a Halliburton cementer. In the engineering training program that they had in those days, you actually stayed in each department or each specialty group for some period of time and you'd work yourself up to the point where you could run the job yourself. ... You were part of the crew, and that was the beauty of it. You got a first-hand taste of what a crew went through. You got a taste of sleeping in pickup trucks. Sleeping between bulk tanks. Getting eaten up by mosquitoes in the marsh. Going offshore with them, getting your food from a helicopter, dropped in a styrofoam box. Seeing alligator eyes looking at you as you head for work on a barge." [13]

One-Stop Shopping

Halliburton Company continued to add divisions in an ongoing effort to create "one-stop shopping" for oil field services. In looking at potential acquisitions, the company was more concerned with providing new services than with increasing gross revenue. Jerry Blurton, vice president of finance and administration, said Halliburton hasn't wavered from its goal of providing complete service to the oil field industry. "Our objective is to be the top one or two companies offering services. We do not want acquisitions just for the purpose of getting revenue. It is usually not very cost-efficient to do that." [14]

As Halliburton swallowed company after company, it inevitably experienced corporate heartburn, said Les Coleman, executive vice president and general counsel. Coleman said Halliburton had to find ways to incorporate different management structures. The results were worth the trouble because the acquisitions increased Halliburton's breadth and depth.

"Over the years when the company was growing very rapidly, from the 1960s to the 1980s, the decision-making was decentralized, and in some cases not controlled very well. But there was a higher premium on catching the business than there was on cost-management. The company acquired an awful lot of stuff, I mean major businesses in most people's books. Acquisitions are a strategic tool to be used in the right circumstances."[15]

In 1972, Halliburton Company added IMC Drilling Mud Inc., of Houston, to its list of subsidiaries comprising the Halliburton Services division. Halliburton had owned 50 percent of IMC since 1968. The company, renamed IMCO following the acquisition, prepared and maintained a complex mixture of barite, bentonite and other chemicals that was known throughout the industry as mud. The mud was pumped into wells to remove drill cuttings, to control well pressures, and to cool and lubricate drill bits.[16]

Halliburton Services set another record when workers performed the deepest

HALLIBURTON CO.

hydraulic fracturing treatment in the history of the process. Almost a quarter-million gallons of fluids were pumped into a 22,400-foot-deep gas well.[17]

Environmental Concerns

In 1966, New York City Mayor John V. Lindsay vowed to banish coal from use in the city after he was forced to declare a smog alert on Thanksgiving Day. Energy plants around the country began switching from coal to oil, a much cleaner fuel. But in 1969, an uncharted fissure leaked about 6,000 barrels of oil into California's Santa Barbara Channel, where a well was being drilled. Daniel Yergin described the slick and the resulting outrage in *The Prize*, a well-written and detailed work about the history and ramifications of oil.

"A gooey slick of heavy crude oil flowed unchecked into the coastal waters and washed up on 30 miles of beaches. The public outcry was nationwide and reached right across the political spectrum. The Nixon Administration imposed a moratorium on California offshore development, in effect shutting it down."[18]

Oil companies responded to environmental concerns in the mid-1970s by finding new ways to both prevent and clean up spills. To protect the Gulf of Mexico, for example, the companies organized the non-profit Clean Gulf Associates (CGA), which contained and cleaned up oil spills. The CGA maintained crews and equipment that could respond immediately to oil spills anywhere in the Gulf. Halliburton was selected as CGA's contractor to buy and stockpile the equipment at strategic locations, provide supervisors to train oil company crews in the use of the equipment, and assist at the scene of an oil spill.[19]

Halliburton developed systems to handle spills in both deep and shallow waters and to

An artist's rendition of IMC Drilling Mud Inc., of Houston, acquired in 1972.

clean beaches. Booms would corral spills and skimmers would suck oil into tanks. To scare wildlife such as birds away from a spill, Halliburton employees devised a propane gun that

was noisy and harmless. Portable rehabilitation stations were developed to clean birds that had unwittingly ventured into the oil.[20] Halliburton also built a 52-foot by 160-foot barge as its premier oil spill cleanup vessel. It was called HOSS, an acronym for high–volume, open-sea system. It was the only vessel of its kind anywhere.[21]

The Halliburton Energy Institute

Training and advanced research remained strategically important to the company's

Left: Several oil spills in the 1960s prompted the Halliburton Company to develop new tools and techniques.

Below: Halliburton crews practice methods to corral oil slicks using booms.

HALLIBURTON CO.

The Halliburton Energy Institute, a hybrid between a college and a resort hotel.

future. In 1976, the company established the Halliburton Energy Institute in Duncan, on a 270-acre campus that was a hybrid between a college and a fine resort hotel. The facility was primarily planned by Bill Elliot . Classes and seminars were offered in subjects related to oil field technology and service, with course titles that included Cementing Technology Workshop, Modern Completion Practices, Hydraulic Fracture Mechanics and Openhole Log Analysis. Instructors were industry experts, including independent consultants and university professors. The institute was open to Halliburton employees, as well as thousands of employees of Halliburton customers, who included the classes as part of their technical and executive training programs. Today, sessions are held throughout the year, excluding December, and most sessions are enrolled to capacity.[22]

Even though the numbers were enlarged by inflation of the currency from the middle 1970s to the early 1980s, the financial growth of Halliburton remained excellent.[23] Throughout its history, Halliburton Company as a whole steadily prospered, even in times of economic, social and political turmoil. Halliburton thrived during the Great Depression, World War II and the post-war economic cycles of boom and recession. However, Halliburton would face its greatest challenge during the devastating recession and the downward spiral of oil prices during the 1980s.

A Halliburton well head crew often rises early and works late to get the job done.

CHAPTER THIRTEEN

From Boom to Bust

"The OPEC cartel lost its control over production and prices; conservation cut far deeper into demand than was forecast; and new sources of petroleum coming on stream have exacerbated supply/demand problems. ... The near-term picture is quite uncertain. No one knows just when energy prices will stabilize."

— Tom Cruikshank, 1985[1]

IN 1979, THE VOLATILE political and social conditions in Iran flared into the Islamic Revolution. Militant students ousted the liberal, pro-West Shah and stormed the American Embassy, starting a hostage crisis that lasted a terrifying 444 days. Strikes occurred at Iranian wells and refineries. Oil companies were terrified they would run out of inventory.[2] Halliburton and Brown & Root employees were evacuated from the region. In America, long gas lines returned, along with "odd-even" days, based on license plate numbers. In *The Prize*, Daniel Yergin described the reaction.

"To the American public, the reemergence of gas lines, which snaked for blocks around gasoline stations, became the embodiment of the panic. The nightmare of 1973 had returned. Owing to the disruption of Iranian supplies, there was, in fact, a shortage of gasoline. Refineries that had been geared to Iranian light and similar crudes could not produce as much gasoline ... from the heavier crude oils to which they were forced to turn as substitutes."[3]

In response to yet another interruption of oil supplies, oil companies stepped up efforts to recover the resource from other regions. Oil production in areas such as the North Sea and Alaska rose substantially and Halliburton broke revenue records in both 1980 and 1981. Net revenue in 1981 was $8.5 billion, an increase of 20 percent over the year before. The company employed 109,000 workers.[4]

But new conservation programs sparked by the shortage and a lingering recession caused a drop in the demand for oil. Furthermore, OPEC's unity was sundered when Iraq attacked Iran in a war that would ultimately claim more than a million lives. Several OPEC nations began to produce oil at an unprecedented rate and the world experienced a glut. Prices fell through the floor and into the basement. The average price per barrel of oil fell from $32 in 1981 to $12 in 1986.

By 1982 the number of drilling rigs, domestic and overseas, had dropped dramatically. For the first time in its history, Halliburton Company suffered a decline in revenue, from $8.5 billion in 1981 to $7.3 billion in 1982.[5] Although company officials were worried, they expected oil revenue to remain stable in 1983. That hope proved wrong. OPEC turned on the oil taps and didn't turn them off, causing prices to drop even lower.

A belt buckle commemorating 89 years of the oil industry in Duncan, Oklahoma, from 1892 to 1981.

Tough competition among oil field service companies contributed to the difficulties, noted the 1983 Annual Report.

"A slow economic recovery in the early part of the year, lower prices for crude oil and the surplus deliverability of natural gas all worked against the oil service industry in 1983. Another factor damaging to earnings was the intense competition among service companies, which led to widespread price-cutting throughout the year."[6]

Dale Davis, director of strategic and business management, was hired in 1982, and recalled the tough times.

"From 1981 to 1986, activity in the United States went from 4,530 rigs down to 663 rigs. We were trying to manage the tremendous decline in crude oil prices. We didn't believe the political world would push that much oil through. How do you help the company survive when you had your whole strategy organized around roughly 3,500 U.S. rigs and 1,500 international rigs, and suddenly you're trying to make the

company survive and be a viable, profitable entity at 600 to 700 U.S. rigs and 700 to 800 international rigs?"[7]

The Information Superhighway

The oil industry showed a slight improvement in 1984, and Halliburton went ahead with plans to update its information and communication systems in Arlington, Texas. Oil field service crews from all over the world were linked to the center, which was manned 24 hours a day, 365 days a year. B.N. Murali, vice president of technology, said the center enhanced the company's ability to exchange information within the company and with customers.[8]

"The biggest technological deal, I would say, is the information technology. Companies like Halliburton who can address these opportunities and take advantage of the technology ... are going to survive. Those who don't, won't be able to survive."[9]

In conjunction with the company's growing emphasis on communication, Halliburton estab-

1979: A second oil shock encourages the United States to begin conservation and spurs the search for alternate fuels.

1985: Destabilized oil prices slow need for Halliburton's oil field services.

1980: OPEC nations flood the oil market as the economy slips into recession.

HALLIBURTON CO.

lished a program known as Resource Management Systems, or RMS. RMS consisted of teams of employees who helped managers and staff improve job performance, cut costs and boost sales, employee productivity and safety.[10] The team-building programs were crucial to the company in a time when the workforce was shrinking. By the end of 1984, the number of Halliburton employees had dropped to 68,000, from a peak of 115,000 in 1981.[11]

Getting Back to Basics

Although the Welex Division was the only segment to post a loss in 1984, the company continued to face difficulties. To divest itself of operations not essential to its core business of oil field service, Halliburton Company sold Southwestern Pipe to a group of that company's managers. It also sold some of the railroad freight car repair facilities run by FreightMaster and most of the assets of

Computers become an important tool in helping Halliburton workers improve job performance and efficiency.

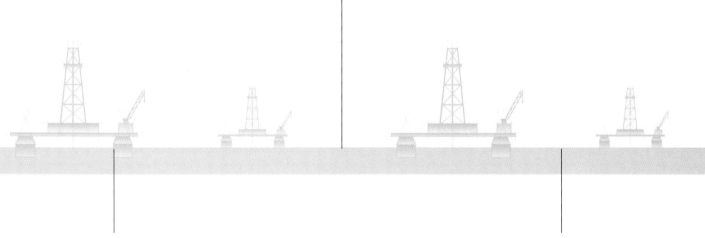

1988: Company officials begin looking for ways to consolidate services.

1986: The Halliburton Company experiences toughest fiscal year in its history.

1988: Halliburton buys Gearhart Industries, world's third largest wireline logging concern.

CEO Tom Cruikshank helped guide the Halliburton Company through 1986, the toughest year in its history.

Premium Threading Services, an unprofitable division of Otis Engineering.[12] By the end of 1985, the Annual Report, once full of confidence and hope, stated that Halliburton faced "severely depressed conditions in all its markets." The uncertain future resulted in a wage and salary freeze for workers and managers. Thomas Cruikshank, in his annual letter to shareholders, wrote:

"When the present downturn in the energy business began to surface several years ago, most observers believed that it was a natural reaction to the hectic, hyperactive period that preceded it. But it has turned out to be a deeper, longer-lasting recession for the industry than most imagined. The OPEC cartel lost its control over production and prices; conservation cut far deeper into demand than was forecast; and new sources of petroleum coming on stream have exacerbated supply/demand problems. ... The near-term picture is quite uncertain. No one knows just when energy prices will stabilize."[13]

The bottom line for 1986 was the worst in Halliburton's history, with a stunning operating loss of $91.8 million. Special write-downs of almost $489 million reflected a steep drop in the value of assets and investments, and brought the total loss to $515.2 million.[14] In mid-1986, the company added a furlough program that required employees to take one week off without pay every eight weeks.[15] By the end of the year the company's payroll had dropped to 47,000.[16] "There was a human side to all this," said Dale Davis. "At one time, when you worked for Halliburton you thought you had a career for life. But the organization as a whole had to change to survive."[17]

The company tightened its belt by consolidating some plant operations and selling off excess equipment, including recently-purchased airplanes. In all, capital expenditures dropped 59 percent.[18]

One of the few bright spots of the year occurred in the People's Republic of China. Halliburton won a government contract to provide onshore oil field service work, making it the first foreign oil field service company to work on mainland China.[19]

Fortunately, the end of 1986 signaled that the worst was over. "Seldom has a company been so severely tested as was Halliburton in 1986," wrote Cruikshank in his annual letter to shareholders. "Our company responded well — albeit at a considerable cost to its human and financial resources."[20]

Tom Cruikshank presided over some of the toughest years in Halliburton's history. Thanks to his commitment to trimming and streamlining, the company returned to profitability in 1987, with income of $48.1 million on revenue that had dropped slightly from $3.9 billion in 1986 to $3.8 billion in 1987.[21] As oil prices inched up, drilling resumed. To better position itself in the recovering oil field service industry, Halliburton purchased a 60 percent ownership in Geophysical Service Inc., a world-leading geophysical contractor. In 1987, Halliburton executives proceeded cautiously, recognizing the global nature of the oil industry, and placing new emphasis on overseas markets.[22]

The company forged ahead in research and development, as it had since the days of Erle P.

Halliburton. In 1987, Halliburton spent $59.9 million on developing such products as a fully automated fracturing system, with more powerful pumps and more precise instrumentation, and a new fracturing fluid, Liquid Gel Concentrate (LGC). Because the fluid was a concentrate, the cost of transporting it was reduced and the customer only paid for what was mixed and used on the job.[23]

An Eye Toward the Future

In 1988, corporate officers began looking for ways to improve the organization of the company. Dale Jones saw that the company could save money and increase efficiency by combining some business units.

"We began to see that major changes were necessary. At that time I said to someone: 'Five years from now you won't recognize this company because it will be a lot different from what it is now.' I just knew that we had to do business differently. I couldn't forecast that the process would be exactly as it was, but we were seeing more opportunities to integrate services. Before then, we had walls between each operation."[24]

Tom Cruikshank hinted at some of the impending changes in the 1988 Annual Report.

"Halliburton entered the 1980s ... organized as a number of strong, relatively independent business units. This decentralized structure was well suited to meet the needs of our expanding business units. ... Now, however, it is clear that we must pull together the collective operating and technological strengths of the company and improve our competitive position in several key areas."[25]

The economic downturn during the 1980s led the Halliburton Company to sell off much equipment, including planes.

HALLIBURTON CO.

Halliburton Company began to consolidate some of its subsidiaries. The company acquired a wireline logging company, Gearhart Industries, and combined it with Welex to form Halliburton Logging Services (HLS). Gearhart's subsidiary, a geophysical company called Geosource, Inc., was combined with Geophysical Service Inc., which had been purchased from Texas Instruments, to form Halliburton Geophysical Services (HGS). Drawing employees and technology from Halliburton Services, Otis Engineering, Welex and Vann Systems, Halliburton formed a new division, Halliburton Reservoir Services (HRS). This new division was a single source for production testing, drill stem testing and reservoir evaluation services. Halliburton was now better prepared to serve a diminished oil exploration industry, and also poised for an anticipated expansion of the business in the 1990s.[26] Total employment for Halliburton and its subsidiaries returned to 61,400 in 1988, with revenues that increased from $3.8 billion in 1987 to $4.83 billion to 1988.[27] Income increased 98 percent, to $93.6 million.[28]

HALLIBURTON CO.

Streamlining

To further streamline the entire company for the future, Halliburton jettisoned the FreightMaster division and the Life Insurance Company of the Southwest in 1989. Tom Cruikshank, by then chairman and CEO of Halliburton, stated that neither company "closely fit Halliburton's current plans for future growth. Our principal objectives relate to more fully developing the company's oil

Equipment was taken from several business units to form Halliburton Reservoir Services. Shown above is a geophysical truck. A freshly painted wireline truck is shown left.

HALLIBURTON CO.

field services and engineering and construction business segments."[29] Halliburton Company in 1989 continued its financial recovery, with revenues increased to about $5.66 billion.[30]

World events favored an optimistic view of the stability of oil prices and supplies. The Iran-Iraq War ended in 1988, which meant an end to the missile attacks on Middle East refineries and oil tankers. The oil production capabilities of the belligerents, damaged during the war, were being repaired, and both supplies and prices were stable. The OPEC nations recaptured much of the market share, lost as a result of embargoes and boycotts, by keeping prices down.[31] In the 1989 Annual Report, Tom Cruikshank offered prescient comments on the world's renewed reliance on Persian Gulf oil.

"These trends will cause the Middle Eastern OPEC countries such as Saudi Arabia, Iraq, Iran and Kuwait to become the dominant suppliers of the world's petroleum supply by the middle of the decade. ... The consequences of these trends will have a very adverse effect on the United States' balance of trade. United States oil production is now falling at an alarming rate with no improvement in sight."[32]

In 1990, the world would learn just how critical that reliance had become. Iraqi dictator Saddam Hussein, seeking to become the region's dominant power, sent troops and armor into neighboring Kuwait.

A Halliburton worker struggles to control a burning well in Kuwait, set afire by retreating Iraqis following their defeat in the 1991 Gulf War.

Fires of Ambition

"One of the things that I sense that is common throughout the Halliburton family is the loyalty that employees have. People are proud of their careers and of what they have been able to do over the years with the company."

— Dick Cheney, 1996[1]

ON AUGUST 2, 1990, a hundred thousand Iraqi troops and tanks roared into Kuwait, seizing oil fields and refineries, and, in the process, trapping 20,000 foreign workers. More than 3,000 of these workers would be used as "human shields," often chained to strategic sites to discourage retaliatory attack. Immediately following the invasion, Halliburton executives rushed to evacuate company employees who had been working in Kuwait. A 24-hour crisis management team was formed to help track workers and their families. The escalating crisis was documented through inter-corporate information transmissions:

August 2, 1990

The following is a summary of our discussion this morning ... on the situation in Kuwait after the Iraq invasion. All of our people are safe as they all live south of Kuwait City. The Iraq army has taken over all the Kuwait government but the ruler and his family are safe in Saudi Arabia.

We have several of our people that are attempting to leave the country by traveling over land through Khafji to the south into Saudi Arabia. Our Saudi agent is trying to help. ... The American and British embassies in Bahrain recommended everyone stay in their houses for now and not evacuate, but our employees that

are trying to leave did not receive this information.[2]

According to a Halliburton transmission later that day, two oil rigs in northern Kuwait were occupied by Iraqi troops who "escorted" five American workers, including two from Halliburton, toward the direction of Iraq. "In summary, our people at the Santa Fe 'rig 6' are reportedly detained, but we evidently do not have confirmation as to the other employees."[3] On August 8, 16 employees were still in Iraq and 10 employees and their families were in Kuwait. Concern was mounting over Iraq's intentions toward Saudi Arabia, where the majority of Halliburton workers and their families were staying.

The situation in Saudi Arabia seems to be deteriorating, and a number of our people are extremely nervous. ... We will do what we can to calm people down, but a lot depends on what is said today by President Bush and by Saddam Hussein, and immediate reactions. ... We have been unsuccessful in our efforts to contact our people in Iraq or Kuwait.[4]

An oil-soaked and exhausted Halliburton worker takes a breather from fighting Kuwaiti oil fires.

A transmission two days later confirmed that the employees in Iraq were "effectively now trapped in Baghdad. ... All borders closed. ... Only Eastern Europeans apparently being let through."[5] Hussein didn't release the 10 workers he was holding at various strategic sites inside Iraq until December 1990. One worker, released December 11, requested a thorough medical exam, "as he has some concerns since he was kept at a plant where radioactive emission could be a problem, he has been advised to pick a clinic of his choice and we will pick up the tab for the expenses."[6] Hussein released all the hostages that December in a last-minute effort to forestall the eventual attack by the U.S.-led coalition forces.

The Waiting Game

From August to January, as the United States underwent the largest military deployment since the Vietnam War, the deadly game of war was one mainly of rhetoric combined with tense waiting. Business had to go on as usual, and that meant reporting to stockholders. Financially, Halliburton was doing well. The 1990 Annual Report stated that oil field work had produced a net income of $197.4 million, a 46 percent increase over 1989.[7] CEO Tom Cruikshank stated in his annual letter that, from an economic standpoint, Halliburton remained strong in spite of the invasion and damage to Halliburton property.

"The invasion of Kuwait by Iraq in August required us to make a $29 million provision for expected losses associated with our business activities in those two countries. ... It is difficult to write a letter to our shareholders this year, a letter you will read some weeks later, and accurately describe the short-term outlook for much of our business. ... We do not believe that the recent crisis in the Middle East will have a long-term adverse impact on our business. ... However, the fact that hostilities have occurred at all serves to remind us of the unpredictable nature of the oil market which drives much of our company's business."[8]

Promises Kept

On January 17, 1991, the initial air strike of Operation Desert Storm was unleashed on Iraq, and thousands of tons of munitions systemati-

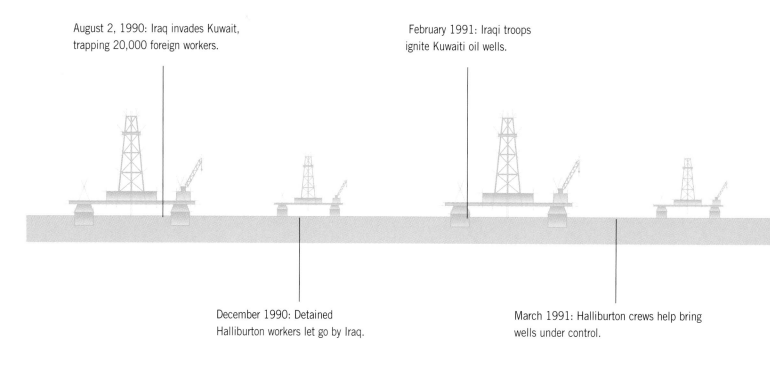

August 2, 1990: Iraq invades Kuwait, trapping 20,000 foreign workers.

February 1991: Iraqi troops ignite Kuwaiti oil wells.

December 1990: Detained Halliburton workers let go by Iraq.

March 1991: Halliburton crews help bring wells under control.

BUSH PRESIDENTIAL MATERIALS PROJECT

cally pounded the Iraqi armed forces. President George Bush and his advisors, including U.S. Secretary of Defense Dick Cheney, had promised that Iraq's aggression would not stand. A defiant Saddam Hussein unleashed his own weapons: obsolete Scud missiles that fell randomly and

Dick Cheney was a member of President George Bush's "Gang of Eight": from left, Deputy National Security Advisor Bob Gates, Chief of Staff John Sununu, Dick Cheney, Vice President Dan Quayle, Bush, Secretary of State Jim Baker, National Security Advisor Brent Scowcroft and Chairman of Joint Chiefs of Staff Colin Powell.

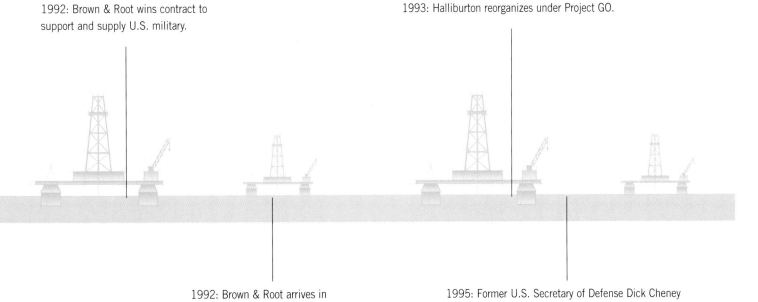

1992: Brown & Root wins contract to support and supply U.S. military.

1993: Halliburton reorganizes under Project GO.

1992: Brown & Root arrives in Somalia to support U.S. Army.

1995: Former U.S. Secretary of Defense Dick Cheney named President, Chairman and CEO of Halliburton.

PHOTOS: HALLIBURTON CO.

usually off-target, and his own promise that he would set Kuwaiti oil wells on fire.

Six weeks of continuous bombardment, blockade and propaganda by coalition forces had largely destroyed Iraq's military capability. When the ground war began in February, hundreds of thousands of coalition troops attacked and flanked the Iraqi Army, which began to surrender to anyone from the West — even journalists, who were unsure what to do with their insistent captives. As the Iraqis retreated, they blew up more than 700 Kuwaiti oil wells and started the spectacular and ecologically catastrophic fires that lit up the sky by night and hid the sun by day.

Red Adair was on the scene to help Halliburton battle the hundreds of burning oil wells. Adair had learned to fight oil well fires in 1936, and had founded his own company in 1959, becoming one of the best known of the often-heroic oil well fighters. John Wayne portrayed Adair in the 1972 movie, *The Hellfighters*. Adair had worked with Halliburton crews for years. He remembered when Hussein's threat to blow the oil wells was made.

"I went to Washington and talked to some high people to get them prepared. 'Let's get the stuff on location so we're ready. ... I've worked with Saddam Hussein before. If he says he's going to do it, he's going to do it.' They said, 'Oh, we got guys that can fly over and parachute and disarm it, and

Above: A tragic and beautiful photograph of the Kuwaiti oil wells burning on the horizon.

Below: A sign warning motorists to slow for camel crossings.

be gone in 15 minutes.' I said, 'You got to be kidding.' The Iraqis would simply wire 50 wells and set a timer. Then set another 50 or so. They all set them together and they're all detonated at the same time. That's exactly what they did. The Iraqis had some good engineers design it and they did a damn good job. But we all worked together and got it done."[9]

Halliburton crews brought 320 wells under control in less time than was expected. More than 190,000 work hours were spent fighting the fires without a single lost-time accident.[9] "It's called teamwork," Adair said. "When Halliburton did something, it was teamwork. There's no other company in the world like Halliburton."[10]

The fall 1991 issue of the *Cementer* provided a vivid account of the conditions endured by Halliburton crews along with other well service companies.

"Empty bunkers strung together by narrow trenches, and half-buried trucks, are evidence of

futile attempts to hide from stealth-age aircraft in the middle of a treeless desert. ... Then everything turns dark — pitch black. It's still mid-day, but the sun can't shine through the dense, black smoke. The smoke is high enough overhead to allow travel along the roads. But all that can be seen are the burning wells, like torches dotting the countryside, and headlights. Two pairs of headlights slowly weave back and forth off the road with what looks like the silhouettes of men standing up over the cabs. They're ordnance disposal teams still clearing the oil fields of mines, unexploded bombs, and abandoned weapons. ... You can hear the roaring of the fires. ... The glow of it lights up the interior of your vehicle. You can't get very close because of the heat, but the bellowing of the flame is loud enough that you have to yell to be heard above it. Soon your glasses, your clothes, and your skin are spotted with droplets of oil falling out of the sky."[11]

More than 60 Halliburton workers helped bring the spraying wells under control, all the time struggling under the intense air pollution. According to the *Cementer*, "early estimates said it would take a year and a half to three years before the last well is brought under control. Now, some of the more optimistic forecasters say that more than 90 percent of the blowouts will have been extinguished and capped within one year from the time the first well control operations began."[12]

Above: Brown & Root worker George Herion, serving as operations manager to ship out ammunition left by U.S. forces after Operation Desert Storm.

Below: A Halliburton crew silhouetted by a burning oil well.

Brown & Root Goes Army

Within days of the end of the Persian Gulf War, the U.S. Army Corps of Engineers selected Brown & Root to assess and repair damaged public buildings in Kuwait. Brown & Root's initial $3 million contract would swell by September to $22 million.[13] On arrival, the company's engineers found debris, vandalism and fires, but little structural damage caused by the Iraqi invasion. Project management would be the main problem, as traffic bottlenecks at the Saudi-Kuwait border slowed the shipment of building materials. Brown & Root would also win contracts to demobilize U.S. Army troops and equipment in Saudi Arabia. As part of its work, Brown & Root would prepare for shipment about 250,000 tons of ammunition and missiles, including enemy-captured ordnance, left in various locations.[14]

Brown & Root's work for the U.S. military was just beginning. Under an Army-initiated program called LOGCAP, or Logistics Civil Augmentation Program, the company would work in concert with the military to plan contingency

Above: Brown & Root employees deployed in Haiti to provide support for the U.S. military in 1994.

Below: Project Manager Jack Avant, wearing the Brown & Root cap, poses with a contingent of Marines who provided security for Brown & Root workers in Somalia.

or emergency operations anywhere that U.S. troops were deployed. It was the first time the U.S. military had ever contracted with a civilian group for such worldwide logistics support planning.[15]

Since the Civil War, private contractors have helped feed, house, or provide other support for U.S. troops, but only after the fighting had begun. Never before had a contractor been asked to help plan for it. However, as part of its defense build-down, the Pentagon was doing away with many of its own logistical support services. The LOGCAP umbrella contract, awarded in 1992, had been highly sought-after, and Brown & Root was proud to win it. For security reasons, however, the company could release few details, including the names of 13 countries they specifically would study.[16]

Within days of getting the LOGCAP contract, the company hurried to provide humanitarian assistance to famine-stricken Somalia in southern Africa as part of Operation Restore Hope. Initial jobs

ranged from building showers and latrines to running a laundry service, operating a landfill, and buying fresh fruit for the troops. As time passed, more complex tasks were assumed, such as providing lighting at the Mogadishu airfield, surveying the water and sewer systems, preparing the port to receive and support ships, and drilling new water wells.[17] A U.S. Army Corps of Engineers official would describe Brown & Root as a provider of "everything from latrines to linguists."[18]

A Brown & Root publication catalogued the arduous tasks: "Imagine supporting 28,000 military troops in a country without a government, a business, a police force, or even one telephone. After traveling halfway around the world to reach the site, you discover that the capital city of one million people gets its water from a single water well, which has no pump. The locals use donkey carts, carrying 55-gallon drums of water, to transport the precious commodity. Add 40 mph winds, 100 degree temperatures, and swirling dust."[19]

Both Brown & Root and the Army had to overcome differences in philosophy, and the most basic problems had to be resolved, explained former Chief Operating Officer Emil Zerr.

"In Somalia, the biggest problem we had was when the Army would come up with these vari-

ous tasks. We'd have to price out an estimate on each of these tasks. Then when they told us to go ahead and do it, they wanted it right away but they didn't have the funds for it. So it became a real problem of trying to meet the demands for the military and be responsive and not get ourselves so deeply committed financially that if the appropriations didn't come through, we'd spend the money and not get paid. [21]

Brown & Root had overcome its declining fortunes, due in part to these new initiatives. By 1991, the company could boast revenues of $3.7 billion, double that of 1987, and involvement in some 800 projects. [22] Its increasing role in "KP" duty for the military meant increased revenue, as the United States continued to deploy troops in other hot spots such as Haiti and, most recently, Bosnia.

Dick Cheney, former U.S. Secretary of Defense and now Chairman, President and CEO of Halliburton, said hiring private companies for logistical support exposes fewer Americans to danger because local people are usually hired to build overseas bases. "You've got Bosnians out there helping to build and maintain the camps in Bosnia rather than put more Americans at risk." [23] Cheney, however, agreed that working for the government can be tough.

"The federal government is always a difficult customer. I used to sit there as Secretary of Defense and sometimes wonder why anybody did business with us because it was so bureaucratic and had so much red tape connected with it." [24]

European Marine Contractors

European Marine Contractors, a joint venture between Brown & Root and Saipem, continued to pay off handsomely, as well as set world records in the pipeline industry. In 1992, the world's largest offshore pipeline, known as Zeepipe, was completed. The 670-mile pipeline stretched from offshore Norway natural gas fields to Belgium. A new level of partnership between Brown & Root and Halliburton Energy Services was reached when both segments cooperated to clean and put the pipeline into operation in 1993. [25]

While EMC worked on the project, the specialist pipeline company was awarded a contract to design, build and test the Europipe and Zeepipe phase II pipelines. The total project cost more than $550 million, the largest contract ever awarded in the offshore industry. According to Halliburton's September 30, 1992 Quarterly Report, the lines are "part of a concerted effort by Norway to become the major natural gas vendor to the European continent within the next few years." [26]

In 1994, EMC won a contract to complete the second-longest offshore pipeline, a 440-mile project for ARCO China's Yacheng field project in the South China Sea. The project was scheduled to begin in early 1996. [27]

The Battleship *Blücher*

In 1993, Halliburton's ability to mobilize against environmental dangers was tested when a battleship, sunk during World War II, began to

Environmental scientists gather water samples in Eastern Europe to test as part of Brown & Root's water quality and pollution control work.

BROWN & ROOT

leak fuel from its bunkers. The German battleship *Blücher* had lain like a giant tomb at the bottom of the Oslofjord since it was sunk in 1940 by Norwegian shore batteries. According to a Halliburton newsletter, the battleship was pummeled by batteries on both sides of the fjord and fatally punctured under the waterline by torpe-does. More than 600 sailors and the equivalent of 20,000 barrels of heavy diesel bunker fuel were trapped in the vessel.

In late 1993, diesel fuel was discovered seeping in ever-increasing quantities from the sunken wreck. An agency from the Norwegian government contacted Rockwater, Halliburton's

Tools of the Trade

SEVERAL YEARS AGO, Halliburton sent a survey to its customers with a simple question: What trends did customers see occurring in the oil industry and what did they require to succeed? The answers were surprisingly simple: Customers responded that the trend is toward smaller oil fields, and their need was to squeeze every drop of oil and gas from these fields in the most efficient manner possible. The survey spurred Halliburton to develop several innovative products, most of which combined operations to save time and effort.

Pathfinder LWD: Introduced in 1995, the Pathfinder Logging While Drilling (LWD) was developed to obtain crucial downhole formation data during drilling, without pulling the drillstring out of the hole. Housed within the drillstring, the LWD system performs logging functions behind the drill bit while the bit turns in the hole.[1]

Scout Sonic Service: The following year, the Scout Sonic Service was added to the LWD, providing full wave acoustic logging while drilling service. The first such service to be commercially offered, the Scout Sonic offered the full array of wireline logging that previously could not be performed until drilling was completed.[2]

Multilateral System 3000: On May 6, 1996, Halliburton Energy Services installed the world's first "full-bore re-entry access multilateral system." This means that lateral reservoirs, at different pressures, can be repeatedly tested, re-perforated and restimulated from

one main wellhead.[3] This is often necessary because formations tend to close up and productivity drops.

Sandstone 2000 Acid System: Although the acidization process developed in the labs of Halliburton increased production in wells, the chemicals used often damaged oil and gas formations by contaminating them with minerals. The Sandstone system minimizes those effects and enhances formation productivity.[4]

PHOTOS: HALLIBURTON CO.

PEE WEE CAREY/HALLIBURTON CO.

Statue of Erle P. Halliburton, erected in 1993 in Duncan's Memorial Park. The statue stands just down the road from his original shops and equipment yard.

that inefficiency and resistance to change was a by-product of the duplicate managements that ran each of Halliburton's subsidiaries.

The consolidation began with Halliburton Services, Otis Engineering, Halliburton Logging Services, Halliburton Geophysical Services, Halliburton Reservoir Services, Halliburton Resource Management, Sierra Geophysics, Halliburton Geodata, Jet Research Center and Smith International's Directional Drilling Systems and Services. According to a company newsletter, the acquisition of Smith International was part of Halliburton's strategy "to provide total well service packages for customers seeking integrated oil field services from a single company."

Each division and company had its own administrative structure: a president, vice presidents, departments for accounting, auditing, credit, treasury, tax, legal, data processing, regulatory affairs and so forth. The various oil-field related companies and divisions were merged into the Energy Services Group, and all of the administrative duties were handled by a central office. Jimmy Cooper, vice president and chief environmental officer, foresaw the need to merge services in the 1980s. When the consolidation began, he helped install the necessary structure. Cooper remembered that he met resistance at first.

"In 1991 and '92, we basically consolidated the computer, the information technology groups, what I call the business applications. We got all the employees on the same payroll system that are not in the U.S. payroll system. It was tough because some unit presidents did not want that to happen. They were independent and could see that they were losing something they did not want to."[29]

In one sense, Halliburton was centralizing services while decentralizing decisions. For example, more decisions would be made in the field by managers. Halliburton began a course of training called Front Line Management Development (FLMD) for district managers and operations managers. According to Ken LeSuer, president of Halliburton Services and one of the executives in charge of restructuring the company, the course would help "transfer the decision-making process

underwater engineering and construction contractor. Rockwater discovered that nearly half of the hull plates' thickness had rusted away. Saturation divers marked areas for drilling locations and Rockwater developed special drilling machines. Rockwater's semisubmersible support ship, SEMI I, controlled operations. It took six weeks and about 120 people to recover the fuel from 82 outboard and 23 inboard tanks.

The operation recovered about 80 percent of the oil, virtually eliminating the threat of oil pollution from the wreck in the waters near Drøbak.[28]

Reorganization

Halliburton executives had begun to consolidate services before the distraction of the Gulf War. It was becoming apparent by the late 1980s and give the front line mangers the tools they need to make sound decisions."[30] LeSuer stated that "we have mostly been judged on how well we carried out the orders and directions of upper management. Now, managers will have the opportunity to make the decisions locally, while being responsible for the results that the decisions produce."[31]

Project GO

In January 1993, Halliburton Company embarked on the biggest reorganization effort in its history: Project Global Organization. Alan Baker, chairman of the Halliburton Energy Services Group, set up a five-member team led by Ken Lesuer, to reorganize the Energy Group. The goal was to form a "fully integrated, seamless organization," explained W.J. Zeringue. "We started bringing other key managers" into the planning group, recalled Zeringue. "The five grew to 25. Grew to 75." Before the project was finished, more than 200 people were working on the restructuring of Halliburton. There were teams in every section of the organization looking at the way they did business and figuring out how to do it better. In the process, inefficiency in administration, production, and service would be eliminated or reduced. Zeringue said the process was not easy because Halliburton Company had been such a dynamic, diverse and independent-minded company for so long.

> "What we would have to do was take care of the redundancy and the inefficiencies that we had with nine separate companies. We had 75 different titles that represented sales in this organization amongst the different companies."[32]

Zeringue said many people in the company were nervous about the project, a feeling that lasted as executives fine-tuned the structure of Halliburton Energy Services, the name of the emerging umbrella organization. But the company was at the forefront of what would be a major corporate worldwide restructuring of services.

> "We bit the bullet and went first. Well into 1994, we still had a lot of consternation and con-

> cern because, quite frankly, we were still affecting people's livelihoods. ... The blue collar portion of Halliburton had been affected quite severely. Going into 1995, we began seeing periods of stability as some of the processes that we had defined were being put into action."[33]

Zeringue explained how the restructuring affected individual Halliburton services. For example, Halliburton introduced horizontal drilling. Within the service, Halliburton offered technology such as steering and measurement tools that help the horizontal drilling process. "What we are doing now organizationally is framing strategies that fit our customers' purposes," he said. Another example is the amount of water that drilling an oil well produces. Disposing of water is a costly endeavor. "We use video to see where the water is being produced, and we can go in and devise a solution to control the water. If we can control the water and lessen the amount that is produced, that's a savings to the customer."[34]

The reorganization had shaken the company, as nearly 2,700 employees had been terminated. As a further consequence, Halliburton had sold its geophysical and natural gas compression units, the "non-core businesses," in the words of chairman Tom H. Cruikshank. A new culture was emerging at Halliburton. It was a leaner company, with multiple levels of management stripped away and employees holding more responsibility for their own and the company's success. There was more communication among employees. And the company would continue to study itself, with an emphasis no longer on cutting back, but instead on improving management and working more closely and efficiently with its customers.

"We have always had a focus on getting the job done properly," commented Robert Nash, senior vice president of Solutions and Services. "There is an expectation on the company's part that our primary focus is to serve the customer's needs."[35]

Dick Cheney Takes the Helm

Following the massive reorganization of the Halliburton Company came another big

Richard Bruce Cheney

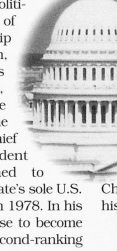

ON OCTOBER 1, 1995, 54-year-old Dick Cheney became president and CEO of the Halliburton Company. With a resume that includes serving as Chief of Staff to President Gerald Ford and Secretary of Defense under President George Bush, Cheney was supremely qualified to take the helm of the complicated and dynamic organization.

Cheney earned his undergraduate degree, and later his masters in political science from the University of Wyoming. A one-year fellowship brought Cheney to Washington, and this experience led to a job as a Capitol Hill staffer. In 1974, Cheney was invited to work in the Nixon White House. In 1975, he was appointed as White House Chief of Staff, serving under President Gerald Ford. Cheney returned to Wyoming in 1977 to run as the state's sole U.S. Representative, and was elected in 1978. In his five terms on the Hill, Cheney rose to become the House minority whip, the second-ranking Republican leader.

In 1989, Cheney was appointed U.S. Secretary of Defense under President George Bush. In this role, he presided over a time of profound change within the military as the Cold War ended and new enemies emerged. He played a pivotal role in Operation Desert Storm, working closely with Colin Powell, Chairman of the Joint Chiefs of Staff.

In his autobiography, *My American Journey*, Colin Powell described Cheney as "a cerebral cowboy, used to wide-open spaces where one did not have to deal with many people. He was a conservative by nature and in his politics, a loner who would take your counsel, but preferred to go off by himself to make up his mind. ... Here was someone else who had learned never to let 'em see you sweat. I enjoyed working with a master of the game."[1]

In his book *The Commanders*, Bob Woodward wrote that analyzing Cheney was something of a hobby among his admirers.

"Even to his closest aides, Cheney was something of an enigma. If they asked him something specific, he generally would give an answer, but he was not one to relax and unburden himself to others. ... Pete Williams even had a name for the loose, unofficial group of people like himself who tried to better understand the inscrutable Cheney by following and closely analyzing his movements: "Cheney-watchers."[2]

change. In 1995, Chairman Tom Cruikshank announced that former Secretary of Defense Dick Cheney, among the leaders who had orchestrated the defeat of Saddam Hussein, would become president and chief executive officer. Cheney arrived at Halliburton with unmatched government credentials: he served in a variety of posts under presidents Richard Nixon and Gerald Ford; he became White House chief of staff for Ford; was elected as the single representative to Congress from Wyoming in 1978 and became House minority whip in 1988. But Cheney achieved the most fame under President George Bush, serving as Secretary of Defense from 1989 to 1993.

Aside from the experience gained in running and streamlining the nation's $270 billion-a-year military establishment, Cheney had experience in the oil industry from constituents and various public policy debates. In a recent interview, Cheney said that looking at Halliburton from within gave him a new perspective.

"I had some general knowledge of the public policy issues and of the industry in a generic sense. But I was struck by the extent of how each company within the industry has its own identity. I used to think that an oil company was an oil company was an oil company. I'm struck by the evolution — revolution is probably a better word — of the industry itself. It's no longer reacting to the good and bad cycles, of making money one year and not the next. We are clearly spending a lot of time trying to figure out how we can provide a broad range of services."[36]

Cheney added that much of the struggle to enter new markets is political, particularly in areas where the politics are still in transition.

"As I look at the projects and proposals that come across my desk, I have been struck by the extent of whether a project goes forward or not is more of a political decision than it is an engineering one. The engineering and technical aspects of it are sometimes relatively easy. The hard part is the politics. For example, developing the resources in the former Soviet Union. There are enormous resources and tremendous poverty. All the elements are there to make you think that obviously people are going want to develop these resources and market these assets and yet, time after time, those projects are thwarted over unresolved political issues that they are still wrestling with inside the former Soviet Union."[37]

In Search of Synergy

Dick Cheney arrived when Project GO was starting to reap dividends for the company. In 1994, the company brought in $174 million in net income, the highest level in a decade.[38]

Cheney said he was relieved that Project GO was implemented before he arrived. "I can't imagine what it was like trying to manage an organization that was really nine separate companies. I find that when I deal with Halliburton Energy Services, there is a very strong sense of being part of a team."[39]

Cheney commented that much of his first year was spent learning about the company and helping to foster cooperation between Halliburton Energy Services and Brown & Root. While Cheney said he was pleased with the results thus far, he noted that opportunities to streamline the company into a more efficient organization still existed. Consequently, ways to regroup Halliburton's energy service units were explored to meet the growing customer needs for complete service.[40]

This regrouping would eventually lead to the creation of a new organization, Halliburton Energy Group, which would become home to the energy service segments from both Halliburton and Brown & Root. The group's mission — to achieve synergy while meeting all of a customer's needs — would be bolstered with the arrival of Landmark Graphics Corporation, a leader in information technologies. Landmark would bring a new dimension of service and efficiency to Halliburton through its use of information-managing products.

Finding The Common Ground

On July 25, 1996, Halliburton announced that its energy segments would work together to develop the Sangu offshore natural gas field, located in the Bay of Bengal south of Bangladesh. Under the agreement with Cairn Energy PLC, Brown & Root is in charge of the surface installation and Halliburton Energy Services is in charge of the subsurface work.[41]

The contract with Cairn Energy, a Scotland-based international exploration and production company, is unique, according to Halliburton Chief Financial Officer Dave Lesar. He explained that Halliburton is in fact a partner with Cairn, with aligned interests and shared risks. Halliburton has a 25 percent interest in the Cairn field, and a long-term agreement to manage it.

"Halliburton provides all of its normal service abilities and gets paid for that service. HES may perform the drilling and stimulation, etc. and Brown & Root may fabricate the platform, etc. Secondly, we are contracted with Cairn to operate and maintain that field for a long time and we are going to get a management fee for that. Thirdly, by taking a 25 percent interest in the field itself we will have an equity rate of turn. At the end of the day, we get a piece of the profit. We took the equity because it really aligns our interests with Cairn. They look at Halliburton as not only as a solutions provider but as a partner. People tend to deal with partners different than they deal with vendors."[42]

Lesar said joint projects between HES and Brown & Root will become the norm as Halliburton continues its mission to weld the two together. He added that Cheney has helped this effort by devising a "shared services" organization. Functions such as procurement, human resources and accounting, traditionally handled individually by segments of Halliburton, have been successfully molded into a cross-company team.

"There are about 11 or 12 operations that can be handled on behalf of Halliburton with common procedures, common policies and common management. We believe this will allow people from Brown & Root and HES to gain training and knowledge, and get the two organizations used to working together. At the end of the day, they are really dealing from a common systems standpoint. I know Dick Cheney feels very strongly that shared services is one of those areas that is really going to continue to drive change throughout the organization."[43]

Integrated Solutions: The Landmark Acquisition

Executives often find themselves drowning in the information they need to make timely and important decisions. It is difficult to weigh the significance of every piece of data, and to synthesize it into useful information.

But in June 1996, Halliburton made sure its customers could properly manage and decipher information gathered by its products. As part of its mission to provide total solutions to customers, Halliburton acquired Landmark Graphics Corporation, which provides leading-edge software systems and service, to transform the immense amount of seismic, well log and engineering data into three- and four-dimensional computer models of petroleum reservoirs.

With its 1,000-employee workforce, Landmark is a pioneer in information technologies that, according to Chairman and CEO Robert Peebler, provides more efficient ways to manage risk and increase revenue. Landmark carved out a new industry and continues to lead the market.

Peebler noted that the acquisition took a mere two weeks to negotiate and finalize, an unusually short amount of time for a major $500 million merger, although the deal was not formally completed until October. Peebler described the acquisition as a logical part of Halliburton's total solutions strategy.

"We had some previous discussions with Halliburton about a potential strategic alliance or even a joint venture in the data management area, and because of that we already knew some of their executives. We had talked with each other enough to be pretty clear on each other's strategy. ... Halliburton realized that the Information Technology component of the industry had a growing importance, and they were really up against Schlumberger, who already had a division with some capabilities in this area. So Halliburton saw an opportunity to gain the leadership position in Information Technology. Landmark fit very well with their integrated solutions strategy."[44]

Hank Holland, executive vice president of Integrated Solutions, noted that Landmark's capabilities and Halliburton's information-gathering tools are a natural marriage.

"We can offer customers a greater breadth of solutions, and Landmark can become the technology underpinning to Halliburton Energy Services. So, when Halliburton drills and completes a well, the data that is captured becomes source data for our products. We can then offer the customer complete field management solutions, including the Information Technology and Data Management infrastructure."[45]

Landmark reported $171 million in revenue in fiscal 1996 and Peebler expects growth to remain strong. Landmark joins Brown & Root and Halliburton Energy Services as a wholly-owned subsidiary of Halliburton Company.

A Better Way to do Business:
The Halliburton Advantage

With the 21st century just around the corner, Halliburton has positioned itself to become what Dave Lesar described as "the biggest and the best" in the evolving energy industry. The efforts so far have paid off

in strong third quarter earnings in 1996, up 20 percent from 1995.

In the company's earliest days, Erle P. Halliburton recognized that the company had to respond to his customers' changing needs. As mentioned earlier, Halliburton's leaders realigned the company in the fourth quarter of 1996. Landmark Graphics, Halliburton Energy Services, Brown & Root Energy Services and a new organization, Halliburton Energy Development, were organized under the new Halliburton Energy Group. Steve Moore, director of Corporate Communication, said this alignment will "get as much synergy as possible" out of the various energy business segments.[46] Halliburton Energy Development was specifically designed to manage "contract-to-produce" jobs similar to the Cairn contract.

A similar change is occurring within Brown & Root. Not only is Brown & Root Energy Services now part of the Halliburton Energy Group, but Brown & Root, Inc. has been further refocused to reflect its two core businesses: Brown & Root Engineering and Construction, and Brown & Root

HALLIBURTON CO.

Services. The latter segment is focused on government-related services, such as LOGCAP. Grouped under Engineering & Construction are all other segments: Forest Products, Chemical, Refining, Gas Processing, Manufacturing and Maintenance. The rationale for these changes was provided in the announcement, made to employees in October 1996:

"In recent months you have seen many changes affecting the way we do business at Halliburton Company. While disruptive and unsettling on the surface, these changes share the common themes of alignment, synergy and customer focus. ... The growth potential for Brown & Root businesses both domestically and internationally is immense. The name, reputation capability and project execution of Brown & Root is well respected throughout the world. We will invest in and build on these strengths. ... The formation of these new units will allow us to eliminate redundancies that have built up over the years. ... We must get more cost effective as a total organization."[47]

These changes in organization are all part of part of Halliburton Company's commitment to its customer-focused mission. From nine separate oil field service companies and one construction company, Halliburton is becoming the "seamless" organization envisioned by Dick Cheney, Lesar, Dale Jones and numerous other executives. These executives develop the plan and communicate the vision, but the company as a whole draws its strength from its workers. It is a quality that was immediately recognized by Cheney, and one that will always give Halliburton the edge over its competitors, no matter what form the company takes in the future.

"One of the things that I sense that is common throughout the Halliburton family is the loyalty that employees have. People are proud of their careers and of what they have been able to do over the years with the company. That's an enormous asset to us, a great advantage. After my time with the military I came to hold a great appreciation for the professionalism of the people I dealt with, the men and women who devoted their careers to the military. And one of the things I am very pleased with is the same sense of professionalism and pride throughout Halliburton. That's a rare commodity you don't often find."[4]

Notes to Sources

Chapter One

1. John P. Harbin, interviewed by the author, December 12, 1995. Transcript, p. 9.
2. "A Quarter Century of Progress," *The Cementer*, Halliburton Archives, July-August, 1949, p. 22.
3. "History of Halliburton Services," Halliburton Archives, unpublished manuscript, author unknown, p. 3.
4. "Erle P. Halliburton: A Product of the American Way of Life," *The Cementer*, July August, 1949, p. 5.
5. *Ibid.*, p. 5.
6. "History of Halliburton Services," p. 4.
7. *Ibid.*, p. 5.
8. *The Cementer*, July-August, 1949, p. 2.
9. J. Evetts Haley, Erle P. Halliburton: Genius with Cement El Paso: Carl Hertzog, 1959, pp. 11-13; Halliburton Archives, quoted in *A Brief History of Halliburton Service (1916-1977)*, by Rex Hudson.
10. J. Evetts Haley, *Erle P. Halliburton: Genius with Cement,* El Paso: Carl Hertzog, 1959, p. 11-13.
11. Vida Halliburton, "The Silent Partner Speaks," *The Cementer*, July-August 1949, p. 5.
12. *Ibid.*, p. 6.
13. *Ibid.*, pp. 5-6.
14. *Ibid.*, p. 7.
15. *A Brief History of Halliburton Services*, p. 11.
16. Corporate Minutes, Vol. I, 1921.
17. "75,000 Jobs Done in Ten Year Period," Duncan *Sunday and Evening Banner*, Duncan, Oklahoma, June 29, 1934.
18. "The Silent Partner Speaks," *The Cementer*, p. 8.
19. *Ibid.*, pp. 8-9.
20. *Ibid., p. 8-9.*
21. "A Quarter Century of Progress," *The Cementer*, p. 23.
22. "75,000 Jobs Done in Ten Year Period," Duncan *Evening and Sunday Banner.*
23. *A Brief History of Halliburton Service (1916-1977).* p. 5.
24. Halliburton corporate counsel Earl Babcock manuscript, *The Good Old Days at Halliburton*, unpublished and undated.
25. *Ibid.*, p. 4.
26. *A Brief History of Halliburton Services (1916-1977)*, p. 6.
27. Corporate Minutes, Halliburton Corporation, Vol. I; quoted in "*The Good Old Days at Halliburton,*" by Earl Babcock, p. 6.
28. *Ibid.*
29. *Ibid.*
30. *The Cementer*, July-August, 1949, p. 23.
31. Corporate Minutes, Vol. I, p. 6.

Chapter Two

1. J. Evetts Haley, Erle P. Halliburton: Genius with Cement El Paso: Carl Hertzog, 1959, p. 21; Halliburton Archives, quoted in *A Brief History of Halliburton Service (1916-1977)*, by Rex Hudson.
2. *The Cementer*, July-August, 1949, p. 24.
3. *Ibid.*
4. Various sources, including Erle P. Halliburton, "We'll Get There Somehow," Duncan *Evening and Sunday Banner*, Duncan, Oklahoma, June 29, 1934. Halliburton Section celebrating the company's 10th anniversary.
5. Edwin Paramore, interviewed by the author November 14, 1995. Transcript, p. 15.
6. *A History of Halliburton Services*, pp. 28-30. Unpublished manuscript, author unknown.
7. *Route 66*, by Michael Wallis, St. Martin's Press, New York, 1990, p. 9.
8. *History of Halliburton Services*, p. 28.
9. *The Cementer*, July-August, 1949, p. 22.
10. *A History of Halliburton Services*, p. 18.
11. *Genius with Cement*, by J. Evetts Haley, quoted in *A History of Halliburton Services.*
12. Vida Halliburton, "The Silent Partner Speaks," *The Cementer*, July-August 1949, p. 5
13. Malcolm Rosser, interviewed by the author, January 18, 1996. Transcript, p. 13.
14. Halliburton Archives, unpublished, manuscript, author unknown.
15. Notebook of H.T. Crain, former Halliburton secretary-treasurer.
16. *The Cementer*, July-August, 1949, p. 27.
17. *A History of Halliburton Services*, p. 26.
18. *Ibid.*, p. 27.
19. "A Walk Through History," p. 8.
20. Corporate Minutes, Vol I, p 70.
21. Earl Babcock manuscript, unpublished and undated, p. 5.
22. Corporate Minutes, Vol. I, p. 100.
23. "Halliburton Formation Testing Device for Testing Productivity of Formations without Setting Casing," 1941 HOWCO Tester and Acidizing Tools Partial List, published by the Halliburton Oil Well Cementing Company, Duncan, Oklahoma.
24. *The Good Old Days At Halliburton*, Earl Babcock manuscript, pp. 8-9.
25. *Ibid.*, p. 12.
26. *Ibid.*
27. *Ibid.*
28. *Ibid.*, p. 13.
29. *Ibid.*
30. *Ibid.*, p. 15.
31. *Ibid.*
32. "The Dispatcher Highlights," an unpublished manuscript, August, 1964.
33. John Harbin, interview, p. 9.

Chapter Two Sidebar

1. *The Cementer*, 1949 25th Anniversary issue, pp. 9-11.
2. *Ibid.*, pp. 9-11.

Chapter Three

1. *Duncan Daily Banner*, November 14, 1948.
2. Harold F. Williamson, The American Petroleum Industry, 1899-1959 (Evanston: Northwestern University Press, 1963), pp. 536–537.
3. *Duncan Daily Banner*, November 14, 1948.
4. Bob Diggs Brown, interviewed by the author, January 18, 1995. Transcript, p. 1.
5. *A History of Halliburton Services*, unpublished manuscript, author unknown, p. 26.
6. *A Brief History of Halliburton Services*, by Rex Hudson, p. 24.
7. "Halliburton Formation Testing Device," described in Howco Tester Catalog and Parts List, published in 1935 by the Halliburton Oil Well Cementing Company, Duncan, Oklahoma.
8. *The Cementer*, July-August, 1949, p. 27.
9. Earl Babcock, unpublished and undated manuscript, p. 23.

10. Malcolm Rosser, interviewed by the author, January 18, 1996. Transcript, p. 14.
11. "Tenth Anniversary of the Halliburton Organization Finds 432 on the Payroll," *Duncan Evening and Sunday Banner*, June 29, 1934, special Halliburton section.
12. Notebook of H.T. Crain.
13. "Multiple Stage Cementing," Export Catalogue Number E-1, Oil Well Cementing Equipment, published in March 1937, by the Halliburton Oil Well Cementing Company, Duncan, Oklahoma.
14. "Full Hole Cementing," 1937 export catalog.
15. Corporate Minutes, Vol. I, pp. 198-200.
16. *A History of Halliburton Services*, pp. 31-32.
17. Corporate minutes, Vol. III, p. 449.
18. *Halliburton Company Profile*, undated, unpublished manuscript, p. 4.
19. Corporate Minutes, Vol. III.
20. *History of Halliburton Services*, p. 33.
21. Corporate Minutes, Vol. III, p. 451.
22. *Duncan Daily Banner*, Oct. 14, 1957.
23. *History of Halliburton Services*, pp. 34–35.
24. Corporate Minutes, Vol. III, p. 452.
25. Corporate Minutes, Vol. II, p. 384.
26. Corporate Minutes, Vol. III, p. 452.
27. John P. Harbin interview. Transcript, p. 9.
28. Malcolm Rosser interview. Transcript, p. 14.
29. *The Cementer*, 25th Anniversary issue, p. 2.
30. *The Cementer*, 25th Anniversary issue, p. 2
31. Bob Diggs Brown interview. Transcript, p. 6.
32. Corporate Minutes, Vol. IV.
33. *The Cementer*, July-Aug, 1949, pp. 28-29.
34. Edwin Paramore. Transcript, p. 10.
35. Corporate Minutes, Vol. IV; directors meetings on July 1 1947 and April 19 1948.
36. Corporate Minutes, Vol. IV, special meeting of directors, April 19 1948.
37. Bob Diggs Brown interview. Transcript, pp.6–7.
38. Harbin interview. Transcript, p. 13.

Chapter Four

1. E.P. Halliburton, "A Tribute to the 25-Year Men," *The Cementer*, July-August 1949, inside front cover.
2. *The Cementer*, "25 Years Service With Howco," July-August 1949, pp. 11-32.
3. Excerpt of article in the *Duncan Daily Banner*, October 14, 1957, p. 7.
4. Edwin Paramore. Transcript, p. 9.
5. *The Cementer*, January-February 1947, pp 4-7.
6. *Ibid.*, p 7.
7. *Ibid.*, pp 18-19.
8. *Ibid.*, pp. 22-23.
9. Bob Diggs Brown, transcript, p. 10.
10. The *Duncan Daily Banner*, June 21 1992, p. 19aa.
11. Rex Hudson, *A Brief History of Halliburton Services*, pp 40–41.
12. Halliburton Oil Well Cementing Company Annual Report, 1957.
13. *Ibid.*
14. "Construction Begins on Technical Center," *The Cementer*, September-October 1952, p. 18.
15. *A Brief History of Halliburton Services*, p.33.
16. *Ibid.*, pp. 32–33.
17. *Ibid.*, p. 33.
18. *The Cementer*, July-August 1949, p.15.
19. The *Duncan Daily Banner*, February 17 1984, p. 5A.
20. *The Cementer*, November-December 1957, p. 21.
21. *The Cementer*, November-December 1957, p. 16.
22. *The Cementer*, November-December 1957, p. 14.
23. Bob Diggs Brown. Transcript, p. 4.
24. Halliburton Oil Well Cementing Company Annual Report, 1957.
25. The Welex Log, Vol. I, #1, July 1965, pp. 1–4.
26. Halliburton Oil Well Cementing Company Annual Report, 1957.
27. *Ibid.*
28. *Ibid.*
29. *Ibid.*
30. *The Cementer*, Fall Issue, pp. 34–35.
31. John P. Harbin interview, transcript, p. 19.
32. Karen Stuart, interviewed by the author, December 12, 1995. Transcript, p. 1
33. Halliburton Company Annual Report, 1960.
34. *Ibid.*
35. *Ibid.*
36. *Ibid.*
37. *Ibid.*
38. *Ibid.*
39. *A Brief History of Halliburton Services*, pp. 41–42.
40. Halliburton Company Annual Report, 1961.
41. *The Dallas Morning News*, September 24 1995, p. 32 A.
42. Halliburton Company Annual Report, 1961.

Chapter Five

1. Dana Blankenhorn, "The Brown Brothers: From Mules To Millions as Houston's Contracting and Energy Giant," *Houston Business Journal*, March 19, 1979, p. 1.
2. *The Houston Chronicle*, Dec. 20, 1942.
3. *The Handbook of Texas*, Vol. 1. Austin: The Texas State Historical Association, 1952, p. 144.
4. *Chronicle*, 1942.
5. *Ibid.*
6. Klempin, Raymond. *Houston Business Journal*. First of a three-part series, Aug. 30, 1982, p. 16.
7. *Houston Chronicle*, Dec. 20, 1942.
8. *Ibid.*
9. *Ibid.*
10. George R. Brown, interviewed by Paul Bolton on April 6, 1968. Lyndon Baines Johnson Oral History Collection. Transcript, p. 2.
11. *Houston Post*, November 16, 1962.
12. Caro, Robert A, *The Years of Lyndon Johnson: The Path to Power*, New York: Alfred A. Knopf, 1982, p. 370.
13. *Chronicle*, 1942.
14. Klempin, p. 16.
15. *Brownbuilder\69: The First 50 Years*. Special 50th Anniversary Issue, 1.
16. *The Houston Post*, Jan. 26, 1963.
17. George R. Brown, interviewed Aug. 6, 1969, by David G. McComb as part of the University of Texas Oral History Project. Lyndon Baines Johnson Library's Oral History Collection. Transcript, p. 2.
18. "Experience Record and Qualifications of Brown & Root, Inc. — Austin and Houston, Texas," dated April 1, 1941.
19. *The Houston Chronicle*, Jan. 23, 1983.
20. Rice University Review, p. 4.
21. George R. Brown biography, dated Jan. 17, 1976, Brown & Root historical files.
22. Blankenhorn, Dana. p. 1.
23. Caro, p. 371.
24. George R. Brown, Aug. 6, 1969 interview. Transcript, pp. 1–2.
25. *Chronicle*, 1942.
26. Blankenhorn, p. 1.
27. *Brownbuilder: 75th Anniversary issue*, 1994, p. 10.
28. Johnston, p. 386.

29. *Ibid.*
30. *Ibid.*
31. Blankenhorn, p. 1.
32. *Ibid.*
33. *Chronicle*, 1942.
34. Caro, 370.
35. Johnston, Marguerite. *Houston: The Unknown City, 1836–1946.* College Station: Texas A&M U P, 1991, 387.
36. *Ibid.*
37. Caro, 372.
38. The Scoreboard, November 1964.
39. "Herman Brown, et al., Appellants, v. O.L. Neyland, Appellee, Brief for Appellants in the Court of Civil Appeals for the 3rd Supreme Judicial District of Texas at Austin," p. 160.
40. Caro, p. 371.
41. Johnston, p. 255.
42. *Ibid.*
43. Shelton, Beth Anne, et al. Houston: *Growth and Decline in a Sunbelt Boomtown*, Philadelphia: Temple UP, 1989, p. 14.
44. George R. Brown, April 6, 1968 oral history interview, p. 2.
45. Charter of Brown & Root Inc., filed with the Texas Secretary of State on July 2, 1929.

Chapter Six

1. Beaubien, *Houston Chronicle*, April 27, 1941.
2. Caro, Robert A, *The Years of Lyndon Johnson: The Path to Power*, New York: Alfred A. Knopf, 1982, p. 371.
3. *Ibid.*, p. 372.
4. George Brown, interviewed by David G. McComb for the University of Texas Oral History Project on Aug. 6, 1969. Lyndon Baines Johnson Library's Oral History Collection. Transcript, p. 3.
5. Caro, p. 372.
6. Klempin, Raymond. *Houston Business Journal*, Aug. 30, 1982, p. 18.
7. *Ibid.*
8. *Brownbuilder/69: The First 50 Years. Special 50th anniversary issue*, p. 3.
9. Beaubien, Ola H., *Houston Chronicle*, April 27, 1941.
10. Adams Jr., John A., *Damming the Colorado: The Rise of the Lower Colorado River Authority, 1933–1939*, (College Station: Texas A&M UP, 1990), p. 67.
11. *Ibid.*
12. *Ibid.*
13. *Ibid.*
14. *Ibid*, p. 68.

15. Banks, James H. and John E. Babcock, *Corralling the Colorado: The First Fifty Years of the Lower Colorado River Authority.* (Austin: Eakin Press, 1988), p. 96.
16. Caro, p. 380.
17. *Ibid.*
18. *Ibid.*, p. 383.
19. *Ibid.*
20. Banks, p. 98.
21. Adams, p. 70.
22. George Brown, interviewed by Paul Bolton on April 6, 1968. Lyndon Baines Johnson Library's Oral History Collection. Transcript, p. 4.
23. Banks, p. 102.
24. *Ibid.*, p. 155.
25. Beaubien, *Houston Chronicle*, April 27, 1941.
26. Banks, pp. 155–56.
27. Beaubien, *Houston Chronicle*, April 27, 1941.
28. Caro, p. 475.
29. *Ibid.*, p. 527.
30. *Ibid.*
31. Gillan, Linda. *Houston Chronicle*, March 2, 1980.

Chapter Seven

1. *Brown Victory Dispatch*, November 2, 1945.
2. Caro, Robert A, *The Years of Lyndon Johnson: The Path to Power*, New York: Alfred A. Knopf, 1982, p. 581.
3. *Ibid.*, p. 582.
4. *Ibid.*, p. 584.
5. George R. Brown. Aug. 6, 1969 interview. Transcript, p. 12.
6. *Ibid.*, p. 585.
7. George R. Brown. Aug. 6, 1969, interview. Transcript, p. 13.
8. The Nueces County Historical Society, *The History of Nueces County*, (Austin: Jenkins Publishing Co., 1972), p. 159.
9. George R. Brown. Aug. 6, 1969, interview. Transcript, p. 12.
10. George R. Brown. Interviewed by Paul Bolton on April 6, 1968, Lyndon Baines Johnson Library's Oral History Collection. Transcript, p. 9.
11. George R. Brown. April 6, 1968 interview. Transcript, p. 9.
12. *Houston Chronicle*, December 20, 1942.
13. Caro, p. 664.
14. *Brownbuilder/69*, p. 4.
15. *Brownbuilder/69*, p. 4.
16. *Brown Victory Dispatch*, November 2, 1945.
17. *Ibid.*

18. *Ibid.*, October 2, 1943.
19. *Ibid.*
20. *Ibid.*, November 2, 1945.
21. *Brownbuilder: 75th Anniversary, 1919–1994*, p. 13.
22. *Ibid.*
23. *Brown Victory Dispatch*, November 9, 1945.
24. *Houston Chronicle*, February 27, 1942.
25. *Brown Victory Dispatch*, August 26, 1944.
26. *Houston Post*, February 28, 1942.
27. *Ibid.*
28. *Brown Victory Dispatch*, July 21, 1945.
29. *Ibid.*, October 26, 1945.
30. *Ibid.*, July 18, 1942.
31. *Ibid.*, November 25, 1944.
32. *Houston Chronicle*, March 22, 1942.
33. *Houston Press*, December 22, 1942.
34. *Time*, January 11, 1943, 76.
35. *Ibid.*, 78.
36. *Brown Victory Dispatch*, November 16, 1945.
37. *Ibid.*, February 19, 1944.
38. *Brown Victory Dispatch*, May 13, 1944.
39. *Houston Chronicle*, "Brown Fits Warships for Combat at New Dry Docks," February 27, 1944.
40. *Brown Victory Dispatch*, April 7, 1945.
41. *Ibid.*, September 14, 1945.
42. *Brown Victory Dispatch*, December 14, 1945.
43. Documents filed with the Texas Secretary of State, December 31, 1942.
44. Caro, p. 743.
45. *Ibid.*, p. 753.

Chapter Eight

1. Fuermann, George. Houston: *Land of the Big Rich.* Garden City, N.Y.: Doubleday & Co., 1951, 120.
2. *Brownbuilder/83*: Winter, 9.
3. "Brown Shipyards to be Active in City's Future." Houston, March 1946.
4. The Scoreboard, May 1963.
5. Dana Blankenhorn, "The Brown Brothers: From Mules To Millions as Houston's Contracting and Energy Giant," *Houston Business Journal*, March 19, 1979, p. 3.
6. *Ibid.*
7. Castaneda, Christopher J. and Joseph A. Pratt. *From Texas to the East: A Strategic History of Texas Eastern Corporation.* College Station: Texas A&M U P, 1993, p. 104.

8. "A Pioneer Among Pioneers." *Brownbilt*, Fall 1972, p. 22.
9. *Ibid.*
10. *Ibid.*
11. *Brown & Root Engineering*, p. 16.
12. *Ibid.*
13. *Brownbuilder*, Spring 1984, p. 13.
14. *Brown & Root Engineering*, p. 16.
15. "Brief Statement on Brown & Root, Inc., Houston, Texas," June 13, 1947.
16. *Brownbuilder: 75th Anniversary, 1919–1994*, p. 8.
17. *Houston Chronicle*, July 2, 1952.
18. Documents filed with the Texas Secretary of State, December 22, 1948.
19. *Ibid.*, December 28, 1954.
20. Johnston, Marguerite. Houston: *The Unknown City, 1836– 1946*. College Station: Texas A&M U P, 1991, p. 385.
21. *Ibid.*
22. *Ibid.*
23. Banks, James H. and John Babcock, *Corralling the Colorado: The First 50 years of the Lower Colorado River Authority*. Austin, Eakin Press, pp. 179-180.
24. *Houston Chronicle*, Aug. 1, 1951.
25. Dugger, Ronnie. *The Politician: The Life and Times of Lyndon Johnson*. New York: W.W. Norton & Co., 1982, p. 292.
26. Howard, Jim. "Battle-broken Tanks Reconditioned Here," *Houston Chronicle*, July 11, 1951.
27. Howard, H*ouston Chronicle*, July 11, 1951.
28. *Brownbuilder: 75th Anniversary*, 1919–1994, p. 10.
29. Blankenhorn, p. 3.
30. Collier, Everett. "Brother Team's Success Story Mules to Millions." *Houston Chronicle*, Dec. 18, 1950.
31. Blankenhorn, pp. 3-4.
32. "Milestones: Rice Stadium," *Brownbuilder*, January-February 1982, p. 14.
33. Fuermann, George. Houston: *Land of the Big Rich*. Garden City, N.Y.: Doubleday & Co., 1951, 120.
34. *Ibid.*, p. 122.
35. Dugger, p. 290.
36. *Ibid.*, pp. 291–292.
37. *The Washington Post*, June 24, 1952.
38. "Brown & Root, Tops in Total Construction in Texas," company advertisement, Houston, March 1952.
39. Dugger, 284.
40. *Franklin* [Louisiana] *Banner Tribune*, February 18, 1958.

41. Articles of Merger filed with the Texas Secretary of State on December 27, 1958.
42. "Milestones: Lake Pontchartrain Causeway." *Brownbuilder*, May-June 1982, p. 7.
43. *Brown & Root Engineering*, p. 41.
44. "There Is Where the Oil Is." *Brownbilt*, Fall 1972, p. 12.
45. Klempin, September 6, 1982, p. 19.
46. "Yanhee Project in Thailand." *The Scoreboard*, October 1963.
47. Burleson, M.T. "Thai Musings," *The Scoreboard*, December 1959.
48. *Brownbuilder: 75th Anniversary, 1919–1994*, p. 21.
49. George R. Brown, interviewed by David G. McComb for the University of Texas Oral History Project, Aug. 6, 1969. Lyndon Baines Johnson Library's Oral History Collection, Transcript, p. 15.
50. *Engineering-News Record*, November 15, 1962, pp. 71, 75.
51. *Ibid.*, p. 71.
52. Gary Morris, interviewed by the author, January 17, 1996. Transcript, pp. 11-13.
53. Overton, Tom. *Houston Post*, July 20, 1980.
54. *Brown & Root Engineering*, pp. 42-43.
55. Fenley Bob, "$68 Million For Curiosity: Mohole Project Originator Says Goal Still 4 years Off "*Dallas Times Herald*, May 14, 1963.
56. *Brown & Root Engineering*, p. 17.
57. *Ibid.*, p. 18.
58 *Engineering News-Record*, November 15, 1962, p. 86.
59. *Ibid.*, November 15, 1962, p. 86.
60. Klempin, September 6, 1982, p. 21.
61. *Brownbuilder*, January-February 1967.
62. Klempin, September 6, 1982, p. 21.

Chapter Nine

1. John P. Harbin, interviewed by the author, December 12, 1995. Transcript, p. 14.
2. Dana Blankenhorn, "The Brown Brothers: From Mules To Millions as Houston's Contracting and Energy Giant," *Houston Business Journal*, March 19, 1979, p. 4.
3. *Engineering News-Record*, November 15, 1962, p. 82.
4. *Ibid.*, November 15, 1962, p. 86.
5. Stephen Zander, interviewed by the author, 1996. Transcript, p. 3.
6. *Brownbuilder: Special 50th Anniversary Issue*, p. 6.

7. John Harbin, interviewed by the author, December 12, 1995. Transcript, p. 16.
8. "Herman Brown: November 10, 1892–November 15, 1962." *The Scoreboard*.
9. *The Houston Press*, November 16, 1962.
10. *Engineering News-Record*, November 15, 1962, p. 75.
11. *Houston Chronicle*, November 17, 1962.
12. Texas H.S.R. No. 108, dated February 7, 1963.
13. *Engineering News-Record*, November 15, 1962, p. 75.
14. Halliburton Company Annual Reports, 1962 and 1963.
15. Harbin interview. Transcript, p. 14.
16. Gary Montgomery, interviewed by the author, January 17, 1996. Transcript, p. 1.
17. Thomas Cruikshank, interviewed by the author, November 15, 1995. Transcript, p. 29.
18. Dale Jones, interviewed by the author, January 17, 1996. Transcript, p. 34.
19. Dale Jones interview. Transcript, p. 27.
20. "Industry: Buying Out a Giant," *Time*, December 21, 1962, p. 69.
21. Draft of speech prepared for offshore industry seminar, September 6, 1968, in Houston. George Brown Executive Files, Box 2.
22. Susan Keith, interviewed by the author, January 16, 1996. Transcript, p. 1.
23. Letter to stockholders and employees, published in the Halliburton Company 1963 Annual Report, p. 3.
24. 1963 Consolidated Annual Report.

Chapter Ten

1. Tommy Knight, interviewed by the author, April 26, 1996. Transcript, p. 36.
2. Klempin, Raymond. *Houston Business Journal*. September 13, 1982, p. 13.
3. George R. Brown, interviewed July 11, 1977, by Michael L. Gillette. Lyndon Baines Johnson Oral History Collection, Transcript, 23.
4. Klempin, September 6, 1982, p. 21.
5. Tommy Knight interview. Transcript, p. 36.
6. Thad "Bo" Smith, interviewed by the author, January 17, 1996. Transcript, p. 2.
7. *Brown & Root Engineering*, p. 42.
8. *Brown & Root Engineering*, pp. 41-42.

9. *Brownbuilder*, May-June 1970, p. 3.
10. George Brown telegram to Robert Gilruth, NASA Manned Space Center, July 22, 1969. George Brown Executive files, Box 12.
11. *Brownbuilder*, May-June 1970, p. 7.
12 .*Brownbuilder: 75th Anniversary, 1919–1994*, p. 27–28.
13. Brown & Root, Inc./Marine, promotional booklet, p. 29.
14. Dr. Jay Weidler, Ph.D., interviewed by the author, April 8, 1996. Transcript, pp. 3-4.
15. *Brownbuilder: 75th Anniversary, 1919–94*, p. 28.
16. *Brownbilt*, Fall 1974, p. 16.
17 Bo Smith interview. Transcript, p. 10.
18. *Brownbilt*, Fall 1974, p. 8.
19. Dana Blankenhorn, "The Brown Brothers: From Mules To Millions as Houston's Contracting and Energy Giant," *Houston Business Journal*, March 19, 1979 p. 4.
20. Klempin, September 13, 1982, p. 14.
21. Brownbilt, Summer 1977, p. 22.
22. "Milestones: Fort Vermilion Bridge." Brownbuilder, Fall 1984, 6.
23. W. Bernard Pieper interview, p. 15.
24. Klempin, September 13, 1982, p. 15.
25. Gillan, Linda. "Brown & Root is a Golden Problem Child for Halliburton Co." *Houston Chronicle*, March 4, 1980.
26. *Brownbuilder: 75th Anniversary, 1919–1994,*
27. Gillan, *Houston Chronicle*, March 4, 1980.
28. *Brown & Root Engineering*, p. 44.
29. Klempin, September 13, 1982, 13-4.
30. *Ibid.*
31. Gillan, *Houston Chronicle*, March 4, 1980.
32. Klempin, September 13, 1982, p. 14.
33. *Brownbilt*, 1980 Annual Report Issue, p. 3.
34. *Brownbilt*, Summer 1977, p. 6.
35. *Brownbuilder: 75th Anniversary, 1919–1994*, pp. 29-30.
36. Gillan, Linda. *Houston Chronicle*, March 4, 1980.
37. *Brown & Root Engineering*, p. 45.
38. *Brown & Root Engineering*, pp. 45-46.
39. Jay Weidler interview. Transcript, p. 17.
40. *Brown & Root Engineering*, p. 46.
41. Klempin, September 13, 1982, p. 14.

Chapter Ten Sidebar

1. Klempin, Raymond. *Houston Business Journal*. First of a three-part series, Aug. 30, 1982, p. 16.

Chapter Eleven

1. Lawson, Michael and William G. Krizan. "Brown & Root Realigns in a Drive for Profits." *Engineering News–Record*, October 6, 1988, p. 26.
2. "Brown & Root Recaptures Number One Spot ... By a Nose." *Brownbuilder*, May-June 1982, p. 8.
3. B.K. Chin, interviewed by the author, April 11, 1996. Transcript, p. 10.
4. *Brown & Root Engineering*, p. 73.
5. *Ibid.*, p. 74.
6. *Ibid.*, p. 73.
7. *Ibid.*, p. 74.
8. Gary Montgomery interview. Transcript, p. 9.
9 .*Brown & Root Engineering*, p. 74.
10. "Do It Right the First Time," *Brownbuilder*, Fall 1983, p. 12.
11. *Brownbuilder: 75th Anniversary, 1919–94*, p. 32.
12. Randy Harl, interviewed by the author, January 17, 1996. Transcript, pp. 9-10.
13. "NSPE Honors LOOP Engineering." *Brownbuilder*, March-April 1982, p. 10.
14. "1,000 Attend Rites for George Brown." *Houston Post*, January 25, 1983.
15. "Builder, Philanthropist George Brown, 84, Dies." *Houston Chronicle*, January 23, 1983.
16. *Brownbuilder*, Spring 1982, Annual Report Issue, p. 3.
17. Shook, Barbara. "Brown & Root Ready to Return to Structure Set Up By Founders." *Houston Chronicle*, July 29, 1983.
18. *Ibid.*
19. *Biography of T.L. Austin Jr.*, dated October 15, 1980. Brown & Root Archives.
20. Shook, "Brown & Root Ready to Return to Structure Set Up by Founders."
21. "Meet Your New President," p. 6.
22. Shook, "Brown & Root Ready to Return to Structure Set Up by Founders."
23. Larry Pope, interviewed by the author, January 17, 1996. Transcript, p. 8.
24. Jack Browder, interviewed by the author, February 9. 1996. Transcript, pp. 6-7.
25. Tommy Knight manuscript revision, July 11, 1996.
26. *Ibid.*
27. Lawson, p. 27.
28. "Louis Austin Passes Baton to Ber Pieper." *Brownbuilder*, 1990, Vol. 2, 4.

29. Peter Arrowsmith, interviewed by the author, April 22, 1996. Transcript, p.12.
30. W.B. Pieper interview, p. 12.
31. Lawson, 26.
32. Emil Zerr, interviewed by Joan Thompson, April 3, 1996. Transcript, pp. 20-21.
33. "Louis Austin Passes Baton to Ber Pieper." *Brownbuilder*, 1990, Vol. 2, 4.
34. *Ibid.*, Vol. 2, 3.
35. Lawson, 26.
36. Lawson, 27.
37. *Ibid.*
38. *Ibid.*, 28.
39. *Ibid.*
40. *Ibid.*
41. Bivins, Ralph. "Brown & Root Site Near Alief Reopens." *Houston Chronicle*, November 22, 1988.
42. "Airco, Inc. Begins Production in Revolutionary War Hideout." *Brownbilt*, 1983. No. 2, pp. 25-27.
43. "Diego Garcia Island: Site of Navy Support Facility Expansion." *Brownbuilder*, Fall 1983, p. 10.
44. *Brown & Root Engineering*, p. 47.
45. "Exxon's Guyed Tower at Home Now in Gulf." *Brownbilt*, 1983. No. 2, pp. 9-11.
46. Jim Jacobi, interviewed by the author, April 8, 1996. Transcript, p. 6.
47. *Brownbilt*, 1983 Annual Special Edition, 43.
48. *Brown & Root Engineering*, p. 49.
49. *Ibid.*, 72.
50. *Ibid.*, 75.
51. *Ibid.*, 72.
52. Bo Smith interview. Transcript, pp. 17-18.
53. "Brown and Root, Inc." Revised by Brown & Root, February 1990, p. 2. Brown & Root Archives.
54. *Ibid.*, p. 10.
55. "Table 4: Brown and Root, Inc., Subsidiaries and Affiliates, 1990." Brown & Root Archives.
56. John Redmon, interviewed by Alex Lieber, May 30, 1996.
57. Antosh, Nelson. "New Chief Picked For Brown & Root." *Houston Chronicle,* July 24, 1990.

Chapter Twelve

1. Ken LeSuer, interviewed by the author, January 16, 1996. Transcript, p. 12.
2. Halliburton Company Annual Report, 1963.
3. *The Cementer*, November–December 1964, pp. 2-23.
4. *Ibid.*

5. Halliburton Company Annual Report, 1967.
6. *The Cementer,* November-December 1968, pp. 22-25.
7. Ken LeSuer, interviewed by the author, Jan. 16, 1996. Transcript, p. 13.
8. Daniel Yergin, *The Prize,* Simon & Schuster, 1991, pp. 605-608.
9. Halliburton Company Annual Report 1973, p. 7.
10. Marion Cracraft, interviewed by the author, December 12, 1995. Transcript, p. 7.
11. Guy Marcus, interviewed by the author, January 16, 1996. Transcript, p. 3.
12. Notes from Dale Jones, July 1996.
13. Greg Loyacano, interviewed by the author, April 9, 1996. Transcript, p. 3.
14. Jerry Blurton, interviewed by the author, January 16, 1996. Transcript, p. 10.
15. Les Coleman, interviewed by the author, January 16, 1996. Transcript, pp. 2-3.
16. *The Cementer,* March-April 1972, pp. 3–7.
17. Halliburton Company Annual Report 1973, p. 7.
18. Yergin, p. 569.
19. *The Cementer,* September-October 1973, pp. 44-45.
20. *Ibid.*
21. *Ibid.*
22. "A History of Halliburton Services," pp. 58–59; Halliburton Energy Institute Calendar 1996.
23. Halliburton Company Annual Report 1977, inside front cover.

Chapter Thirteen

1. Halliburton Company Annual Report 1985, p. 2.
2. Daniel Yergin, *The Prize,* Simon & Schuster, 1991, pp. 686-691.
3. *Ibid.,* p. 693.
4. Halliburton Annual Report, 1981 p. 3.
5. Halliburton Company Annual Report 1982, p. 2.
6. Halliburton Company Annual Report 1983, p. 2.
7. Dale Davis, interviewed by Joan Thompson, April 3, 1996. Transcript, pp. 3-4.
8. Halliburton Company Annual Report 1984, pp. 10-11.
9. B.N. Murali, interviewed by the author, January 16, 1996. Transcript, p. 20.
10. *The Cementer,* March-April 1984, pp. 16-17.

11. Halliburton Company Annual Report 1984, p. 2.
12. *Ibid.*
13. Halliburton Company Annual Report 1985, p. 2.
14. Halliburton Company Annual Report 1986, p. 2.
15. Halliburton Company Annual Report 1987, p. 5.
16. Halliburton Company Annual Report 1984, p. 2.
17. Davis interview. Transcript, p. 4.
18. Halliburton Company Annual Report 1986, p. 2.
19. 1986 Annual Report, p. 2.
20. Halliburton Company Annual Report 1986, p. 2.
21. Halliburton Company Annual Report 1987, p. 3.
22. *Ibid.,* p. 9.
23. *Ibid.*
24. Dale Jones interview, transcript, pp. 10-11.
25. Halliburton Company Annual Report 1988, p. 2.
26. *Ibid.,* p. 9.
27. *Ibid.,* p. 26.
28. *Ibid,* p. 2.
29. *The Cementer,* Spring, p. 23.
30. Halliburton Company Annual Report 1989, pp. 2-3, 6.
31. Yergin, *The Prize*, pp. 769-771.
32. 1989 Annual Report, p. 2.

Chapter Fourteen

1. Dick Cheney, interview by the author, May 1, 1996. Transcript, p. 26.
2. Halliburton transmission from Jim Dryden to Len Maier, August 2, 1990.
3. August 2, 1990 transmission.
4. August 8, 1990 transmission.
5. August 10, 1990 transmission.
6. Transmission from Guy Marcus, December 11.
7. Halliburton Company Annual Report 1990, p. 2.
8. *Ibid.*
9. Red Adair, interviewed by the author, April 26, 1996. Transcript, p. 14.
10. *Ibid.*
11. *The Cementer,* Fall issue, pp. 6-7.
12. *Ibid.*
13. Tarricone, Paul. "The Incredible Shrinking Rehab." Civil Engineering, p. 44.
14. *Brownbuilder: 75th Anniversary, 1919–94,* p. 36.
15. *Ibid.,* p. 37.
16. Kiely, Kathy. "Cutbacks Boon for Local Firm." *The Houston Post,* June 6, 1993.

17. *Brownbuilder: 75th Anniversary, 1919–94,* 37.
18. Kiely, "Cutbacks Boon for Local Firm."
19. "Brown & Root Supports Relief Effort in Somalia." *Brownbuilder,* No. 1, 1993, 3.
20. *Ibid.,* pp. 4-5.
21. Emil Zerr, interviewed by Joan Thompson, April 3, 1996. Transcript, p. 8.
22. "Brown & Root Credits 1991 Success With Outstanding Project Execution." *News & Views,* a Brown & Root employee newsletter. March 1992.
23. Dick Cheney interview. Transcript, p. 13.
24. *Ibid.*
25. The *Cementer,* Spring 1991, pp. 16-19.
26. 1992 Quarterly Report.
27. 1994 Quarterly Report.
28. 1993 Quarterly Report.
29. Jimmy Cooper, interviewed by the author, January 22, 1996. Transcript, p. 2.
30. The *Cementer,* summer 1992, p. 11.
31. The *Cementer,* Spring 1993, p. 29.
32. Zeke Zeringue interview. Transcript, pp. 12-13.
33. *Ibid.*
34. *Ibid.*
35. Robert Nash, interviewed by the author, January 16, 1996. Transcript, p. 3.
36. Cheney interview. Transcript, p. 16.
37. *Ibid.,* pp. 20-21.
38. *Ibid.*
39. *Ibid.*
40. Brandon Lackey, interviewed by Alex Lieber, June 5, 1996.
41. Dave Lesar, interviewed by Alex Lieber, September 5, 1996. Transcript, p. 4.
42. *Ibid.*
43. Lesar interview, transcript, p. 5.
44. Robert Peebler, interviewed by Alex Lieber, September 5, 1996. Transcript, p. 2.
45. Hank Holland, interviewed by Alex Lieber, August 25, 1996. Transcript, p. 5.
46. Steve Moore, interviewed by Alex Lieber, November 6, 1996, by telephone.
47. Memo to Halliburton Company employees from Dave Lesar, October 24, 1996.
48. Cheney interview, transcript, p. 7.

Chapter Fourteen Sidebar: Dick Cheney

1. Colin Powell with Joseph E. Persico, *My American Journey,* p. 426.
2. Bob Woodward, *The Commanders,* Simon & Shuster Inc. pp. 34-35.

Index